Praise for *The Influential Christian: Learning to Lead from the Heart*

"In *The Influential Christian*, Mike Andrews takes us on a journey in leadership and learning, by asking whether we would like to have an influence on other people. In guiding us to answer the question for ourselves, Mike explores the multifaceted virtue of empathy, by showing how influence is formed through practices that allow us to grow both internally and in our relationships with others. As members of Christian communities, Mike calls on us to learn from Jesus, the ultimate exemplar of empathy, as we grow from his divine influence on us and manifest that influence on others. This is a provocative read."
—Jonathan C. Augustine, senior pastor of St. Joseph AME Church, Durham, NC, and author of *The Keys Are Being Passed*

"Michael Andrews's fine book knows how to put first things recognizably first. Influence is about witness, not words, and the imitation of Christ is to fully embrace love as the architecture of our hearts. This book helps us take seriously what Jesus took seriously. You will be fortified by this journey."
—Gregory Boyle, founder of Homeboy Industries and author of *Tattoos on the Heart* and *Barking to the Choir*

"When it comes to matters of the heart, there is no better guide than *The Influential Christian*. Mike Andrews's modern take on Christian teaching presents an empathic approach to developing seekers in the faith. In a precisely developed narrative, this book unlocks ways to develop meaningful connections with Christ, from a place deep in the heart, through generous, persistent, and influential love."
—Ellen Clark Clémot, senior pastor of The Presbyterian Church of Chatham Township, Chatham, NJ

"In this biblically rooted, highly practical guide, Michael Andrews offers a clear and helpful way for followers of Jesus to develop a lasting, transformative influence grounded in empathy and the way of love."
—Michael B. Curry, presiding bishop of The Episcopal Church and author of *Love Is the Way* and *The Power of Love*

"Christian faith is a way of life—a way of being in the world together that enables all of us to thrive and to flourish. Michael Andrews's splendid book, *The Influential Christian: Learning to Lead from the Heart*, is a rich and wise description of the many ways Christians can learn this way of life and

participate in it. I commend it heartily! I also encourage readers to gather with one another in their congregations, study groups, homes and workplaces to draw upon its wisdom and to practice the kind of life together to which it calls us. It will enrich your lives greatly."
—Craig Dykstra, emeritus professor of practical theology at Duke Divinity School, past senior vice president for religion at Lilly Endowment, and author of *Growing in the Life of Faith*

"Michael Andrews makes a convincing case for centering empathy as a virtue essential for influencing and teaching people and communities. Engaging a wide array of resources across a long historical arc, he offers an authentic pathway accessible to people who learn in various ways. *The Influential Christian* is a valuable resource for all who long for a flourishing world."
—David Emmanuel Goatley, Ruth W. and A. Morris Williams Jr. Research Professor of Theology and Christian Ministry, Duke Divinity School, and author of books including *Were You There?*

"Mike Andrews has written an important book on a crucial topic: leading from the heart to the heart of others for the sake of faithful Christian education and formation. Too often we think of educating people as if they are 'brains on sticks'—here, Mike shows beautifully the power of spiritual and emotional development and human connection for education, formation, and leadership. A wise and insightful book!"
—L. Gregory Jones, dean emeritus at Duke Divinity School, president of Belmont University, and author of books including *Embodying Forgiveness*

"Grounded in Christian spirituality, this book brings inspiration to everyone who wants to have influence. It invites us to be truly and empathetically present with others, to reflect deeply and passionately, and to live and act from our hearts. These notions are elaborated with much care and depth, both theoretically and practically. The messages that this book conveys are both timeless and urgent and have important implications for teachers and coaches/mentors."
—Fred A. J. Korthagen, professor emeritus of Utrecht University, The Netherlands, specializing in teacher education and coaching, and author of books including *Practicing Core Reflection*

"*The Influential Christian* is a wonderful book filled with stories and wisdom gleaned by the author from leading theorists and practitioners from around the world. Michael Andrews has woven a wide array of quotes from the

Bible and Christian leaders that clearly show how one can lead from the heart. His insights and guidelines on empathy are superb. I highly recommend this book for anyone who has a calling to truly and deeply care and support others."
—Michael Marquardt, professor emeritus of George Washington University, co-founder of World Institute for Action Learning, and author of books including *Leading with Questions* and *Optimizing the Power of Action Learning*

"Working from within a Christian perspective, Michael Andrews offers a number of wise reflections about virtue, empathy, practices, trust, influence, and many other crucially important topics, all ultimately in the service of helping us to grow in character and become more and more the people God desires for us to be. Dr. Andrews rightly notes that 'character development is more of a journey than a blueprint.' His book is a valuable resource to take along for the ride!"
—Christian B. Miller, A. C. Reid Professor of Philosophy, Wake Forest University, and author of *The Character Gap: How Good Are We?*

"Dr. Mike Andrews offers an insightful leadership tool with this book. Leadership *is* influence, and Mike has written a comprehensive, yet pragmatic guide to assist in understanding how Christian influence is lived out in our lives as well as its impact on others. I highly recommend adding it to your library."
—Keith O'Neal, lead pastor, Destiny Christian Center International, Muncie, IN

"The guiding principles in this book pierce the hearts of those who influence the life of others. Character and integrity are extremely important components in the personality of the leader, and empathy is transferred from the heart of the teacher to the heart of the learner. I am convinced that the use of this material will serve as a resource for both Christian Education and secular education in the future. The principles discussed in this book can be a game-changer, as we seek ways to influence cultural assimilation in a diverse society. This is an outstanding resource to educate, train and disciple individuals to become ministry leaders and witnesses for Christ."
—Toney Parks, senior pastor of Mt. Sinai Baptist Church, Greenville, SC, and professor of ministry at Erskine Theological Seminary

"Thanks to Michael Andrews who gave us *The Influential Christian*. It supports readers who want to build impactful and helpful behavior in themselves and others. Michael did his homework in gathering and weaving together stories from notable leaders, great ideas, and Scripture passages into a resource that is a pleasure to read and can transform us from the inside. This book is so loaded, one time through won't do it. It's a read-and-reflect-on-bite-sized-chunks resource for learning the most important life skills. His teaching can help with what my favorite psychiatrist suggests as a primary goal in life, 'to be the kind of people in whose presence good things happen.'"

—Jim Petersen, Pastor Emeritus, ret. Licensed Professional Counselor, author of *Why Don't We Listen Better? Communicating & Connecting in Relationships*

"The older I get as a minister and a man, the less enamored I become with the career-building and name-making 'resume virtues,' and the more enamored I become with the 'eulogy virtues.' These are the virtues we hope people will remember at our funerals such as love, kindness, generosity, approachability, and the like. With this hope in mind, my own daily prayer is that God will grant me character that exceeds my abilities, and humility that exceeds my influence. I am thankful for this wonderful book that Michael has written, which serves as a compelling road map for how to get there."

—Scott Sauls, senior pastor of Christ Presbyterian Church, Nashville, TN, and author of books including *Jesus Outside the Lines* and *A Gentle Answer*

"What a refreshing study about how to become a more influential person! With solid research and winsome sensitivity, Mike Andrews emphasizes the value of empathy at a time when this virtue is sorely needed. This book will make you a more faithful leader and, more importantly, a more caring, Christ-like person."

—Andrew Taylor-Troutman, pastor of chapel in the Pines Presbyterian Church, Chapel Hill, NC, and author of *Gently Between the Words: Essay and Poems*

"Michael Andrews understands the peculiar character of leadership in Christ's name. This book shows an experienced Christian educator's wisdom at work and gives practical guidance for how we can better influence fellow Christians for more faithful participation in Christ's mission."

—Will Willimon, professor of the Practice of Christian Ministry at Duke University, United Methodist Bishop, retired, and author of books including *Pastor* and *Accidental Preacher*

THE INFLUENTIAL CHRISTIAN

THE INFLUENTIAL CHRISTIAN

Learning to Lead from the Heart

MICHAEL W. ANDREWS

Alban at Duke Divinity School

ROWMAN & LITTLEFIELD
Lanham • Boulder • New York • London

Published by Rowman & Littlefield
An imprint of The Rowman & Littlefield Publishing Group, Inc.
4501 Forbes Boulevard, Suite 200, Lanham, Maryland 20706
www.rowman.com

86-90 Paul Street, London EC2A 4NE, United Kingdom

British Library Cataloguing in Publication Information Available

Library of Congress Cataloging-in-Publication Data

Names: Andrews, Michael W., 1955- author.
Title: The influential Christian : learning to lead from the heart /
  Michael W. Andrews.
Description: Lanham : Rowman & Littlefield, [2021] | Includes
  bibliographical references and index.
Identifiers: LCCN 2021019622 | ISBN 9781538151723 (cloth) | ISBN
  9781538151730 (paperback) | ISBN 9781538151747 (ebook)
Subjects: LCSH: Influence (Psychology)—Religious aspects—Christianity. |
  Empathy—Religious aspects—Christianity. | Leadership—Religious
  aspects—Christianity.
Classification: LCC BV4597.53.I52 A53 2021 | DDC 248.4—dc23
LC record available at https://lccn.loc.gov/2021019622

CONTENTS

FOREWORD

Rev. Dr. Shakeema North

To the Christian leader aspiring to be influential:

At Covenant House New York, an organization committed to providing housing and support services to youth experiencing homelessness, our work is guided by our mission to serve the young people with absolute respect and unconditional love—and to be visible signs of God's presence in their lives. Many of the young people we serve at Covenant House have experienced varying levels and degrees of trauma. While engaging them in our space, eliciting change by building positive relationships has become essential in our ability to give kids the resilient hope necessary to start them on a path to healing.

I recall a couple of unforgettable conversations with young people early on in my tenure at Covenant House. On one occasion, a group of us walked from the site to Madison Square Garden for the Big East college basketball championship game. As we approached our destination, a young lady ran up and began to walk beside me. Then, out of the blue, she looked over at me and said, "You know, God put you here for a reason." "What made you say that?" I asked, surprised by her comment. To which she said again, "God put you at Covenant House for a reason." Accepting her words as divine confirmation, I responded, "I think so too," with the blessed assurance that God's hand was upon the work I was doing. On another occasion, a young person came to my office to discuss an issue he'd been experiencing. After we spoke, he looked at me and told me that he thought I should "be a pastor," to which my response was, "I am."

The ability to build the type of connection that influences resilient hope and healing in the lives of the people we've been called to serve requires that we develop the inner character essential to being viewed and respected as trustworthy leaders. The depth of our character determines the depth of our influence, and when we nurture genuine connections with both an open mind and an open heart, we never have to announce our titles or wield power to get results. We will be known by our fruit, and the love of Jesus will be seen in us, even when we don't mention his name.

With this book, Dr. Michael Andrews shifts the paradigm, providing you, the Christian leader aspiring to be influential, with the tools necessary to create a productive learning environment. He guides you in developing a heart-centered approach to leadership that uses empathy as a sustainable strategy to cultivate the type of character development that will impact your teaching ministry in ways that manipulation cannot. He helps you see the value of mutual collaboration and shared expertise, such that you will learn how to identify with the feelings and perspectives of others, acknowledging their lived experiences and trusting them as experts in their own lives. Taking it a step further, the questions for group discussion provided at the end of each chapter and the personal stories of proven influencers woven throughout provide you with unique opportunities to learn with and from other leaders who continuously work to lead with the heart and mind of Christ.

As a Christian leader aspiring to be influential, you'll find very few books that bridge the gap between sacred and secular models of care in the way this book does. Using Christian ethics—Christ's way of being *with* people—as the cornerstone, Dr. Andrews masterfully links the practical application of Christian empathy: empathic reception, empathic reflection, and empathic response, with basic tenets of evidenced-based practices, like motivational interviewing. In doing so, he provides you with an approach to teaching and learning that integrates clinical expertise, expert opinion, and expert application that has proven to be effective and is guaranteed to withstand the test of time.

As Dr. Andrews says in the title of this book, the key to becoming an influential Christian is to learn to lead from the heart. The power to uproot and tear down, build and plant—to be influential—is demonstrated when your presence shifts the atmosphere in life-giving, life-affirming, and life-changing ways.

If you genuinely aspire to be an influential leader, whether in traditional or church adjacent spaces, this book will help develop you into the type of leader worth being around.

Rev. Dr. Shakeema North
Vice President of Youth Development, Equity, and Inclusion
Covenant House New York

INTRODUCTION

Would you like to be influential? A person of influence has certain qualities of personal character that affect other people deeply and consistently. Someone with this kind of character values people, reflects upon their needs, and then takes appropriate action. Today we watch leaders in all professions and vocations grapple with their own moral behavior: "Do as I say and not as I do!" At the same time, all levels and reaches of society yearn to be known and appreciated. No message is timelier than the persistent call for virtuous character, but how will that call be answered?

This is a guide for ordinary people who want Christ to equip them to imitate him, whether or not they view themselves as engaged in ministry. The spiritual practices presented here are aimed at connecting with the power and presence of God's Spirit, and the specific skills that constitute these practices foster more effective patterns of engagement with people. Whether or not you're a Christian, this book can provide insight into the kind of inner character that will draw people together. Here is an approach that goes deep into what makes us worth being around. Building character is much more than completing a checklist of self-improvement initiatives— it is about our identity and our integrity.

Several people were important influences in my life long before I thought about my own role as an influence on others. I grew up in a relatively homogeneous, self-sufficient environment and didn't expect anyone outside my family to take much interest in me. However, there were some teachers, managers, and church leaders who modeled open and perceptive thinking, and they introduced me to the value of community and the priority of personal relationships. I enjoyed learning in a church environment, and that is where I began teaching. Eventually I started training other church teachers, and I was fascinated with trying new teaching methods. I began to realize that the most important component of excellence in teaching is the quality of a person's inner character. Through my continuing work with new teachers in the church, stimulated by my doctoral research at Duke University Divinity School, I came to understand that the most significant personal factor in a teacher's character is empathy. Influential people emulate God's loving concern in order to encourage other people. God uses connections between people, together with his Spirit, to guide and transform his followers. This book is the result of my own progress toward learning about influence and the practices that make it work.

Our journey toward a better understanding of influence begins in Chapter 1 with a focus on the heart and how our inner character is central to our lives. In Chapter 2, we will explore how empathy plays a significant role in creating the kind of environment that fosters the development of character. Functioning like a classical virtue, empathy is a quality that enables certain practices to produce spiritual results. Empathy contributes to our own individual maturity, and it sustains the well-being of our entire community. Chapter 3 will explore the nature of Christian practices and identify some specific ways to build influential character. These practices are not primarily focused on what we do by our own power, but instead "they become arenas in which something is done to us, in us, and through us that we could not of ourselves do."[1] They are a means for connecting human behavior with God's purposes and power. Chapters 4 through 6 will then present the key elements of those practices, which depend on the qualities of empathy. The skills of reception, reflection, and response will each be applied to the pursuit of Christian influence. Finally, Chapter 7 will examine how this form of personal preparation and development affects various aspects of Christian growth. These very practices and skills can significantly improve the way church members are trained to minister to one another and to people outside the church. We will see what it can look like when empathic practices and skills come together in Christian environments.

Between the chapters, I tell the stories of individuals who exhibit the practices and skills that demonstrate the value of becoming an influential person. They all have learned through a variety of experiences to develop inner character in themselves and in others. As they have collaborated with others and built strong relationships, they have seen their influence make a difference. They exemplify the results of empathy in action.

My goal is to show that the path to become a more influential person is available to anyone—adult learners, current teachers, potential teachers, pastors, neighborhood role models, and others. The benefits also extend into family situations, providing some new ideas on how to communicate between husbands and wives, between parents and children, and between siblings. Other leaders and interested collaborators—in public schooling, professional advancement, organizational leadership, and civic policy—also recognize the importance of encouraging and developing commendable character. Most groups desire an environment that builds trust and connects people. Developing influence based on empathy is an approach to seeking the value that all people offer.

I am abundantly grateful for the many who have influenced, supported, and contributed to this book. God has been gracious, and his Spirit has been kind. Foremost among the encouragers is my wife, Beth, whose assurances and insightful feedback have helped me articulate the thoughts of my heart. My doctoral advisors at Duke University Divinity School, Dr. Greg Jones and Dr. David Odom, expanded my thinking with grace and acuity, sharing with me their wisdom regarding leadership. My fellow Doctor of Ministry cohort members at Duke motivated me to think about the church's ministries in terms of empathy and spiritual practices. Johnathan Richardson and Simon Stokes walked with me as the seed of this work grew and blossomed. The professors at Duke Divinity School and at Erskine Theological Seminary have been a great treasure; I am especially grateful to Dr. Terry Eves, whose passing in 2019 was a reminder to me that holy friendship is stronger than death. I mention several authors and friends in this book, and I appreciate the influence they have all had on me. My spiritual family at Holland Park Church has supported my teaching and leading for many years, and they have been patient and encouraging while I experiment with educational methods.

I am grateful to Alban at Duke Divinity School, especially Nathan Kirkpatrick, for appreciating the value of Christian influence and supporting this book. Rowman & Littlefield's publishing editor, Natalie Mandziuk, has believed in this project from the beginning and has provided indispensable suggestions. Ashley Festa, my developmental editor, shared her writing expertise by offering myriad ideas that have improved the organization of this work and sharpened its content.

This book is dedicated to my parents, Marvin and Jean Andrews, who taught me to be curious and to love learning.

1

CONNECTING HEARTS

M ost of us want to be heard and understood. We may not think of
ourselves as leaders, but we find ourselves trying to influence others
that one path is better than another or that a particular decision might be
the way to go. In that sense, we all have a propensity to teach others, even
without a formal, authoritative role in hierarchical structures. A framework
in which Christians learn to exhibit and increase influence is one that cultivates mutual collaboration and spiritual growth. This manner of thinking
can shape the way any group of people journeys together and develops
communal perspectives, behaviors, and affinities along the way.

Popular portrayals of influence usually focus on enabling you to get
something you want. The preparation they provide consists of better ways
to market yourself or your product, so others buy into your proposal or
your leadership. Indeed, there are myriad pundits who regard themselves as
social influencers, providing advice about every possible topic. However,
influence based simply on persuasion and presentation techniques works
in one direction—guiding others toward what you have to offer. It may
produce an *impact* or an *impression*, but it remains either superficial or temporary. Genuine influence is much deeper. It doesn't depend upon positional authority or marketing ability. It's built upon personal relationships.
The approach to influence I'm going to describe consists of developing and
relying on certain spiritual practices and interpersonal skills available to anyone. Our influence isn't a flashy product or idea. It is about simply offering
ourselves. The late congressman John Lewis wrote that the most significant
lesson he ever learned is that "the true work of social transformation starts
within."[1] The real power of our influence emanates from who we are and
what we represent.

People with influence have found ways to connect with others through shared values, goals, experiences, and relationships. These kinds of connections help develop an individual's inner character (often referred to as *heart*). Character is always grounded in a guiding narrative—the big story that gives meaning and direction to life. For Christians, that big story is the gospel of Jesus Christ. Adopting this narrative and trusting in God's Spirit for growth provides the foundation for developing a Christian's character and influence.

The aspect of Christian character that most affects influence is the ability to *connect hearts*, bringing people together to share what is most significant in their lives and to encourage each other. When Christians participate together, new ways of learning are created that nurture transformation into Christ (Ephesians 4:15). The ability to connect with others in this way is often referred to as *empathy*—understanding and sharing the feelings of someone else for that person's benefit. This sort of influence is a way of *being with* people. Becoming a Christian influencer requires being open to the influence of others. We don't persuade by pushing our opinion onto people, but rather by our own sincere openness to change. We can coach each other to become leaders if we ourselves are attentive to both God's Spirit and how we communicate. This is how growth and change are possible.

Influence is by its nature a quality that functions in community, and connecting with others makes life more interesting than trying to manage everything alone. The key to tapping into this influence is the development of personal character through collaboration with other Christians and with the Spirit of God. When the positive aspects of empathy are used to highlight the significant features of leadership, we discover some basic skills we can use to create connections. Providing new opportunities for people to collaborate and to gain strength from the Lord will enable all of us to grow together as influential Christians.

Every form of cooperative human activity includes specific practices that guide individual and collective behavior. Sports teams establish a set of plays to direct the players on the field. Churches follow liturgies that move worship along. Cruise ships provide schedules of activities and entertainment. Orchestras rehearse musical pieces with particular instrumental sections and with the entire group in order to blend and coordinate their sound. Schools provide classes in which students learn together by completing and discussing assignments. For Christians, there are spiritual practices that are shared activities of the church. These practices—like baptism, reading Scripture, or praying—define a Christian's identity and offer opportunities for the person to grow into that identity. Some practices, when viewed through a lens of empathy, cultivate character and develop a deeper form of influence.

The first building block of influence I will present is a practice of being fully available and supportive to people. I call it a practice of *formative presence* because it's an engagement in which people are changed. Just as Jesus's demeanor led others to assess their relationship with him, so the nature of our own role and identity likewise affects people in definitive ways. This practice of formative presence develops character because it's incarnational—an expression of genuine embodiment. The essential character of *who we are* is embodied in our presence, so our identity is both revealed and developed through this practice.

A second critical practice involves *resilient trust*, which encompasses the sort of behaviors that build and sustain integrity. Jesus demonstrated both truth and grace in a paradoxical combination that made him both reliable and transparent. Do you remember how often Jesus healed people and then charged them with a responsibility to be faithful? Like the people he encouraged, we become trustworthy through many small acts of honest, compassionate engagement. Relationships of trust are always tested with adversity, and resilience is strengthened by being anchored in Christ and faithful in community. Both of these practices (formative presence and resilient trust) are patterns of communal action in which the benefits of God's presence and power are made available to every participant.

We can understand character development as based upon formative presence and resilient trust along with three underlying skills of empathy that help individuals develop connection with God and with people. The first of these skills is *reception*, which is a collaboration between people that communicates acceptance and understanding. Reception begins with listening and evokes honest dialogue, opening up ways to share empathy. Yet, as significant as listening and dialogue are for influence, they are just the beginning.

The second empathic skill is *reflection*. It's the component of learning in which underlying assumptions are examined, leading to shared meaning-making activities. Questioning and feedback lead to processes of analysis, synthesis, application, and evaluation. As a result, reflective individuals and groups share in the mutual development of integrity, identity, and social conscience.

Finally, a skillful *response* is an action that expresses accountability with collective wisdom. Christian character is displayed in certain kinds of action that demonstrate both moral intelligence and the guiding presence of God's

Spirit. Character-based influence is a matter of creating responsible connections in which people are open to each other and supportive of everyone's growth. People learn from each other by sharing and examining thoughts, feelings, behaviors, intentions, and values. A community of character becomes a community of influence.

The remainder of this chapter introduces some reasons for pursuing empathic practices and skills. Christians can be more effective witnesses by engaging in practices and behaviors driven by empathy. Since God aims for the heart, so should his disciples.

AIM FOR THE HEART

People are most effective in personal encounters when they embody truth and grace. For Christians, that might sound obvious, but we often forget who controls our ability to influence others. The apostle Paul embodied God's truth and grace as he groomed his beloved friend, Timothy, for a pastoral ministry of helping and teaching others. Timothy needed *training* in addition to the *gift* of teaching God gave him. The pursuit of godliness requires both personal effort (1 Timothy 4:7–8) and spiritual enablement (4:14), and Timothy was instructed to "put these things into practice" (4:15).

My own experience with developing influence and character stems from my interest in learning about life skills and from my calling to lead adult education in a Christian context. As a young person, I did not consider myself an influence on anyone, and I was definitely not interested in becoming a teacher. However, God's Spirit opened my eyes and heart to both the beauty of the gospel message and the value of the people around me. Admittedly, my interest was initially in some of the more technical aspects of God's Word, but as I began to help equip others for teaching, I realized that Christians need more than a curriculum. As I talked with people about teaching, the response I heard most was a desire for something more than study guides. These folks weren't looking for techniques but rather asking how they might be equipped to influence and lead people. Eventually I concluded that what was missing from the preparation of teachers was guidance in becoming the *kind* of people who influence other people. Influence is a matter of reaching into our hearts, our whole inner being, not just sharing thoughts. The preparation of inner character begins with who we are and then determines what we should be doing. God shapes our inner character according to his plan. And he aims for our hearts, not just our heads.

When I was a young adult learning to serve in the church, I had several role models. Terry Smith, one of the leaders in a small congregation in New Jersey, demonstrated the significance of depending on the Lord in all aspects of life. When he would occasionally preach on a Sunday that I was leading worship, I always asked about the focus of his message so I could select some related songs and readings. I discovered over the years that Terry really had only one main subject: Jesus Christ. He offered a variety of insightful perspectives from the Bible, but his subject was always Jesus. Not the issues of the day. Not the controversies in the church. Just Jesus. Realizing this made my preparation for leading worship easier. I knew the worship on those Sundays would especially emphasize Jesus. I eventually adopted that model in my own teaching: I'm never finished preparing a lesson until it's truly centered on my Lord Jesus. My teaching style is not the same as Terry's, but I grew to emulate his heart for Christ. When my heart connects with Christ, my influence connects with other people in ways that curriculum materials alone cannot achieve.

Leadership training resources for public schools, churches, and business programs often focus solely on the methods and techniques for managing groups and don't guide the ongoing character development of the leader in relation to the community. Something more profound than these methods and techniques is required to shape people's hearts. The well-known Christian counselor Jay Adams asserts, "When your goal is to mold the character of an individual, you pursue that task much differently than when your goal is to enable him to answer questions."[2] My objective for showing how to develop influence in this book is different from most mainstream educational tools because I'm focusing on connecting hearts together rather than detailing a sequence of do-it-yourself tasks. Character development is more of a journey than a blueprint, and we will need significant help from God and from our community in order to pursue it.

The only change that will make a lasting difference is a change of heart. Scriptures that explain the change God seeks often refer to the heart (Ezekiel 36:26) because it is all-encompassing. When we speak of the heart, we mean thoughts, emotions, beliefs, and desires. That's why Jesus says the heart harbors the deepest parts of a person's life (Luke 6:45). Influence is about creating change, and real change is centered in the heart.

All people have different experiences, perspectives, sensitivities, and ambitions, so any group will contain some degree of diversity in the members' thoughts, feelings, and desires. The influential Christian expects and appreciates diverse contributions, knowing unity is possible when communication is expressed with grace. Approaching people in love for their own sake requires character anchored in God's nature—full of compassion and grace, slow to anger, abounding in love (Psalm 86:15). God is the epitome of empathy. In order to become like Christ, exhibiting God's nature, the Holy Spirit must change us. Many of today's approaches to Christian education create a fervor to motivate people to live better lives, while God's own power is regarded more like a background effect than as the essential means for changing hearts. The apostle Paul, however, recognized that transformation requires a reliance upon the Holy Spirit: "My speech and my proclamation were not with plausible words of wisdom, but with a demonstration of the Spirit and of power" (1 Corinthians 2:4).

This task of transformation requires greater reliance upon God's Spirit and greater engagement and preparation of people to connect with each other. The church community is where this preparation happens. The local congregation adopts a narrative—the story of God's promises fulfilled in Jesus Christ—that is formative for every member. The church shares a common purpose that guides every Christian to commit to God's plan. In order for the church to connect us together, we must depend upon the Triune God and also upon each other as his chosen people.

LEARNING IS LEADING

The popular motivational speaker Simon Sinek identifies two distinct types of influence: *manipulating* a change in behavior and *inspiring* a change in behavior.[3] He says the reason for the pervasiveness of manipulative approaches in sales and marketing is that manipulation works. People are temporarily influenced by slick marketing. However, manipulation is a strategy for producing a transaction rather than developing loyalty. Sinek proposes that inspiration is more effective than manipulation because the influence lasts longer and the connection between people is deeper. Inspiration is driven by a sense of purpose—asking *why* the influence is needed—and people learn from each other which purposes help them the most. Let's explore the nature of learning as a precursor to understanding the nature of influence.

Character development involves growth in ways that affect how one thinks and feels, accompanied by a deepening of relationships with people and with God. Growth involves learning, and learning follows some form of influential guidance or teaching, even if initiated by our own experiences. Christians rely on God's Spirit to be the main guide, and other people help provide direction. We learn what we are prepared to learn, and the results are influenced by the people and experiences in our lives. The sort of learning that shapes the heart touches the deepest layers of personal identity and readiness for change.

Scientific research supports this idea that our learning depends on our influences. Some of the most exciting advancements in our knowledge about behavioral change are coming from the field of neuroscience. Research on learning and memory has revealed that when people repeat an activity, neural networks in the brain also repeat their corresponding activity. Canadian psychologist Donald Hebb observed that "neurons that fire together wire together."[4] In other words, the pathways in our brains that guide our bodies in certain behaviors are like trails through the forest. The more they are traveled, the more accessible they become, increasing the likelihood that others will follow the same path. This is why repeated behaviors become easier and more likely to occur—they become habits. It also means that changing our actions has an impact on our brain development at any age; our behavior is not predetermined by genetics, and change is indeed possible. As we communicate our experiences with one another and make sense of what we know, we activate new neural networks. Not only that, but people nearby observing our changed behavior have a corresponding change in their neural networks.[5] Our brains naturally mirror the behavior we observe, helping us to imitate others and learn from them. The influence we have on people is a deep sharing of neural engagement, and we usually don't even notice it's happening. Without our own awareness, we influence each other and lead others in their growth.

The Bible also supports this idea that our learning depends on our influences. The New Testament model of discipleship offers a paradigm for the spiritual development of inner character. This model relies upon voluntary, personal relationships between individuals and in community, with a commitment to sharing life and learning together. The Bible clarifies that, while some people may have specific gifts or positions of teaching, all Christians are called to influence and stimulate each other to work together (Hebrews 10:24). A variety of spiritual practices contribute to this model of influence; for example, acts of service, worship, forgiveness, generosity, hospitality, prayer, and sharing Scripture are ways of helping one another grow spiritually. The apostle Paul wrote letters to Timothy explaining that being a leader and a teacher in the church is about holding on to faith and good conscience, cultivating a relationship with God, nurturing God's gifts, honoring leaders, and living a holy life. Teaching and learning are not a matter of chattering and posturing among people; they are instead a serious pursuit of God's gifts (Ephesians 4:11–13).

Spiritual practices are an essential element of the believer's journey with Christ, and they are driven by a transformation of the heart. First, God establishes a new relationship with a person through faith in the sacrifice of Christ. Commonly referred to as justification, this change occurs at the beginning of one's spiritual walk. Then the life-giving action provided by Jesus Christ in and through the Holy Spirit continues to help believers grow and develop. The ongoing transformation is often called sanctification or holiness. Both justification and sanctification are brought about through faith. While both are enacted as part of an individual's new birth, sanctification is also characterized by an ongoing application of grace that nurtures personal holiness. In justification, sin is pardoned once for all time, and in sanctification, sin is increasingly conquered by the Spirit to enable righteous living. Spiritual growth is a process of learning and change.

Contrary to some theories of learning development, character development does not typically follow predictable stages. Author and educator Parker J. Palmer explains that the inner landscape of a person's life is a combination of interdependent intellectual, emotional, and spiritual paths. Palmer stresses that relational community is vital for spiritual formation: "Through the other we learn much about ourselves."[6] The communal aspect of character development is necessary because changes that impact faith and maturity are difficult to achieve alone.

I have often observed Christian teachers come to the realization that they learn from the very people they are attempting to teach. No one is without influence. People continually influence each other, despite and because of the differences between them. The voices of other people grow the effectiveness of each person's influence.

The voices of the learners are especially significant in the context of oppressed or underrepresented peoples. Paulo Freire was a Brazilian educator who believed educational processes could be used either as a tool for perpetuating the status of a dominant culture or for lifting those who have been disadvantaged to another level. Educational systems and church institutions in America are now recognizing similar issues of authority and power as they attempt to influence social justice. In Freire's groundbreaking work, *Pedagogy of the Oppressed,* he explained that students are not merely receptacles to be filled by a teacher and indoctrinated by an educational system. Instead, he said people must find ways to share influence with each other across cultural and class boundaries. The people with limited opportunities are the ones who "must find themselves among the emerging leaders" because the oppressive culture needs to learn from them.[7] In a later work, Freire asserted,

To teach is not *to transfer knowledge* but to create the possibilities for the production or construction of knowledge. . . . It is essential therefore, from the very beginning of the process, that the following principle be clear: namely, that although the teachers or the students are not the same, the person in charge of education is being formed or re-formed as he/she teaches, and the person who is being taught forms him/herself in this process. In this sense teaching is not about transferring knowledge or contents.[8]

So far we see that influence involves learning—discovering and examining ourselves, others, and our situations. It entails openness and reflection. Influence is a multidirectional activity in which each participant learns from others. In fact, it may be difficult at times to know who's leading and who's following. As people come together to share their experiences, they inevitably share themselves. The personal values of the participants are mutually weighed and appreciated as contributions to the group's values. One need not assimilate or compromise one's values with everyone in the group, but an appreciation of how the disparate values interwork within the group is important. A group that learns together discovers that each member influences the others by actively engaging with those who have different values and understanding their beliefs and assumptions.

Spiritual practices help Christians create a sense of meaning by sharing space with other people and with God's Spirit. In these practices, we reflect on the range of experiences in the group and discern how we will live in Christ. The learning processes in the church should open our hearts to the Lord in his grace and mercy as the pattern for our behavior. Some practices, like baptism and eucharist/communion, are embodied in the sacraments of the church. Encounters with the broader community shape other practices like hospitality, prayer, and service. Celebration is emphasized in practices like praise, singing, and giving generously, while submission is the focus of fasting and meditation. Our desire for God is expressed in reading Scripture and testifying to God's greatness, and our experiences of contrition or adversity are represented by confession, lament, and forgiveness.

People's lives are often messy, and the spaces in which they discover what is meaningful to them about God's presence vary with the complexity of their experiences. My particular journey has included the stresses of job changes and health issues, and I've found direction in the midst of those trials by following simple routines and practices that focused my attention. Even prostate cancer was a source of significance in my life because I faced the challenges with supportive friends and specific activities like reading, walking, and praying. Although we may think our practices are necessarily linked to specific religious spaces, the reality is that our spirituality is embodied and performed in all of the spaces where we live. Spiritual change in my life has never been spontaneous, and it has always been affected by the influence of people and activities in ordinary spaces. The practices listed in the previous paragraph are places to begin opening our hearts to be influenced—so that we can also learn to be an influence.

Author and theologian Henri Nouwen speaks of the spiritual life as characterized by movement and change. He describes it as a journey that begins by reaching for our inner selves, stretching outward to fellow humans, and then searching for God.⁹ These three areas of our lives are vital aspects of our spiritual influence, so I will adopt them as a guide for how to apply the biblical narrative to our personal growth. However, I believe they should be considered in the opposite order. For the development of inner character, it's best to begin with our submission to the Lord, move toward greater collaboration within community, and then finally examine ourselves. In this way, Christ is the center of our growth in character and influence, allowing us to understand better how all of our experiences of community and individuality can move us toward Christ. The chapters that focus on specific empathic practices and skills will reflect this movement, tracing each empathic behavior from Christ's heart to the community's heart to the individual's heart.

AN EMPATHIC APPROACH

Empathy is the quality that engages the heart in all of its dimensions. Our hearts represent our inner character, the root of our ability to influence people. Since our behaviors originate from what is inside us, it's important for us to understand and direct those inner workings. Therefore, I am using the perspective of empathy to examine the workings of the heart. An exploration of the nature of empathy will highlight the practices and skills of influence.

I hope that as I attempt to exercise empathic behaviors in this book, you will see greater value in being open to new ideas and encounters. Reflection on the significance of these discoveries, together with the guidance of the Holy Spirit, will lead us in responding to what we learn. We are all growing in our ability to influence people, and our openness to each other will increase along the way. The desired outcome of this work is more connection—with the hearts of people and of God.

I've chosen to demonstrate empathic practices through the experiences of a variety of influential individuals. Several of these people come from within my circle of learning in the upstate region of South Carolina. I invited them to share their personal stories and explain what is important for influencing people. Their stories appear between the chapters in order to amplify the message being conveyed in the corresponding section of the book. As I interviewed each one, I centered the conversation on one question: *How would you like to have an influence on other people?* The ensuing dialogue drew upon their experiences, their roles in community, their motivations, and their encounters with people. Their wisdom can help us in our own encounters to connect hearts together.

I have learned about influence by modeling my character after people who exhibit empathy in normal routines of their lives. My background is in engineering and other analytical interests, so empathy was hardly my native language. I like to solve problems and puzzles, and my emotional capacity was not one of my top concerns as a younger person. I love to learn new things, and this openness has helped me interact with people in various contexts that involved satisfying international customers, supporting my team of employees, volunteering for service opportunities, and nurturing my marriage relationship. In every one of these contexts, there have been individuals who encouraged me to look beyond myself and outside my comfort zone. As I found avenues into Christian ministry, I recognized that I love people and I enjoy seeing people with different backgrounds work together. Opportunities for teaching and preaching in New Jersey, New Mexico, and South Carolina surprised me with a new awareness of what God was doing around me and in me. I'm convinced the Holy Spirit has worked through honest, insightful friends—including my patient wife—to open my eyes and help me listen. I believe God wants to be present in each of us so that we take the initiative to reach out to people around us.

QUESTIONS FOR GROUP DISCUSSION

One possible way to begin a discussion about connecting with people is to read Ephesians 4:1–16. Some members of your group may benefit from further study of the Holy Spirit's role in equipping Christians to be an influence. The most important part of this discussion is sharing and hearing each person's story about influencing people and connecting with them.

1. What are some ways you consider yourself to have influence—either as an individual or as part of a group?
2. Who has been a significant influence on your life? How was this person's presence and guidance part of your progress to where you are today?
3. What are some activities you do (or have done) from the heart?
4. How does it feel to be connected with people? What are some instances in which you have connected deeply with others?
5. What are some spiritual gifts that help you connect with people and with God? What are some activities that are necessary to use those gifts? (see 1 Timothy 4:11–15).
6. How might one go about improving or transforming one's character?

REGARDLESS OF WHERE YOU
COME FROM, THERE IS HOPE

Jerry Blassingame likes to start things. He likes to see people change and grow. That's why he launched a nonprofit organization that helps men return to society from prison. "There's nothing like seeing a guy who has served [in prison] ten or fifteen years, who has no hope on day one, and at the end of the year at graduation [from our program], he's getting ready to move into his own place. . . . That's what I love about this job: You actually get to see change."

Jerry's own life is an example of what he hopes to see in others. He has chosen to live in hope rather than in trauma. Surviving a childhood burdened by violence and poverty, Jerry became a Christian in the county jail. He likes to say, "God captivated my heart and won me over." Previously unfamiliar with the church, Jerry was discipled by other prisoners. He found the God of the Bible as someone he could trust, and he has continued to engage with the Lord daily in devotionals and journaling.

While in prison, Jerry decided he wanted to create a business in which he could connect with people, building a better future for people through empathy and trust. The name he wanted to use for that venture, Soteria, is the New Testament Greek word translated *salvation.* Jerry was released from prison after serving three years of a twenty-year sentence, and he created Soteria Community Development Corporation in Greenville, South Carolina. "I just kept my eye on Jesus and the plan he gave me, and everything just followed. He has never failed me one time." Soteria CDC is a faith-based organization that helps almost three hundred clients each year with services that include financial literacy, job training (especially in woodworking skills), job placement, affordable housing, and educational services. Every client who enters the program receives mentoring from someone in the community, and Jerry works with many of them personally, encouraging them in their faith and daily journaling. The success rate for participants in Soteria's program is astounding: Less than 4 percent of those who graduate from Soteria's yearlong program ever return to prison—compared with South Carolina's 27 percent recidivism rate. Some of the graduates have started their own businesses in as little as three years after the end of their incarceration.

Jerry loves one-on-one engagement, connecting with individuals where they are. He focuses on providing his clients with daily structure and walking with them as they rebuild their lives. He helps people work hard and find success, knowing that the larger community respects those qualities. The men who come to Soteria often need positive father figures in their lives, and Jerry treats them like family. He gives them opportunities to tell their stories, to grow in faith, and to develop new skills. Jerry's influence is from the heart—he has the credibility of someone who has traveled the same path they have. As he says, "Regardless of where you come from, there is hope."

2

INFLUENCE GUIDED BY EMPATHY

We can all point to particular people who have been a model for our own lives. The presence of such individuals shapes the way we feel as well as the way we think; as a result, we receive direction for our desires and our beliefs. One of my uncles was such an influence when I was a pre-teen. My father's brother, Harlan, offered me a window into worlds that were different and unique. His interests in music, art, and travel directed me toward perspectives that were much broader than my early interests in math and the sciences. By welcoming me into his interests and stirring my curiosity, he shaped my thinking in critical ways.

I remember Harlan playing piano beautifully, and he would occasionally modify an arrangement to see what I thought about the result. I especially recall the emotional lift of "Autumn Leaves," as arranged by Roger Williams. Harlan would sometimes alter the tempo or add some scalar runs, and then he would ask me how it affected the mood of the song. I was enthralled by the ability of the music to affect what I felt. Moreover, I was attracted to his guidance because he appreciated my opinion and my participation. Harlan was also the one who introduced me to Stanley Kubrick's film *2001: A Space Odyssey*. Even though I was a sci-fi fan, the significance of that movie was way over my head. Harlan helped me think about its meaning and didn't act like my thoughts were immature. My world was so small in comparison to his, but he would tell me about places he had traveled and show me the curious pieces of art he had collected—some depicting people who were very different from me. Although he could have easily disregarded my interests, he instead made an effort to connect with me for my benefit. Harlan had such an influence on me that music, art, and travel became significant elements of my own adult life. He showed that he cared about my thoughts, intentions, and values, even though at the time I hardly grasped the meaning in the things he shared with me.

When Christians employ the qualities of empathy, they are more likely to facilitate inner growth in themselves and in their colleagues. This transformation of the heart is achieved by God's Spirit in concert with the individual's conviction and faith, together with commitment and obedience. Every dimension of what is called the heart—thoughts, emotions, beliefs, and desires—is altered such that the result is indeed a new person, a *new creation* (2 Corinthians 5:17). The makeover begins with new life and continues in growth toward maturity in all of those same dimensions of the heart. The path of transformation takes place in community because our progress toward becoming like Christ depends not only on the working of the Holy Spirit and our own devotion, but also on the efforts of many who provide the guidance and nurture we need. Growth occurs when people connect with each other and with the Lord Jesus in ways that influence the heart, with the necessary result that helping one another along this journey is much more than a mental exercise. The goal is connection that creates wholeness, bringing us to fullness in Christ (Colossians 2:10).

What does it mean to be connected with other people and even with God himself? In a society like ours that attempts to distinguish and disconnect our reasoning, our emotions, and our relational behaviors, how is it possible to engage our whole selves with others, especially those who seem alien to our experience? The inspiring speaker and author Brené Brown describes this kind of connection as "the energy that is created between people when they feel seen, heard, and valued; when they can give and receive without judgment."[1] When there are opportunities for encounters of the heart, people appreciate and learn from each other. In this way, we influence one another. "Connection, along with love and belonging, is why we are here, and it is what gives purpose and meaning to our lives."[2] It's important to understand how empathy creates connection in a Christian context. Empathy is a virtue, and like other virtues it can take on extreme forms. Empathy can also operate as a focal lens that will show more clearly how to cultivate greater influence. Empathy prepares us by developing godly character in ourselves and in those whom we influence.

UNDERSTANDING EMPATHY

The essential characteristic of empathy can be described as "the ability to identify with the feelings and perspectives of others . . . and to respond appropriately."[3] Empathy offers space for a person's thoughts, feelings, behaviors, intentions, and values to be fully understood and engaged in for that person's sake. It is often described as "walking in another person's shoes," but the concept entails more than trying to fit myself with my own perspectives and feelings into someone else's situation. It's a matter of looking through the other person's eyes with their viewpoint. In order to exhibit empathy toward others, we must recognize that everyone is complex and sees the world through that complexity.

Psychologists have defined *empathy* in two significant ways: (a) a cognitive awareness of the thoughts, feelings, perceptions, and intentions of another person; and (b) a vicarious emotional response corresponding to another individual's internal state. Scholars make this distinction between cognitive awareness (thoughts) and affective awareness (feelings), separating the two types of empathy into perspective-taking versus emotional-matching. However, the separation of intellectual and emotional functions may reveal more about our Western Enlightenment cultural heritage than about empathy itself. A cognitive conception of what is going on inside a person requires an emotional awareness as well as a rational analysis. An affective mirroring of someone's feelings requires some degree of discernment in order to comprehend the basis of those expressions in specific social contexts.

Marriage is one context in which both thinking and feeling come together—and often clash. My wife and I continually sort through the rational logic and the visceral emotion that accompany any number of topics as we try to discern why each of us reacts differently from the other. Although we can see that cognitive and affective aspects are both valuable, the particular "hot buttons" for a given subject often create an imbalance. Just because I think the color is blue or that my behavior was warranted doesn't mean that another person sees it the same. What we know and what we feel are often complicated in relationships because we make assumptions about each other. One of the significant aspects of this study of empathy is the intention to embrace both its emotional and rational components, along with a relational aspect that's important for an empathic response.

The confusion about cognitive and affective elements is but a part of the problem with understanding empathy. The word *empathy* is relatively new, first coined in 1909 by E. B. Titchener to describe an act of imagining what it would be like to be someone else.[4] Before this word was created, its older sibling, *sympathy*, bore some of the same meaning that's accorded to affective empathy today. In contemporary use, the two words are often contrasted, with *sympathy* viewed as an understanding of

Sympathy   **Empathy**

Popular Distinctions Between Sympathy and Empathy

someone else's emotion (without actually feeling it yourself) and *empathy* described as a visceral sharing of an emotion with someone. The popular view is that sympathy is primarily a cognitive recognition of the distressed person's condition and that empathy is a mutual sharing of the emotional condition. It's like the difference between understanding someone else's dislike for bananas—especially if I happen to like them myself—compared with understanding someone's pain from a paper cut. The first one I can acknowledge, but the second one makes me grimace. The accompanying figure represents this distinction. In such a framework, the additional term *compassion* is often used to describe a desire and a suitable action to alleviate distress or bad feelings. The definition of *empathy* I will use is a combination of all of these effects. It is a shared understanding as well as a shared feeling. In this balanced engagement between the individuals, there's great potential for valuing and supporting each other. My intention is to expand the meaning and application of empathy.

Adopting a broader scope for our understanding of empathy can help us see why empathy is important in many contexts. It's sometimes described as feeling *for* another person, but other contexts may emphasize feeling *as* the other person does or sharing an emotion along *with* them, and still others may entail a feeling produced *by association* with the other person in a particular situation.[5] These various postures of engagement make a huge difference in what is communicated between people. When someone expresses a deep concern in a group situation, there are some fairly predictable responses: One person will invariably rise up to resolve the "problem" or share a similar concern, expressing feeling *for* the concerned individual. Another participant is likely to move into proximity with the troubled person, attempting to share the feeling *as* that individual feels it. Someone else might express support and encouragement verbally in their desire to be present *with* the concerned individual. Sometimes emotion will involuntarily move the empathetic person, producing a sensation felt *by association* with the distressed individual. All of these responses are valid forms of empathy, and the appropriateness of the specific action varies with the situation.

Several contemporary authors claim that humans are hardwired for empathy, and this conclusion is usually attributed to the discovery of mirror neurons in the brain.[6] However, there is great complexity in the way empathic tasks operate across the entire brain. Although there has been scientific progress in distinguishing the areas of brain activity corresponding to affective and cognitive forms of empathy, it's still not clear whether different forms of empathy produce consistent patterns of neural activation. Furthermore, individuals do not all respond in the same way to observations of emotion in other people—especially when there are social, spatial, or temporal differences between those people. The emotion one feels may be produced by processes of imitation, imagination, recollection, or transference, and in any case the congruence and accuracy of one's emotion relative to the other person may vary. Then there's an additional layer of complexity when we consider how empathy operates between groups of people rather than between individuals. Collective practices for sharing both understanding and emotion are especially important in our era of tense, partisan communication. In order to become influential in our relationships, empathy must play a significant role.

ATTRIBUTES OF EMPATHY

Empathy is complex because it touches people deeply. When I think of someone who exhibits empathy, multiple characteristics invariably come to mind. For example, my favorite teachers in school were very attuned to the dynamics between students, but they were seldom sidetracked because they had a broad perspective and big goals for the class. They demonstrated personal humility by encouraging learning within the group, yet they persistently focused on the purpose of the classroom activities and pushed the

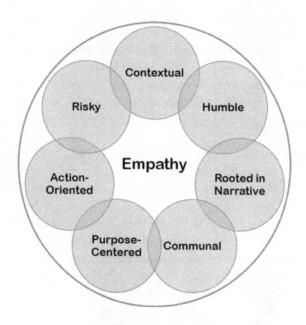

Attributes of Empathy

boundaries of our knowledge. Several important aspects of empathy are summarized in the diagram.

Empathy Is Contextual

The mutual connection of individuals, in thoughts as well as feelings, is cultivated in shared situations. Every situation requires discernment of both the events and the setting of those events. Researcher and author Karla McLaren says empathic skills help one to "understand the usually unspoken and hidden rules of social interaction so that you can respond in a socially sensitive way."[7] There can be no genuine appreciation of the other person's thoughts and feelings without a grasp of the context. It is within specific environments that we discover the wholeness we seek. Therefore, our awareness of what is happening around us is often the best starting point for developing empathy. Various exercises in mindfulness or meditation are appropriate places to begin.

A biblical example of this feature of empathy is found in Abigail, who recognized the dire circumstances her husband, Nabal, had created (1 Samuel 25). As soon as she heard that Nabal had been inhospitable and insulting to David and his army, and she realized David might annihilate her family, she took it upon herself to gather an abundance of provisions and humbly present them to David. Abigail offered to bear the guilt of the offense herself, and she appealed to David to restrain from taking vengeance. She understood what the context required in order to save her family and to persuade David to relent. From a position without authority, Abigail used contextual empathy in a powerful way to turn a bad situation into a positive outcome.

Empathy Is Humble

Throughout the history of humanity, the humble or meek person is rarely described as possessing any kind of strength or power. In fact, humility was not even regarded positively until the beginning of the Christian era. Nevertheless, God himself "adorns the humble with victory" (Psalm 149:4) and rewards them with wisdom (Proverbs 11:2). Unlike the attitude exhibited by most of the world, God stands with those who are weak and lowly, elevating them by sharing his strength.

Humility is a "willingness to hold power in service of others."[8] By devoting resources and status to others, humble people become influential. Jesus is the one who flipped the attitudes about humility upside-down, redefining the very notion of greatness (Matthew 18:1–4). He's the messianic Servant who encourages the oppressed and comforts the brokenhearted (Isaiah 61:1; Luke 4:18). His redemptive love put humility on the list of virtues from that time forward, and in his example we see humility as part of empathy.

Over a century ago, South African writer and pastor Andrew Murray described humility as being "the root of every virtue."[9] His basis for this assertion was the incarnation of Christ, which demonstrated the emptying God did for us all. This humility of God in Christ becomes our salvation because his redeeming work was accomplished for us. Therefore, a humble heart that approaches God accepts the gift of incarnation, casts off the reign of self, and lets God be all in all. When we are filled with God's Spirit rather than ourselves, we are free to be humble toward others. Empathy depends upon the humble heart, indicating to us the way we should value others above ourselves. This new understanding of meekness versus greatness helps us understand what Jesus meant when he said, "Blessed are the meek, for they will inherit the earth" (Matthew 5:5).

One time when Jesus traveled outside the Jewish territory, he encountered a Canaanite woman who interceded for her suffering daughter (Matthew 15:21–28). Jesus emphasized his priority for reaching the Jews, and in her humble acceptance of that precedence, he commended her great faith. Another notable example of humility was Jonathan, the son of King Saul, who was next in line to inherit the nation. However, Jonathan also knew that his friend David had been anointed by Samuel to become king. Jonathan loved David and made a covenant with him (1 Samuel 20:16–17), supporting David's claim to the throne above his own. Who among us has acted with humility when someone else was chosen instead of us for a prestigious role? Jonathan demonstrated empathy not only toward his friend, but also toward the God who raised up someone to be king instead of him.

Empathy Is Rooted in Narrative

The ability to empathize is based on more than an awareness of the context. It's also the result of one's attachment to a larger perspective. One of the misconceptions about empathy in our contemporary culture is the belief that it's simply a matter of individual behavior. However, empathy is about connecting people and discovering the narratives that live in and through us. The story to which I attach myself ultimately sets the course for my perception of who I am and what I will do. It also establishes the framework in which I influence people. Empathy cannot function properly without a guiding narrative—an overarching interpretive account—that calls upon the history, traditions, and culture of the group of people that seek to have a connection. Robert Bellah, a sociologist who has studied the need for connection in our society, says,

> A community is involved in retelling its story, its constitutive narrative, and in so doing, it offers examples of the men and women who have embodied and exemplified the meaning of the community. . . . The stories that make up a tradition contain conceptions of character, of what a good person is like, and of the virtues that define such character.[10]

We know what it means to be part of our community by listening to its stories and by paying attention to the character of the people in that narrative. We are naturally empathetic toward our group's stories, and when we also extend empathy toward other groups, we find ways to connect our history with theirs.

The Christian story involves empathic practices. They are particularly noticeable in the parables of Jesus that exemplify pieces of the larger story in which Jesus saw himself.

- A despised Samaritan helps an injured Jew (Luke 10:30–37), depicting Israel's role in God's plan to bring together the nations.
- A shepherd searches for a lost sheep (Matthew 18:12–13; Luke 15:3–7), demonstrating God's perseverance in rescuing his people.
- A father welcomes his wayward son and encourages his other son (Luke 15:11–32), exemplifying the grace of God in offering forgiveness and hope to everyone.
- A king sympathizes with an indebted servant, but punishes him for not extending the same grace to others (Matthew 18:23–35). God shows patience and grace to those who humble their hearts.

For believers in Christ, empathy is not merely an individual behavior, but rather an affirmation of, and a commitment to, the story of Jesus Christ and the church. This story presents Jesus empathizing with us in our weakness and offering mercy and grace.

Not all groups and societies share the same story, but all of them have some sort of guiding narrative. As philosophers and psychologists have attempted to scrutinize the meaning of empathy and theorize about the concept, some have attempted to disconnect empathy from a narrative that empowers it. They regard empathy as either an involuntary, uncontrollable feeling or as a proficiency people develop and control solely for their own benefit. However, even these notions of empathy interpret it in light of certain assumptions—particularly about individualism. Empathy may be minimized by a narrative of personal freedom and independence, but it's the high-level perspective that gives empathy such a definition. There's always a larger, interpersonal perspective on what is good for humanity that guides empathic behavior, even if it's not obvious. The Christian perspective values connection and cooperation and is based on the good news that God exhibits the attributes of empathy in his kingdom through Christ Jesus.

Empathy Is Communal

Christians have a story, and that story is shared with the community of believers. The communal structure of empathy is significant because it supplements the cognitive and affective characteristics with a *relational* aspect that transcends the individual self. This social engagement is similar to playing in a musical group. Each member has a particular part to play in harmony with the others, and each one shares in the ownership of the total result. Likewise, the apostle Paul spoke of the church operating as a body with many members exercising a variety of interrelated functions (Romans 12:3–8). This unity-in-diversity creates an environment that encourages every citizen to contribute distinct spiritual gifts to the common good rather than to presume everyone must conform or assimilate in order to be accepted. In other words, the community is more complete and capable when a broad range of people contribute themselves to its growth.

Community was important to Mordecai, the cousin and adoptive father of the main character in the book of Esther. He identified with a minority group in Persia, the Jewish exiles who didn't return to Jerusalem. Mordecai is probably best known for helping to thwart Haman's schemes against the Jewish people, but before that event he exposed a conspiracy against Emperor Xerxes, who is referred to in the Bible as Ahasuerus (Esther 2:21–23). Mordecai supported the welfare of the people in Susa and the stability of the current government because the prophet Jeremiah had earlier told the exiles to care for the places where they were sent (Jeremiah 29:7). This act of communal empathy was significant enough to the Persian administration to note it in the government records (Esther 6:1–2). Empathy in community is especially important because people are watching.

Empathy Is Purpose-Centered

Empathy has a purpose tied to its narrative. The Christian's objectives are to love God and love our neighbor. In light of empathy, the purpose can be restated as imitating Jesus Christ and seeking good for others. The apostle Paul reminded the church to "look not to your own interests, but to the interests of others" (Philippians 2:4). We exhibit empathy because our purpose is centered in Christ rather than in ourselves. Christ is the standard for our behavior, and our personal preferences do not define our ethics. We imitate Jesus, who "humbled himself and became obedient to the point of death—even death on a cross" (Philippians 2:8). A sense of purpose is what gives meaning to life, and for the Christian who asks the deep questions regarding identity and values (such as "Who am I?" and "How should I live?"), that purpose is rooted in service to the Triune God.

When the Lord summons someone, the biblical response is often, "Here I am." Abraham, Isaac, and Jacob, as well as Moses and the prophets

Samuel and Isaiah, all accepted God's purposes with these words. It's significant that a humble young woman named Mary, when she was told she would give birth to Jesus, responded in the same manner (Luke 1:38). She listened to the angel and understood that message to reveal how God's purposes were being fulfilled in her. She demonstrated empathy toward God by trusting him to accomplish his will. She didn't yet understand everything that would happen, but she allowed herself to be the means for it to happen. God's will is the ultimate basis for empathy.

Empathy Is Action-Oriented

Empathy is a choice to connect with another person both emotionally and intellectually. That choice is often a precursor to an action that reinforces the choice. Empathy requires doing things in various situations that provide necessary experience for becoming empathetic. Our prayers for growth and our choices to act with empathy result in further opportunities to exhibit empathy. By our actions we influence people, and because of our empathy we are also influenced by them. Thus, the ongoing cycle of choice and action boosts the effect of the influence. For the Christian, such actions are a response to the love of God expressed in Christ Jesus, cultivating empathic character in the same way spiritual practices develop other dispositions of character.

Moses was born at a time when the pharaoh of Egypt felt threatened by the growing population of enslaved Israelites. In order to reduce their strength, Pharaoh imposed greater burdens and ordered the Israelite baby boys to be killed (Exodus 1–2). Moses' mother laid him in a waterproof basket she placed along the bank of the Nile River. When Pharaoh's daughter came out to bathe in the river, she noticed the basket and had empathy for the child. She knew this was a Hebrew boy, and she hired the boy's mother to nurse him. Later, Pharaoh's daughter took in the boy as her own son, naming him Moses. The daughter of Pharaoh knew her father had commanded the extermination of Hebrew boys, but when she saw this particular baby, she had empathy and took action to rescue him. She then displayed further empathy by raising Moses in the royal household. Her empathy indicated the right course of action for her to take. Similarly, we may find ourselves in situations that call for assisting someone who is considered by others as undeserving of help. Empathy motivates action, and the action often provides additional opportunities for expressing empathy.

Empathy Is Risky

Opening oneself to another person requires relinquishing control. There is a risk in this sort of openness because it's for the other person's benefit, not mine. I may want something for the other person that they do not achieve. My empathy may produce a different result. There have been occasions when I as a manager listened attentively to an employee's aspirations and provided an opportunity I thought was a fitting match. Then the person struggled and stumbled. My empathy may have been influential, but it could not produce the outcome I envisioned. Even though I had the other person's interests in mind, I was not seeing the opportunity from that person's perspective. If the focus is truly on the other person, constraints on the outcome must be relinquished. This makes empathy feel messy and unpredictable, but the amount of influence I have is due to my empathic behavior, not to the outcome. The irony of personal influence is that it requires opening up oneself to the influence and control of others.

The development of empathic influence rarely moves in a single, linear direction. It's a shared growth in which people move together toward a result, and seldom is it tidy and organized. However, the riskiness of empathy can offer opportunities for influence that are otherwise unavailable, as in working with an adversary toward a win-win solution. Imagine people who are ideologically opposed joining together with a common goal. For example, consider what is necessary in the United States for the two main political parties to agree on almost anything. Even on an individual level, subjects such as abortion, gun safety laws, and property rights are almost impossible to discuss. Expressing empathy means paying attention to ideas I may not like and having regard for the person who expresses those ideas. Empathy in the presence of disagreement is often disarming and calms the conversation to a point that people can begin to understand each other. A constructive dialogue seldom happens unless empathy is present. When I am willing to step off my soapbox, my conversation partner may choose to do the same. When I am willing to explore my assumptions, my conversation partner may choose to do the same. It's only then that win-win solutions can be considered. Of course, the vulnerability of this encounter must be accompanied by certain boundaries to maintain safe and healthy differentiation with respect to the other person in order to avoid detrimental emotions or behaviors.[11] Nevertheless, the most creative solutions are usually the result of influence coming from multiple, even unexpected, directions.

After Saul encountered Jesus on the road to Damascus and became a disciple, Barnabas introduced him to the apostles in Jerusalem (Acts 9:26–30). The Christians were afraid of Saul, and after his life was threatened, he was sent home to Tarsus. After a while, the gospel spread to non-Jews in Antioch, and Barnabas recognized that the Lord was doing the very thing for which Saul had been chosen—taking the name of Christ to the Gentiles (Acts 9:15). Therefore, Barnabas went to Tarsus to get Saul—later to be called Paul—and take him to the work in Antioch (Acts 11:25–26). Barnabas had a gift for connecting people and discovering how God was using them. He took a risk with Saul and commended him to the other disciples as God's instrument for reaching the Gentiles. His empathy for Saul was risky because many of the Christians in Jerusalem did not trust Saul. Barnabas demonstrates for us how to look for what God is doing. He empathized with a believer who was not being accepted by other Christians. Barnabas risked his own reputation by encouraging someone for a mission many did not think was appropriate. When have you been called upon to risk something for a fellow believer?

Summary: Empathy as a Virtue

In all of the characteristics described above, empathy is a virtue, and this realization confirms the importance of pursuing empathic character. Moreover, the pursuit of empathy as a virtue offers us a path to learn and develop it like other virtues. It is not, as some contemporary authors suggest, an involuntary, innate behavior determined entirely by genetics or environment.

In ancient Greek culture, the term for *virtue* meant "that which causes a thing to perform its function well"—thus, human virtue would be that which enables people to live well according to their purpose.[12] It's the capacity for living life at its best—not merely as the preparation for living such a life, but as the actual living of that life. Virtues are guiding qualities that function as both a directional compass and a preparatory exercise. The underlying assumption is that such a virtuous life has a purpose, and actions—specific practices—that are aligned with the purpose produce benefits that are fulfilling for the individuals. Empathy exists as a virtue in a Christian context where the objective is to imitate Christ.

You may not see empathy appear explicitly in any list of virtues, but the essential nature of empathy is well represented in other virtuous qualities of character. The New Testament lists various virtues as the gifts of the Spirit and as the fruit of the Spirit. Descriptions of gifts and fruit that relate to empathy include love, honor, joy, hope, patience, hospitality, truthfulness, kindness, compassion, goodness, righteousness, humility, gentleness, forgiveness, self-control, peace, forbearance, and faithfulness. The supreme Christian virtue is love. Jesus Christ commanded his disciples to "love one another. Just as I have loved you, you also should love one another. By this everyone will know that you are my disciples, if you have love for one another" (John 13:34–35). Jesus's statement is consistent with God's commandment to Israel to "love your neighbor as yourself" (Leviticus 19:18), which is the basis of the so-called Golden Rule: "Do to others as you would have them do to you" (Luke 6:31). Jesus is referring to empathic acts of service, not merely to the avoidance of treating people badly. There are critics today who claim that the Golden Rule is about projecting one's own feelings and thoughts onto the needs of another person, but the admonition in the Bible expresses a deeper intention to treat others with empathic love. This manifestation of empathy is a representation of God as one who invites people to join with him and contribute their feelings, thoughts, and actions. It's a matter of relating to one's neighbor *as if* one were that person, as expressed in the rabbinic maxim, "Do not judge your fellow until you have stood in his place" (Mishnah Pirkei Avot 2:4).[13]

Empathy helps us to communicate with others on a deeper level and understand them more completely. Most people relish the satisfaction of being accepted and appreciated. When our relationships function in this manner, we accept each other and know we are accepted for who we are.

DISTORTIONS OF EMPATHY

There are unhealthy behaviors associated with empathy that must be recognized and avoided. Since empathy functions like classical virtues such as courage, temperance, and justice, it can tend toward either a positive balance or a negative extreme. The Greek philosopher Aristotle gave us our traditional understanding of virtues, and he described *virtue* as "a mean between two vices, one of which is marked by excess and the other by deficiency."[14] The most excellent, beneficial way to live a virtuous life is to exercise the characteristics of a virtue that do not stray into either an excessive embodiment or a paucity of that virtue. The human tendency is to carry a good thing too far, and our vices are usually outsized expressions of virtues. Most people desire a healthy degree of balance, despite the pressures and inclinations to adopt extreme positions.

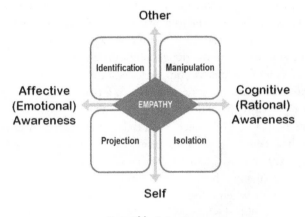

Empathic Extremes

As we consider the nature of empathy as a virtue, it's possible to imagine a two-dimensional graph that lays out the range of empathic operation. As shown in the diagram, the first axis represents the distinction between cognitive awareness (thinking) and affective awareness (feeling). Both aspects are required for empathy to be beneficial, but we often emphasize one over the other. Emotional connection alone, without appropriate discernment, can create situations in which empathy becomes biased and unrestrained. Rational judgment alone, without adequate emotion, fosters coercion and insensitivity. The second axis of empathic behavior is based on the distinction between awareness of oneself and awareness of the other person or group. A focus entirely on the self creates distance between people while excessive emphasis on the other person or group eliminates healthy boundaries. The distinction between self and other is not about being an introvert or an extrovert. It's about our awareness of ourselves and others. Both introverts and extroverts may exhibit empathy that's either balanced or distorted in one of the four extremes. You can probably imagine some of the negative results if we drift into any of the four empathic extremes. Healthy empathy consists of a balance of these qualities, and one's influence with others is greatest in that healthy state.

Identification

One of the necessary ingredients of healthy empathy is the ability to differentiate between oneself and the other party. Without a well-defined sense of self, a person tends to have an unhealthy connection with the other person or group, landing in the upper half of the empathic extremes matrix. Since the left half of the matrix emphasizes emotional responses, the upper-left quadrant represents an extreme in which a person becomes enmeshed in the other's identity. This distortion of empathy is evident when people demonstrate both a lack of choice and a lack of boundaries. A phrase that's commonly heard from them is "I have to . . .", and they find it almost impossible to say "no" to a request. People who struggle with this extreme have difficulty allowing others to work without their help. They frequently use the pronoun *we* when referring to someone's actions, as when a parent explains that "we did our homework." Many helicopter parents demonstrate this category of behavior.

The Scottish philosopher and economist Adam Smith observed over two centuries ago that there is a form of fellow-feeling that can come upon people automatically, involuntarily, and instantaneously.[15] An observer identifies so closely with another person that the observer reflexively shares the other person's emotion. As a result, the observer cannot distinguish who is feeling the emotion. The observer's lack of differentiation between *self* and *other* causes the observer to invade the space of the one who originally exhibited the emotion and form an unhealthy attachment to that person—an attachment that sacrifices one's self-definition and self-regulation. This condition has also been observed to cause fatigue and burnout in both the people who are giving care and those who are receiving it.

Manipulation

The upper-right quadrant of the empathic extremes matrix, with its emphasis on cognitive awareness and the other person, represents the capacity to grasp someone else's thoughts without any sharing of emotion. Yale psychology professor Paul Bloom argues for empathy that's strictly cognitive, but he acknowledges that it can be abused: "Successful therapists and parents have a lot of cognitive empathy, but so too do successful con men, seducers, and . . . bullies."[16] This extreme form of empathy tends to manipulate people's emotions and attitudes, and many marketing schemes follow this approach. You can spot this extreme when people appear to know your situation but ignore how you feel about it. Most of us like to be in an advisory role, but people in this category do not connect with others emotionally. They may express certainty about what's best for you. Some common phrases heard from them are, "What you need is . . ." and "Let me help you with that."

The ambitious exploitation of people is not a new phenomenon, and it has often been observed that institutions, governments, businesses, churches, and individuals behave in ways that coerce people. The ones with the power may view their actions as empathetic while the recipients may view those actions as oppressive coercion. The reason for the disconnect is that the empathy lacks affective awareness, resulting in a manipulative distortion. Even in those cases where people are being helped, a form of *toxic charity* develops when the recipients are not fully engaged in the actions on their behalf.[17]

Paulo Freire observed this phenomenon in the Brazilian educational system several decades ago. The government used the educational process to subordinate the peasants by perpetuating a colonialist class system. It was a form of manipulative empathy that appeared to help the lower classes while leaving their situation unchanged. Freire labored for the literacy of the poor, which was necessary in order for them to be eligible to vote and increase their self-dignity.[18] His ideas were largely ignored in the United States, where the educational system has continued to divide students into economic and racial classes. The influential Christian recognizes that empathy can be used negatively to manipulate people, so we must be aware of how our best efforts might unintentionally perpetuate the disadvantages some people experience.

Isolation

The lower half of the empathic extremes matrix emphasizes the self over all others. When thinking takes precedence over feeling, the condition is sometimes manifested as a *passive empathy* that removes itself from responsible action toward other people. In the lower-right quadrant of the diagram, emotions and diversity both carry negative connotations. People in this category may care about those who are close or similar to them, but they don't reach out very far. They tend to exhibit stoic and strictly rational behaviors, responding defensively to many encounters. People who constantly explain themselves and correct others may fall into this category. Teachers who operate in this way usually focus on dispensing knowledge rather than paying attention to the needs of the learners. I'm reminded of the image of a university class in which the material was transferred from the teacher's notes to the student's notes without passing through the mind of either. The teacher may be concerned with the success of the students but not with building any sort of relationship with them.

Developing empathy and influence requires a capacity for attentive compassion that is impossible when maintaining an emotional distance. Since a strictly intellectual understanding of empathy cannot fully engage others, it ultimately isolates the individual from the potential benefits of deep personal relationships. Furthermore, whenever there is fearful suspicion or a power dynamic between people, empathy may be pushed toward the lower-right quadrant of the matrix. For example, White people sometimes assume the prerogative of judging the validity of concerns expressed by people of color—without appreciating the reality of those concerns. Powerful people—of a higher social class, more educated, with greater wealth, with more prestige—tend to pay less attention to social contexts and the need for perspective-taking. Isolated people are often more inspired by themselves than by others because they have few connections with others.

Projection

The popular author Stephen Covey tells a story about someone going to an optometrist for help with eye problems. The doctor listens to the complaint and then takes off his own glasses and hands them to the patient. He says he has worn this pair of glasses for ten years and they have helped him tremendously. Of course, the patient's vision is not improved, but the doctor insists the glasses work great and the problem must be that the patient is not trying hard enough.[19]

People who function in the lower-left quadrant of the matrix emphasize emotional responses and ignore the distinctiveness of the other person's circumstances. They tend to assume the other person feels as they would in a similar situation. This preference for our own perspective or a familiar viewpoint is a form of projection psychologists refer to as *in-group bias*. Projection is a distortion of empathy that focuses only on our own conditions and thereby distorts our judgments regarding what other people are doing and the choices they are making. Furthermore, when we project our own thoughts and feelings rather than understanding what a person is going through, we tend to ignore the extent to which our assumptions and actions may contribute to making the other person's situation worse. When I'm only focused on my own feelings rather than the other person's difficulties, I'm likely to say or do things that hurt rather than help that person. People operating in this category are likely to be heard projecting their own feelings onto others: "I know just how you feel." They may offer their own similar experiences, but these stories can be easily perceived as an attempt to *outdo* or *one-up* the other person.

When we project our own feelings, thoughts, biases, and preconceptions onto others, we assume that they should behave as we would—that they are working with the same resources and networks we have. We may be trying to "walk in their shoes," but we are merely wearing their shoes without comprehending what their situation is like for them. That person has a different perspective, and we are in danger of projecting our own attitudes, fears, and desires. This is why there's a tendency to blame victims for their adversity rather than recognize the effects of social, economic, or cultural factors. Furthermore, psychologists have observed that the unpleasant characteristics we project onto others are often the negative traits we dislike in ourselves. As a result, we who teach and preach are apt to emphasize the problems we ourselves face as individuals. Coaches, educators, and health professionals also have a tendency to assume that their own experience and knowledge will enlighten and strengthen everyone, regardless of differences. We may think we are looking through other people's eyes, but that's not entirely possible. What we can do is appreciate and respect the perspectives we hear from others—especially when those perspectives differ from our own. Healthy empathy consists of listening and supporting other people in their situations without imposing ourselves upon them.

Summary

In order to understand the distinctions among these four categories of empathic extremes, let's consider how some known characters exhibit these observable traits. For example, in the *Peanuts* comic strip created by Charles Schulz, the humor is often developed by contrasting the perspectives of some diverse personalities.[20] Charlie Brown is perhaps the least stable emotionally, and he's persistently anxious about what others think of him. As evidenced in the perennial gag with him trying to kick a football that Lucy withdraws, Charlie Brown cannot set healthy boundaries for others' behavior; thus, he's an excellent example of *identification*. Lucy van Pelt also exercises an awareness of others, but it informs her assessments and actions rather than her emotions. It's no accident that she is cast in the role of psychologist, because successful therapists strongly exhibit cognitive empathy. In her case, this trait is also evident in her bullying and presumption, and it's what makes her an example of *manipulation*. The character Schroeder is attractive to Lucy, perhaps because he's also a thinking, rational individual. However, he is much more focused on his own desires and preferences—especially the music of Beethoven—than on hers. Schroeder does not see himself as responsible for the friendship with Lucy, and for this reason he represents *isolation*. One of the interesting relationships between characters is the attraction Peppermint Patty has for Charlie Brown. Her image of him is largely fabricated in her own mind, as demonstrated by her calling him "Chuck." In this way, she does not differentiate between her reality and his reality. Her extreme version of empathy is *projection*. So, is there a *Peanuts* character who expresses healthy empathy? The one whose insecurity is most obvious (his attachment to his blanket) appears to be the most well-adjusted. Linus van Pelt, Lucy's brother with the security blanket, shows concern for both his own well-being and the needs of others. And despite his youth, Linus often exhibits the most mature blend of intellectual and emotional perspectives. The revised diagram illustrates how these characters align with the empathic extremes matrix we used earlier.

The four quadrants of the matrix are all distortions of healthy empathy, and most speakers or authors who oppose the use of empathic behaviors are reacting to these unhealthy manifestations. Virtuous empathy is found in a balance of cognitive and affective awareness as well as a balance between one's sense of self and a sense of the other party. I have not addressed the possibility of behaving *without* empathy, because I agree with Karla McLaren that such a condition—psychopathy or sociopathy—is relatively

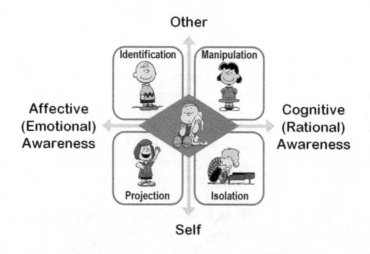

Other

Identification   Manipulation

Affective (Emotional) Awareness ← → **Cognitive (Rational) Awareness**

Projection   Isolation

Self

Peanuts **Characters Exemplifying the Range of Empathy**

rare. Many of those who have been labeled as low-empathy may be either coping with hypersensitivity, such as people on the autism spectrum, or exhibiting some of the unhealthy extremes that have been presented here.[21]

One of the benefits of viewing empathy as a virtue is that this perspective helps us understand the deceptive nature of distorted empathy. Seldom are individuals aware of the level of their empathy or how far they are from a healthy, centered empathy. Although a full examination of the means to achieve a wholesome balance is outside the scope of this study, I'll make a few suggestions about movement from the extremities of the matrix toward the center. Movement in a *cognitive* direction from the *affective* side of the matrix toward the center requires learning what others are actually thinking—not just feeling—about their own behavior. In the reverse direction, movement from the *cognitive* side of the matrix toward the center occurs as a result of building or improving relationships in such a way that we're more engaged with the actual feelings—not just the ones we make up in our heads—accompanying others' behaviors. On the vertical axis of the matrix, moving out of the region of *self* toward the center, in the direction of the *other*, requires that we humbly accept responsibility for our own actions, thoughts, and emotions. Then we must find ways to make the other person or group more familiar to us. Those who wish to move away from an extreme identification with the *other*, toward the center and toward *self*, must learn to reflect critically on personal relationships and establish boundaries that differentiate *self* from the *other*. Later chapters will expand on these brief recommendations to describe some helpful skills related to practices guided by the virtue of empathy. In the next section, I will explain how empathy can act as a guide.

EMPATHY AS A FOCAL CONCEPT

I'm an amateur photographer, and because my wife and I enjoy hiking, my camera work is mostly outdoors, where lighting is often a challenge. Although most cameras provide sufficient options to accommodate a variety of conditions, I occasionally need some additional help in setting up the desired scene. Specialized lenses and filters offer a means for modifying the view captured by the camera. For example, a polarizing lens allows only light rays traveling in one direction to enter the camera, thus reducing the reflections from normally scattered light. I can then view and photograph my intended subject in a controlled context that prioritizes the direction of light. As a result, the images are sharper and not hampered by glare.

Similarly, it's possible to consider a subject like influence in a way that prioritizes a specific concept like empathy. The lens used to examine the subject constrains the perspective so that certain attributes of the image are either heightened or diminished. Assuming that the lens does not distort the veracity of the image, we would expect particular aspects of the subject to be highlighted in a way that an unfiltered view might not reveal.

Any virtue can be used as a lens to view a given subject. As an example, consider how a court of law depends on the virtue of *justice* as a lens that reveals what is most significant about the case at hand. As each witness is cross-examined, the jury, the attorneys, and the judge are measuring the stories being told by any evidence of justice. I've served on a few juries, and I've observed that the focus on justice is often muddled by the attorneys' objectives and by the jurors' personal experiences. We usually think we are examining the evidence objectively and can determine innocence versus guilt, but the jury only gets to see the evidence and explanations presented to them—filtered through the attorneys' selective presentations and their own past experiences. The defendant and the plaintiff often have very different perspectives on the same event, and each attorney suggests a particular way of seeing it.

As another example, consider how the virtue of *mercy* acts as a focal concept in the observance of Jubilee (Leviticus 25:8–55). Although justice, obedience, and inheritance were common themes associated with the celebration, the messianic focus of Jubilee is on mercy (Isaiah 61:1–3). By directing the practices of Jubilee toward mercy, the elimination of sin, debt, and enslavement became concrete forms of forgiveness and liberation. Eventual freedom from the pressing bondage of evil and death was conceivable in the small personal steps any individual could take. Jesus emphasized the freedom of the people and the land rather than the supposed rights of the wealthy. The example of the biblical Jubilee highlights the importance of the narrative and purpose behind the understanding of mercy. No group other than Israel has attempted such an embodiment of mercy because God's people have a unique story.

In the Christian context, the ultimate picture of empathy as a virtue is the incarnation of Jesus Christ. God becoming human is the definitive picture of what is meant by *being with* people. Immanuel—"God with us"—is the foremost image of empathy (Isaiah 7:14; Matthew 1:23). The coming of Jesus communicated God's plan directly and clearly. God demonstrated that he intimately identifies with humanity. When empathy is the lens on Christian activity, the narrative behind the activity becomes evident: The incarnation of Christ is revealed in practices that emphasize God's purpose for humanity. The lens focuses on the way the cross of Christ changes people's lives. As a result, we see more than simply the people and the situations around us; we also see the effects of the Holy Spirit making Christ visible. Christ gives an identity to the church that's driven by God's purposes rather than secular motivations that commoditize performance and results.

In order to examine the nature of influence in the Christian context, we will view it in light of the virtue of empathy—specifically as evidenced in the incarnation of Christ and the presence of the Holy Spirit in the church community. This approach will help us understand better how the heart of a Christian is shaped by empathic practices.

EMPATHY AND INFLUENCE

Someone who demonstrated significant empathic influence in my life was my professor of Hebrew at Erskine Theological Seminary. I pursued a Master of Divinity after retiring from my telecommunications career, and Dr. Terry Eves taught several Old Testament language courses. I listened in awe as he lovingly spoke about biblical characters and events, relating their situations to both ancient and modern contexts. Terry was someone who expressed genuine interest in the concerns, beliefs, and desires of both his students and his fellow faculty. He often devoted time to helping his students grow spiritually as perceptive interpreters of the Bible. His skills of listening and reflection guided me to explore my own relationship with difficult texts and with many situations calling for biblical wisdom. His warm, empathic concern shaped the manner in which I approach people today. With his guidance, I came to appreciate the complex reality that God had placed his Word in the hands of humanity, much as God had entrusted the incarnation of his Son to the world. Terry's love for the Word and his commitment to his students were contagious, and to this day in every class I teach, I consciously carry *with me*—as an incarnation of empathy—the image of his influence.

A person's inner character—what I'm calling *heart*—is an accumulation of habits that produces and is eventually guided by certain dispositions or virtues. Tom Lickona speaks as both an educator and a psychologist when he writes, "Character matters—in every sphere of society. . . . At the end of the day, the most important measure of a society is not its economic wealth, its technological genius, or its military might; it is the character of its people."[22] The essence of empathic influence consists of connecting hearts together in an environment of shared character development. Influential Christians are engaging themselves with others and connecting other people together. There are many ways in which people exercise influence, but they all are based on the ability of people to connect to the character of other people. The connection assumes a narrative (in this case, the Christian story) and is made effective through practices that align us and give us purpose. The necessary learning process for developing empathic skills requires concrete, repetitive exercises of interacting with God, community, and individuals.

New habits and experiences are physically possible because the brain has a neuroplasticity that enables the pathways for thoughts and memories to change. Moreover, changes in behavior are spiritually possible because we have assistance from our Creator. Just as we become healthier when in communication with people, so also we discover peace and fullness in contact with the Lord. Our actions shape our thinking and feeling, and our personal relationships help direct those actions. The empathic practices we adopt are vital for our mental and physical well-being, as well as for the health of the relationships we have with others.

Empathy as a virtue can be learned by imitating Christ and his follow-ers, directed by God's Spirit. Stanley Hauerwas, theologian and professor of ethics at Duke University, maintains that the help we need is available in Christ: "Christian virtue is not so much initiated action but response to a love relation with God in Christ."[23] We are formed in the image of Christ as both God's gift and our calling. Explaining God's empathy in the fifth century, Cyril of Alexandria described Christ as "blending Himself, as it were, with our nature . . . in order that . . . He might enable man to share and partake of the Nature of God."[24] Christians develop the virtue of empathy by engaging in various practices of imitating Christ, who embod-ies the empathy of God.

In this chapter, I have examined the nature of empathic behaviors and how they operate. I've described empathy as the capacity to identify with the feelings and perspectives of another person to such an extent that the individual feels understood and affirmed. Such an activity creates a safe and respectful environment for sharing thoughts, feelings, behaviors, intentions, and values. The importance of understanding empathy as a virtue is that we can view it as an element of a larger narrative related to God's love. Empa-thy can be used as an effective lens for revealing God's ongoing story in the lives of the people whom we support and encourage. In the ministries of the church, the virtue of empathy gives precedence to the incarnation of God's Son in every encounter. The central purpose of becoming an influ-ence is the same as God's purpose for humanity: *Immanuel*—God with us.

QUESTIONS FOR GROUP DISCUSSION

A good way to introduce a group to the subject of empathy is to read and discuss the parables in Luke 15. Also read Philippians 2 and discuss how our empathy toward others is an imitation of what Jesus Christ did for us.

1. Why do you suppose God's new creation requires transformation of the heart?
2. What is empathy? What are some different ways people define it?
3. Describe some of the pros and cons of "walking in another person's shoes."
4. How does the context of an encounter affect the way you interact with a person?
5. What are some of the stories (family, culture, Bible, etc.) that have shaped your identity?
6. What happens when you open yourself up to others? What happens when others open themselves up to you?
7. What are some examples of emphasizing either rational, cognitive judgment or emotional, affective connection in an unbalanced way?
8. How aware of others are you? What is it like to tune in to their feelings? How does it affect you to discern their thoughts?
9. What are some limits on how open or vulnerable you are willing to be?
10. What are some situations in which people have power over you? When do you have power over other people?
11. Which character in the *Peanuts* comic strip are you most like? Explain why you relate to this character.
12. How does it help you to know that Christ is *Immanuel* ("God with us")?

PEOPLE TOGETHER SERVING DAILY
(PTSD) FOR GOD

David Nardone served in the Marine Corps for sixteen years. During that time he developed post-traumatic stress disorder and tried to deal with it in unhealthy ways. He sought help for substance abuse while still in the military, and after his discharge he received additional assistance to address his anger issues related to PTSD. The Department of Veterans Affairs and Upstate Warrior Solution both offered him support and encouraged him to reach out to other veterans. In 2016, David launched Fellow Countrymen, a nonprofit organization that provides shelter for veterans experiencing homelessness. He began with two beds in a donated facility, serving thirteen veterans during a two-year period. God used David's efforts to rebuild struggling lives. Working together with United Housing Connections in Greenville, South Carolina, Fellow Countrymen expanded to a capacity of ten beds in 2019. Federal funding for pandemic-related assistance provided opportunities for further expansion in 2020.

David values honesty, transparency, and humility, and he tries to encourage other veterans to also develop those qualities. He admits he doesn't have things all figured out: "There's no way to really explain how to serve homeless people in a quick and easy [way]. . . . You've got to have empathy; you've got to have compassion." He appreciates working with people who are willing to let God's Spirit guide them. For several years, he worked one-on-one with disadvantaged veterans to arrange housing, counseling, and jobs. As David helped them, he recognized in their behavior the person he had once been, and he knew how to support them and direct them into counseling. David hopes that people will see his willingness to serve God as inspiration to get closer to the Lord. He says, "I'm only here to try to lead you by example in serving the Lord."

David is inspired every day with a mission to serve God and other people. He is thankful for his family's support in his recovery. He praises the Lord for providing every resource he and his clients have needed. In early 2019, David realized he was again being called to step out in faith because the needs were greater than he could personally handle. His passion to help more people was beginning to overwhelm him, so he added staff to create a small leadership team. He believes that clients trust his organization because it is Christ's ministry, "a team put together by [Christ] to do his work." David has realized the way to battle post-traumatic stress disorder is with another kind of PTSD: People Together Serving Daily.

3

INFLUENCE FORMED
THROUGH PRACTICES

When the lens of empathy is held up to the various activities encompassed by the ministries in the church, which aspects come into view in a significant way? The church has often understood its influence as being manifested in particular forms of teaching, including preaching, Bible classes, liturgy, catechisms, and the affirmation of confessional statements. Do these express the full range of Christian influence, or is there more? This chapter begins with an examination of how influence is based on a combination of learning and teaching, followed by some scrutiny of Christian practices. In this context, I pose the question of whether influence is expressed and cultivated in spiritual practices. The result of this study consists of two spiritual practices that highlight the qualities of empathy.

Although traditional teaching methods have been a primary means for influencing people, there are significant limitations. I grew up thinking of teaching as an assigned role given to an individual for the limited purpose of facilitating a forum for the transfer of information. When I have been in that role myself, I felt the burden of being expected to be proficient in my knowledge and flawless in my presentation. Perhaps such expectations have contributed to the current environment in which relatively few people seek roles as nonprofessional teachers—even in the church. Maybe we resist the idea of teaching being a gift. It's a gift that was difficult for me to accept. Yet I know God's Spirit helps us in special ways. Teaching is a serious endeavor that's not to be taken lightly (1 Timothy 4:16), but Jesus encouraged all of his disciples to be *like him* as a teacher (Matthew 10:25). Everyone is an influence and therefore teaches others. The author of the book of Hebrews laments that the entire church has missed opportunities to be teachers (Hebrews 5:12). Only Christ is the true teacher, and everyone else learns from him and imitates him (Matthew 23:8–10). Therefore, we must understand the dynamic between teaching and learning—the correlation between teachers and learners—so that we can clarify who in the church should be regarded as an influencer and what that role entails.

The biblical concept of learning is grounded in knowing and respecting the Lord God (Deuteronomy 10:12–13). This is the basis of wisdom. The principle of learning from the Lord and embodying his instruction is prominent in the Psalms. There is delight in learning and obeying God's ordinances in order to declare them in the presence of others (Psalm 119:79, 171–175). God is the source of all truth, and the role of the learner in the Judeo-Christian context has been not only to accept instruction but also to pass it on to others—to children, to fellow Jews or Christians, to foreigners and outsiders, and even to all the world. A key aspect of learning is to be able to embody and communicate what is received.

Greek culture after the Classical Period (fifth and fourth centuries B.C.) largely adopted Plato's idea that learning primarily consists of recollection. Knowledge was thought to be a process of drawing upon the intrinsic contents of our memories, rather than the acquisition of new concepts. However, most Jewish and Christian writers have described learning as a process of receiving instruction, gaining familiarity, and appropriating knowledge through experience or practice. Jewish wisdom literature declared that learning must precede speech or teaching (Sirach 18:19), and most people learned about Jesus and about God's plan in the context of group meetings (Acts 16:13–15). A Christian's transformation is achieved in relationship with the Triune God and with people who demonstrate practices that reflect Christ. Therefore, a Christian teacher might be anyone who appreciates and engages with those who are learning. The process of learning emphasizes that the Lord provides the message and entrusts people to represent the implications of that message.

Empathy is fundamentally relational because it is a means of identifying with people's feelings, thoughts, and perspectives. Therefore, empathy as our lens highlights God's story operating in the intersecting lives of people. Jesus is with us, and we are with each other. Father Gregory Boyle, who ministers to gang members in Los Angeles, is fond of saying, "The strategy of Jesus is not centered in taking the right stand on issues, but rather in standing in the right place—with the outcast and those relegated to the margins."[1] Jesus's identity as Immanuel—God with us—reveals the empathic behaviors that help develop Christian character and influence.

UNDERSTANDING PRACTICES

Practices form a significant part of every cooperative human endeavor. Sometimes we call them disciplines, and sometimes we call them exercises. For example, there are business practices, mindfulness exercises, healthy disciplines, and ordinary daily routines. These activities range from mundane tasks to obscure sacramental rituals, and many lists of them are available. I will emphasize spiritual practices, which I will define more concretely after examining three possible perspectives.

The first perspective considers Christian practices as *socially meaningful, independent actions* that create space for theological reflection in the midst of ordinary routines. Without relying too heavily on traditional norms, individual practitioners are empowered to discover ways to feel connected to community and to engage in something that transcends themselves. Some examples include humanitarian relief efforts, participation in social movements, and fund-raising for specific causes. The second perspective draws directly from ancient spiritual disciplines and exercises in which people engage for the purpose of *drawing nearer to what is sacred*. The authority of particular institutions, such as monastic groups, lends dignity and integrity to spiritual exercises that have long been central to church life. In this case, spirituality depends on communal expressions of sacramental activity. Religious practices such as eucharistic and baptismal rituals are in this category, along with specific approaches to pursuing holiness. The third perspective focuses on *communal development of solidarity and mutual benefit*. Moral and political philosopher Alasdair MacIntyre defines social practices in the context of human virtues.[2] They are activities that connect a person with the purposes of a larger ethical community and its structures. Craig Dykstra, a senior fellow in Leadership Education at Duke University Divinity School, emphasizes the spiritual benefits of communal practices. He describes the practices of the Christian faith as "habitations of the Spirit" because they create a space for experiencing the presence of God:

> They are not, finally, activities we do to make something spiritual happen in our lives. Nor are they duties we undertake to be obedient to God. Rather, they are patterns of communal action that create openings in our lives where the grace, mercy, and presence of God may be made known to us. They are places where the power of God is experienced. In the end, these are not ultimately our practices but forms of participation in the practice of God.[3]

This final perspective on practices includes the Christian community participating in the life of God. The Lord empowers people with the presence of his Spirit, and spiritual practices prepare people for encountering his presence.

This examination of influence anchors Christian practices in the relationship with Christ, connecting a person with the immanent presence and power of the Holy Spirit. The relationship with God's Spirit makes the practices spiritual. By this definition, spiritual practices affect believers in the following ways: establishing their identity, demonstrating their identity, and blessing their identity. For example, practices of prayer, submission, and baptism are a participation with God in his redemption as he forms us in his image. Practices of worship and singing demonstrate the Christian's devotion and gratitude to God. Practices of meditation and reading Scripture provide blessings of illumination and comfort. We engage with God and with other people in ways that make us new, visible, and valued. Regarding such practices, theologian and author Richard Foster asserts in his widely acclaimed book, *Celebration of Discipline,* that "the inner attitude of the heart is far more crucial than the mechanics for coming into the reality of the spiritual life. . . . [Practices] allow us to place ourselves before God so that he can transform us."[4] The apostle Paul encouraged the church in Rome "to present your bodies as a living sacrifice, holy and acceptable to God, which is your spiritual worship" (Romans 12:1). As we commune with God and with each other, we are strengthened and equipped to live sacrificial lives.

UNDERSTANDING INFLUENCE

The influential Christian is someone who connects hearts together. In some cases I connect myself with others, and sometimes other people connect with each other because of my influence. The result is a web of connectivity shaped by many people beyond those who are my closest contacts. First, think about the people with whom you feel deeply connected. For me, that would be my wife and a few close friends. Then consider how these people are closely connected with others due to your influence. One person shares with another the depth of their dependency on God, and the Spirit of God may then be invited to also work in the other person's life. As spiritual practices draw us into the heart of God and our empathy draws us close to other people, our influence nurtures new and deeper relationships. In order to understand how influence functions, we will look at some scriptural considerations, some contemporary perspectives, and a few unexpected twists in the Bible.

Biblical Perspectives

In the New Testament letter to the Ephesians, Paul helps us see how influence germinates and grows in the church (3:16–19):

> I pray that, according to the riches of his glory, he may grant that you may be strengthened in your inner being with power through his Spirit, and that Christ may dwell in your hearts through faith, as you are being rooted and grounded in love. I pray that you may have the power to comprehend, with all the saints, what is the breadth and length and height and depth, and to know the love of Christ that surpasses knowledge, so that you may be filled with all the fullness of God.

Paul's objective in reaching out to these Christians is to strengthen them— so that each might be supported "in your inner being." This terminology is echoed by Peter when he refers to the "inner self" in 1 Peter 3:4 (ESV)—which can also be translated "the hidden person of the heart." Both apostles are describing the person's inner character that is shaped and guided by God's Spirit. Paul is praying that their character will be grounded in love, empowered by the Holy Spirit, and filled with the love of Christ and God's abundance. Since he's writing to Christians here, Paul is not praying for their conversion; he's praying that they may become mature, embracing all that God wants them to be. This is the sort of preparation necessary for Christians to develop influential, godly character, and it's the ultimate objective for the practices we want to pursue.

Let's ponder for a moment how Paul led people into this glorious relationship with God. In his explanation to the Ephesian church, he emphasized that the blessing is granted by God through his Spirit and that it happens as they are "grounded in love . . . with all the saints." Paul regarded them as already special, calling them "saints"—meaning "holy ones." Therefore, their practices mostly consisted of infusing their relationships with greater love. In his letter to the church in Corinth, Paul explained to the church how love works (1 Corinthians 13): Love is not only the supreme virtue—it exhibits empathy in all situations toward all people. We are all connected by love. In chapter 12 of the same letter, Paul uses the human body as his model for this connection. The body has many members and many functions empowered by a diverse assortment of spiritual gifts, but it is nevertheless one body and it is Christ's body.

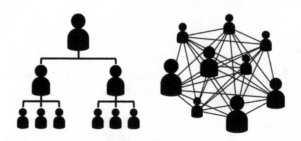

Hierarchical and Non-Hierarchical Networks

The parts of the body—the church working together as a unit—learn from each other how to grow and what it means to steadfastly stay connected to Christ. Notice how this works in hierarchical versus non-hierarchical networks. When one person is in control, all instruction, communication, and influence is relative to that individual. But in a non-hierarchical network, every participant has access to all the other members. The church as conceived in the New Testament is mostly non-hierarchical, but Christ is the central focus, and every member of the church interacts with each other as well as with him. In fact, the church is the body of Christ, so Jesus Christ is *the entire network*, not just the top position. The Son of God is the primary source of influence, and everyone else supports all the members of the network.

Contemporary Perspectives

One of the popular ways to understand influence is found in the classic DiSC personality assessment.[5] This tool is used to discuss people's behavioral differences. Teams can learn how to work together better by understanding the members' motivations, communication needs, and approaches to dealing with conflict. Four primary strengths are identified: Dominance, Influence, Steadiness, and Conscientiousness. In this context, influence refers to a strong inclination toward openness, collaboration, enthusiasm, and relationships. These are excellent descriptors of some key aspects of personality, and all four of the DiSC categories are capable of exhibiting influence by connecting people's hearts together.

Individuals who exhibit strengths in the Dominance style behavior may appear to show a lack of concern for others, but they enjoy challenges and are often willing to take risks and initiate change. They bring people together and offer new opportunities. The Influence style of behavior is motivated by relationships and values free expression among the members of a group. As leaders, they tend to be supportive, helping others quickly belong to the group. However, they may lack enough structure to sustain their influence. People who are mostly in the Steadiness category are usually driven to seek stability in their situations, and they are deliberate in pursuing collaborative goals. They may appear to avoid change, but their influence comes from their awareness of others and their good listening skills. Finally, those who excel in Conscientiousness place a priority on planning and accuracy. As leaders they may seem overly critical toward others, but they usually work creatively toward clear, diplomatic solutions. Their influence is often a result of how their objectivity and reliability benefit others.

All four of these categories include people who can be influential in the lives of others. Their differences lie in how they achieve and sustain connections between people. Also, since an individual's profile of DiSC categories can change with time and situations, it's important to be aware that a shifting environment can affect one's behavior and influence. For example, my profile is quite different in relaxed conditions than it is in stressful conditions. This is a good tool for observing how influence works across personality differences, but it doesn't provide a sufficient road map for attaining or sustaining influence. For that we need our lens of empathy.

Another fashionable depiction of influence appeared several years ago as a circle within another circle.[6] The inner circle represents the range of things one can possibly affect, such as where to live, what to buy, and what to read. The outer circle encompasses all of those issues that affect one's life but lie outside of one's control, like the weather, national politics, the economy, professional sports, world events, and most peers. One version of this model adds an innermost circle of control, making a distinction between direct effects and indirect effects. Regardless of which version of the model I use, when I'm functioning within my circle of influence or control, my language is positive, affirming, and solution-oriented. However, whenever I focus mostly on my circle of concern, my language will tend to be blaming, accusing, and reactive. As I am proactive in regard to my own influence, my behavior impacts more people in positive ways, and the capacity of the inner circle may increase. However, if I persist in being reactive, the circle of influence may diminish. As in the previous paragraph, this is a tool for observation rather than a guide for how to develop my

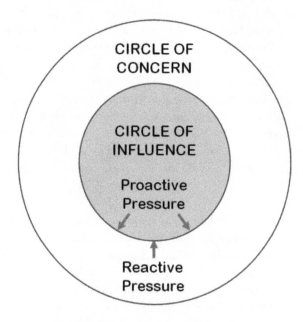

Circle of Influence

circle of influence. Empathic practices that develop new and deeper relationships can extend the circle of influence.

Some Surprises

Using empathy to focus on the nature of influence reveals three unexpected results when we look at the New Testament. These surprises have to do with the concept of schooling, the perception of leaders as a select group, and the terminology we use. First, Jesus did not establish a school in the sense that we consider places of learning today. Educator and theologian Robert Banks points out, "It was not *preparation* of the Twelve *for* mission that was uppermost in his mind, but *engagement* of the Twelve *in* mission."[7] Jesus's goal for his disciples was not solely to make them teachers; he sought to develop their spiritual character so they would exhibit the presence of

Christ and the Spirit in their lives and pass their transformative learning on to others. Even though schools and teachers were familiar concepts among the scribes in the first century, neither Jesus nor the apostles used that model for growing the kingdom. Jesus's relationship with his disciples was expressed through hospitality, prayer, sharing meals, sharing ministry, and caring for those in need. Jesus focused on practical life applications and experiences. The apostle Paul recognized himself as a teacher, but he saw himself as a servant of the gospel (Colossians 1:23) and he described his work as a ministry of reconciliation (2 Corinthians 5:18–19). He was mainly interested in the *pattern of influence* that helped people mature in Christ. The early church's practices emphasized building relationships for the purpose of joining people to Christ.

A second unexpected result of looking at the empathic aspects of guiding others is that practices of relationship are often conducted by those who have no official position. While it is true today that pastors, shepherds, missionaries, worship leaders, and congregational staff are responsible for many of the processes in the church, the New Testament model for church leadership has very little hierarchy. A larger variety of disciples conducted the ministries of the early church. When there was a particular need, people were identified to address that need (Acts 6:1–6). Pastoral leaders were not authoritarians, but examples for the congregation to imitate. In reality, the entire church should be equipped for ministry, requiring that leadership roles be distributed among the church members. Will Willimon, a well-known preacher, author, professor, and former bishop in the United Methodist Church, recommends that pastors "give away ministry to the laity and sit loose on the organizational reins of the church in order to foster lay initiative and empowerment."[8] A significant feature of empathic influence is the sharing of leadership between clergy and laity, between shepherds and sheep, between men and women, between old and young, and between people who embody other human differences. As a result, all Christians are encouraged to become mediators of God's grace and truth. This shift in the nature of church leadership requires greater attention to the calling each believer experiences from God, which includes discernment of God's gifts and each person's sensitivities. Not everyone is called to teach in the traditional sense, but everyone has a responsibility to represent Christ to others. The practices of influence we are looking for are those that nurture the shared responsibility we have for and with each other.

A third unexpected result of viewing influence through the lens of empathy involves semantics. The range of biblical terminology usually associated with teaching is more about instruction than connecting people, and empathic connection is instead expressed with the term *compassion*. Paul refers to the Christians' "compassion and sympathy" (Philippians 2:1) with the first term emphasizing gut-level, affective concern and the second emphasizing cognitive concern. Paul tells them they should have the same love and the same mind as Christ (2:2), which means that their presence should exhibit the very heart of Christ. Furthermore, the church is to be a place where each member dwells in safety and humility with the others, seeking the growth and blessings of one another (2:3–4). When the end goal of an activity is *loving* people rather than merely teaching them, that activity is a genuine spiritual practice of influence. Our Lord transforms us and enables us to give ourselves to one another. (2:5–13).

Identity and Integrity

Paul's letter to the Philippian church describes practices of identity and integrity that are key to influential character. The identity of the Christian is bound to Jesus Christ, and we have the same mind as our Lord (Philippians 2:5–13). As he offered himself humbly for others, so our attachment to him is exemplified in regarding others above ourselves. Similarly, the integrity, or wholeness, of the Christian is evidenced in the way life is structured around Christ. We work out our salvation knowing God is working in us. His power changes us as we devote our lives to him. Therefore, we can be blameless and innocent even in the midst of a corrupt and selfish society. Paul says we "shine like stars in the world" when we cling persistently to Christ (2:15). Author and educator Parker Palmer explains further how these qualities work: "*Identity* lies in the intersection of the diverse forces that make up my life, and *integrity* lies in relating to those forces in ways that bring me wholeness and life rather than fragmentation and death."[9]

My identity is formed in community with those whom I embrace, and it reflects my choices regarding the people whom I want to imitate. There are various groups I associate with, and my identity may be formed in any or all of them. Oftentimes we are surprised that one group has influenced our sense of self more than others we thought we valued. For example, does our affinity for a group devoted to sports or politics set our priorities at odds with Christian ideals? We tend to talk about people and things we value, whether it's the new boat, a recent award, a project team, the long-awaited trip, family events, or a Christian ministry. Those areas of life that we desire others to know about us may indicate some significant aspects of our identity.

Integrity is a bit different from identity, but it is nevertheless formed in community. Integrity is reflected in the collection of people who embrace me, and the individuals who support me usually do so because they are drawn to something I represent. However, they are not all drawn to the same aspect of my character because my own identity is based upon multiple influences in my life. Thus, the broader group presents me with a mirror of all that I value and promote. They may not be the same as I am, but their association with me is due to the sort of integrity they see in me. We seldom talk about the things that constitute integrity because our assumptions about ourselves and others often go unexamined. However, by observing what people generally expect from me, I can judge through their eyes what I appear to stand for. Whereas my identity lifts up those whom I value, my integrity reflects that which others value in my life.

The image of lifting up one another challenges most traditional norms of teaching and influencing—even in the church. Paulo Freire observed, in a context charged with racial inequities and politico-economic tensions, that education is much more effective when our identity and integrity are shaped by love, respect, and reconciliation:

> It is fundamental for us to know that without certain qualities or virtues, such as a generous loving heart, respect for others, tolerance, humility, a joyful disposition, love of life, openness to what is new, a disposition to welcome change, perseverance in the struggle, a refusal of determinism, a spirit of hope, and openness to justice, progressive pedagogical practice is not possible. It is something that the merely scientific, technical mind cannot accomplish.[10]

A desire for mutual enrichment among diverse people creates new possibilities for growth that surpass the limits of simple knowledge transfer. The ways we walk together, share together, and construct meaning together take many forms, including prayer, instruction, worship, hospitality, recreation, service, and sharing Scripture. Therefore, as I describe two specific spiritual practices of building influential character, it's important to remember they are not unique and distinct from other Christian practices.

In the following sections, I will describe two practices that follow the pattern of mutual enrichment with specific attention to the formation of identity and integrity. They are summarized in the accompanying diagram. A practice of *formative presence* highlights the incarnational nature of the Christian's role and identity, and a practice of *resilient trust* establishes a framework for building and sustaining integrity. Both of these are genuine spiritual practices because they are patterns of communal action in which

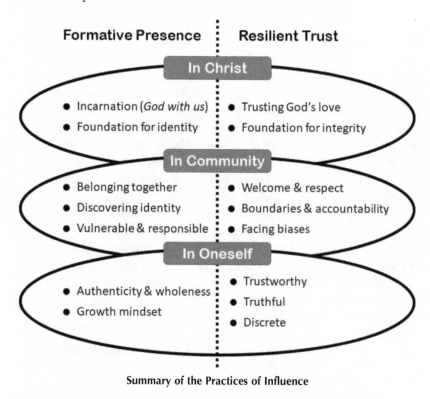

Formative Presence ⋮ Resilient Trust

In Christ

- Incarnation (*God with us*) ⋮ ● Trusting God's love
- Foundation for identity ⋮ ● Foundation for integrity

In Community

- Belonging together ⋮ ● Welcome & respect
- Discovering identity ⋮ ● Boundaries & accountability
- Vulnerable & responsible ⋮ ● Facing biases

In Oneself

- Authenticity & wholeness ⋮ ● Trustworthy
- Growth mindset ⋮ ● Truthful
    ⋮ ● Discrete

Summary of the Practices of Influence

the benefits of God's presence and power are made available to us. My objective in discussing these specific forms of influence is to understand some skills that help every Christian develop empathy.

THE PRACTICE OF FORMATIVE PRESENCE

Our definitive example of empathy is the incarnation of Jesus Christ. The sort of connection we want to have with people is exemplified by the Son of God, who "became flesh and lived among us" (John 1:14). When Nicodemus the Pharisee came to consult with Jesus (John 3:2), he said, "Rabbi, we know that you are a teacher who has come from God; for no one can do these signs that you do apart from the presence of God." To be in the presence of Jesus is to be in the presence of God, the most holy place.

God's presence is formative because he creates and he redeems. He changes our identity and makes us new. His presence in us allows our influence on others also to be formative. Because we are in Christ, we seek to imitate Jesus, following the guidance of the Spirit. In order to represent

Christ, we must pay attention to him, to his message for us, and to the people around us. We must know *whose* we are as well as *who* we are in order to re-present what he has already shown us. In order for the practice to be formative, we need to be with people and connect with them. Each of us is both a formative agent for others and the one being formed by others. This connection with others—happening in the presence of the Lord—is what makes our influence effective.

In his famous psalm of contrition, David pleaded with God to remain present, restoring to him the joy of salvation and the desire to obey, so that David might teach others about God's ways (Psalm 51:11–13). David perceived God's presence in the sheer joy of the relationship and in the guidance he received from God's Spirit. God's presence was welcomed, and it was feared. It's a place for listening (Acts 10:33) and also for speaking (2 Corinthians 2:17). God revealed the essence of his presence to Moses with the proclamation in Exodus 34:6–7,

> The LORD, the LORD, a God merciful and gracious, slow to anger, and abounding in steadfast love and faithfulness, keeping steadfast love for the thousandth generation, forgiving iniquity and transgression and sin, yet by no means clearing the guilty, but visiting the iniquity of the parents upon the children and the children's children, to the third and the fourth generation.

When people encounter the Triune God, it's a life-changing event. This is a *formative presence*. Being in close proximity to the Most High transforms our identity. Jesus's presence was likewise formative, as seen on the road to Emmaus (Luke 24:13–35). After an extended conversation, the disciples shared a meal and a prayer that opened their eyes to Jesus's presence. Moreover, Jesus did not leave his disciples alone, but he sent the Holy Spirit to provide them with truthful guidance. This same Spirit still exhibits God's presence in believers today, equipping, guiding, strengthening, and advocating for us.

When I was an engineering project manager in a major telecommunications company, I helped many product designers complete their projects in a timely manner. Sometimes I would notice a person tense up as I approached. I recognized that my attitude and posture set the tone of the discussion; when I was relaxed, the conversation was much calmer. Also, the conversation would be smoother when I chose to shelve my desire to get data and instead focused on the worker's perspective—finding out more about her interests and frustrations, even including events outside the job environment. I received the information I needed without creating anxiety. It's much better to open with "What's happening?" than with "Are you finished yet?" Most workers are already concerned about doing their assignments well and don't need additional pressure. The main thing they need is the assurance that managers and other leaders are willing to support them. I am present with people when I am *with them* and *for them* rather than only representing my own agenda.

William Kahn, an organizational psychologist known as the "father of employee engagement," provides some helpful research regarding the way people occupy the roles they are in, and he demonstrates what it means to be fully present with another person.[11] Kahn identified three psychological factors that determine whether people will engage themselves in their role: (1) the *meaningfulness* of the interaction with fellow workers and the sense of identity they derive from the work; (2) the emotional *safety* of involvement due to the personal relationships, the group dynamics, and the prevailing norms; and (3) the *availability* of personal resources one can offer without being overburdened. Personal presence is formative when the connections between people—regardless of their roles or relationships—emphasize their value, their well-being, and their ability to contribute.

Educational consultants Laura Weaver and Mark Wilding describe five practical dimensions of engaged teaching useful for developing skills of influence.[12] The five dimensions constitute some of the most significant aspects of a practice of formative presence:

- *Cultivating an open heart* refers to the capacity to demonstrate compassion, authenticity, and vulnerability toward others.
- *Engaging the self-observer* means developing a capacity for self-awareness so that one's own thoughts and behaviors are observed and reflected upon.
- *Being present* refers to being alert and relaxed in the moment in order to effectively engage with others.
- *Establishing respectful boundaries* refers to taking responsibility for oneself and one's role with an intention to clearly define and communicate the limits of engagement.
- *Developing emotional capacity* is a matter of enhancing emotional intelligence and emotional boundaries in order to improve the overall well-being of the participants.

These dimensions are significant factors in our relationships. Our presence influences people in formative ways when we are sufficiently connected with Christ, with the people we influence, and with our own identity.

Identity in Christ

The practice of formative presence underscores the importance of belonging to Christ, the one who reveals God to us and to the world. God is the one who first demonstrated in the incarnation of Christ how presence functions, so we must first attend to our identity in Christ. God's practices of faithfulness, justice, and reconciliation, exercised through his Spirit, initiate the patterns we follow. The Spirit transforms us, and we understand God's presence through the Spirit dwelling in and with us. Our lives demonstrate that we believe God is ultimately in charge and deserves our allegiance more than authorities in the world.

There have been times when I knew God was at the helm of my life. Toward the end of my career in telecommunications engineering, the company started downsizing, and I was on the list of people to go. Office politics drove the decision, so there was little opportunity for negotiation within that environment. As tempting as it was to participate in the local head games, I made a conscious decision to look instead for God's plan, and he led me to focus my energies on supporting the team members who would continue the project in my absence. Most of my peers expected me to simply walk away from my responsibilities, but I continued to be an advocate for the project team, and I managed to procure some necessary resources. That got some attention because I focused on the team's benefit rather than my own. I still had to find another job, but in the meantime I had some influence because I chose to represent my identity in Christ.

When Jesus announced his mission, he framed it in the context of both Scripture and the local worshiping community in his hometown. There were no great fanfares, public announcements, or major productions—just an ordinary Sabbath reading in a rural synagogue. He was handed a scroll, and in his reading (Luke 4:18–19), he quoted from the book of Isaiah:

> The Spirit of the Lord is upon me, because he has anointed me to bring good news to the poor. He has sent me to proclaim release to the captives and recovery of sight to the blind, to let the oppressed go free, to proclaim the year of the Lord's favor.

It's no wonder the hearers were amazed. The carpenter's son was announcing the fulfillment of Jubilee! Here was the mission Jesus established for himself—to change the world in humble, personal ways by his influential presence alone. Many people did not believe it was possible then, and many still don't believe it today. Even John the Baptist and his disciples were perplexed, so Jesus told them that "the blind receive their sight, the lame walk, the lepers are cleansed, the deaf hear, the dead are raised, the poor have good news brought to them" (Luke 7:22; compare Isaiah 35:5–6). The apostle Paul understood Jesus's mission as one of reconciliation, restoring people to God and to each other, despite the apparent impossibility of such claims. This is the mission that informs our practices: God's people are a formative presence in the world because God is healing and reconciling relationships using his people's words, emotions, and actions.

Identity in Community

When Father Gregory Boyle asked for Mother Teresa's diagnosis of the world's problems, she replied that we have "forgotten that we belong to each other."[13] People want to *belong*. Meaningfulness is usually found in togetherness. The Christian community invites people into relationship with a purpose: God is making the world new. Author and theologian Henri Nouwen points out, "We are not primarily for each other but for God. . . . Therefore, the Christian community is not a closed circle of people embracing each other, but a forward-moving group of companions bound together by [God's] voice asking for their attention."[14] Nouwen struggled personally with finding purpose and connection to Christ, resulting in his move from a tenured position at Harvard to become the pastor for L'Arche Daybreak in Toronto, helping the community of people with disabilities. In his own vulnerability, he found his identity in working with a community of vulnerable people. His love for the residents was formative for them, and the presence of a few residents was formative for Nouwen. A Christian who practices formative presence emphasizes the value of God's presence making people's identity new by being connected to Christ.

Paul's relationships with Titus and Timothy illustrate how formative presence works in community. Titus worked as a fellow brother, much like the connection between apprentice and master. Timothy was more like a son to Paul than an apprentice, so the relationship may have been deeper than with Titus. The training Paul gave both of them concentrated on real situations in ministry. Paul sent them out to churches where their presence would benefit the congregations and also their own spiritual growth.

Paul describes Timothy's preparation for ministry in terms of several significant aspects of formative presence. Paul focused on nourishing him by faith and sound teaching (1 Timothy 4:6). Paul encouraged him to exercise godliness because it has potential for benefiting both the present life and the life to come (4:7–8). Paul told him that "the things you must insist on and teach" (4:11) included setting an example by Timothy's own speech and conduct, exemplifying love, faith, and purity (4:12). Timothy supplemented his personal behavior with the *reading*, the *exhorting*, and the *teaching* (4:13). The second term, *exhorting* (also used in Hebrews 13:22), refers to the presentation of a message that inspires and strengthens. The role of the third component, *teaching*, is to establish the message in the hearts of the listeners. Timothy cultivates these acts of preparation in two ways: His conduct flows from the spiritual gift given to him, and he gives himself to carefully pursue godly conduct. The result will be the salvation of both Timothy and his hearers (1 Timothy 4:16). Paul's approach to training Timothy focuses on godliness in both proclamation (the words spoken) and embodiment (the conduct exhibited).

An important part of being a formative presence is learning with other people in community. Indeed, there would be no place for teaching if there were no learning. The influencer is first a learner and then progresses into a role of motivating others to develop and express their own comprehension of the subject. Anyone who influences another person has an especially significant function in guiding a learner on a spiritual journey. The influencer brings something to the preparation that's not already there, something that's a gift to the recipient, transcending the subject material. In other words, the gift of teaching is much more than a gift the teacher receives; it's also a gift of grace the teacher *offers*.[15] The role of the influencer is often to function metaphorically as a midwife, to help learners bring forth and nurture new ideas.

The communities in which we learn and practice formative presence include our neighborhood, our family, our church, our school, our workplace, our friends, our volunteer groups, and specific affinity groups that focus on sports, education, entertainment, politics, exercise, etc. The practice of formative presence is incarnational by nature, which assumes an embodied presence, but the pandemic-related anxieties of 2020 caused many gatherings to become disembodied. The available internet technologies have opened up many virtual opportunities for community, but online engagement presents several challenges. I have observed that videoconference sessions require more planning and attention by the leader, often requiring a technical expert as co-leader. A significant challenge for the facilitator is to avoid the temptation of slipping into a traditional pastor-dominated or lecture-oriented teaching method. Practicing formative presence in an online context requires openness to every participant's needs while moderating the flow of discussion so that everyone has near-equal voice. Sal Khan, an educator and the founder of Khan Academy virtual learning, observes that the most effective online leaders make themselves available to learners in smaller, more informal sessions.[16] The key to spiritual formation in any kind of community is to offer one's complete attention to and full support for others.

Identity formed in community includes both an open heart and respectful boundaries, two of the five dimensions of engaged teaching. These characteristics form a paradoxical pairing of vulnerability and responsibility. Paul introduced a similar conundrum when he told the church to "bear one another's burdens" (Galatians 6:2) but that "all must carry their own loads" (6:5). Without healthy boundaries, our hearts will be overwhelmed and will eventually shut out relationships. God designed us to love each other while maintaining our own wholeness, and that requires our identities to be both connected and distinct.

When my wife and I moved to South Carolina after having worked in the Northeast for many years, we were amazed at how naturally transparent many of the longtime South Carolina residents are. There are many opportunities to be a presence for the benefit of someone else. For example, I've been in line at a store and heard the person next to me share a list of personal medical concerns. My responsibility in a situation like this is to hold the other individual's burden carefully with my presence. What makes my presence formative is giving them space to grow while also being willing to grow along with them.

Identity in Oneself

Most of us who are teachers hope our students will bring their *whole selves* to class, which means we as leaders must be willing to do the same. The extent to which we are open with others depends on our own personal wholeness and vulnerability (the *emotional capacity* dimension of engaged teaching). Our ability to be authentic with others begins with how we relate to ourselves regarding our presumptions about race, gender, age, class, wealth, education, and sexual orientation. As we allow ourselves to be known, we begin to truly know ourselves, and our world enlarges.

Our identity—our concept of self—profoundly affects everything in our lives. Jesus said that the way we view our lives may be more important than anything in the whole world (Matthew 16:26). In particular, one's attitude toward change and growth will determine how one perceives success and failure, learning and achievement, leadership and followership, conflict and reconciliation. Carol Dweck, professor of psychology at Stanford University, asserts that everyone has adopted one of two mindsets—a *fixed mindset* that believes our qualities are carved in stone, or a *growth mindset* that believes our characteristics can be cultivated and changed. Explaining how accurately each type assesses itself, Dweck says,

> If, like those with the growth mindset, you believe you can develop yourself, then you're open to accurate information about your current abilities, even if it's unflattering. . . . However, if everything is either good news or bad news about your precious traits—as it is with fixed-mindset people—distortion almost inevitably enters the picture. Some outcomes are magnified, others are explained away, and before you know it you don't know yourself at all.[17]

The practice of formative presence presumes that we expect growth and change—in ourselves as well as others. None of us is a finished product. The apostle Paul told Timothy that everyone would see his progress, but it would require Timothy to pay close attention to his practices (1 Timothy 4:15–16). Thus he would become a self-observer (one of the five dimensions of engaged teaching).

Challenges to Formative Presence

The practice of formative presence is an approach to empathic influence that engages our relationships with God, community, and self. The important focus of the practice is growing in the life we have in Christ, enabled by the Spirit of God. In order for the practice to yield good fruit, certain distractions should be avoided. Significant obstacles arise when we give excessive attention to our *fears* and our *results*.

Those who influence others know their practice entails change, and change causes people to face their fears. There are deep awakenings, startling discoveries, difficult decisions, and conflicts over fundamental beliefs. Leaders are seldom prepared for the questions, worries, and accusations that engaged group interaction often precipitates. Fear comes upon us when we feel like our responsibility, integrity, or security is on the line. Fear of exposure, failure, or shame can weaken our courage to take risks. In our fearfulness, our ability to be fully present is diminished, and that, in turn, makes our formative practice less effective. The antidote to fear is love. "There is no fear in love, but perfect love casts out fear" (1 John 4:18). Parker Palmer, the well-known educator, suggests that teachers have opportunities to mitigate fear by reclaiming the connectedness fear destroys:

> Each time I walk into a classroom, I can choose the place within myself from which my teaching will come, just as I can choose the place within

my students toward which my teaching will be aimed. I need not teach from a fearful place: I can teach from curiosity or hope or empathy or honesty, places that are as real within me as are my fears. I can have fear, but I need not be fear—if I am willing to stand someplace else in my inner landscape.[18]

A second obstacle to formative presence is that church growth is often regarded as a competition for improving membership statistics and results. It's easy to get distracted from the objective of spiritual transformation to focus instead on how many people are being added to the rolls. When education becomes a means for perpetuating the status quo or for manipulating an outcome, even spiritual disciplines can turn into ways to address and repair problems instead of approaching God. Ironically, an emphasis on measured outcomes via standardized testing is considered a best practice in many school systems. Similarly, churches often use teaching materials that are promoted for building membership results. However, formative presence is not about putting bodies in chairs or creating a production line, but rather, it is about getting hearts engaged and connected. When we observe educational authority distancing itself from the learners themselves, the solution is to reconnect with people. Jesus is our primary example of formative, incarnate presence, and he found ways to connect with the lowliest people in society. As Father Gregory Boyle explains,

> Jesus was not a man *for* others. He was one *with* others. There is a world of difference in that. Jesus didn't seek the rights of lepers. He *touched* the leper even before he got around to curing him. He didn't champion the cause of the outcast. He *was* the outcast. He didn't fight for improved conditions for the prisoner. He simply said, "I was in prison."[19]

A practice of formative presence encompasses those actions that make Christ known and accessible to those who need his touch. Such behavior may or may not be evangelistic, but it will look like Jesus. Regardless of the context, we will demonstrate the characteristics of empathy by opening our hearts while respecting the complexity of other people and their situations. We learn to be completely present with others for their benefit. In an educational environment, listening takes priority over talking. In a professional situation, another employee's idea may be more important than our own. In a church setting, leadership emerges from unexpected quarters. Every instance is different, but our presence consistently reflects Christ. As we exercise habits in which we call upon the Holy Spirit to change people and situations, we ourselves are formed into examples of empathic character.

THE PRACTICE OF RESILIENT TRUST

The previous section described the practice of formative presence, which develops *identity* in the church community. This section will introduce a practice aimed at cultivating *integrity*. Integrity means *wholeness*, and as Palmer says, "By choosing integrity, I become more whole, but wholeness does not mean perfection. It means becoming more real by acknowledging the whole of who I am."[20] Integrity is an important concept in Hebrew wisdom literature, and the specific Hebrew word refers to purity, innocence, or completeness. The Hebrew word *shalom* is used in similar ways, often with a broader connotation of wholeness, well-being, and peace. The opening verses of Psalm 26 connect integrity with wholehearted trust and confidence in God:

> Vindicate me, O LORD, for I have walked in my integrity, and I have trusted in the LORD without wavering. Prove me, O LORD, and try me; test my heart and mind. For your steadfast love is before my eyes, and I walk in faithfulness to you. (vv. 1–3)

A practice of resilient trust is a representation of God's dependability as expressed through our behavior. It's a steadfast commitment to truthfulness and love in order to imitate Christ and increase solidarity with people. This sort of trust is a mutual interdependence with others that consists of much more than simple transactions. Trust means making yourself vulnerable to another person or group in such a way that their actions potentially expose your relationship to risk or uncertainty.

In one of her popular presentations, author and speaker Brené Brown examines the "anatomy of trust," which she also refers to as the "BRAVING Inventory":[21]

- *Boundaries:* Respecting personal boundaries and being willing to say no; asking about what is acceptable when it's not clear.
- *Reliability:* Doing what we say we will do; being honest about competencies and limitations so we can deliver on our commitments and balance our priorities.
- *Accountability:* Taking responsibility for mistakes, apologizing, and making restitution.
- *Vault:* Keeping personal information confidential and not sharing inappropriately.

- *Integrity:* Choosing courage rather than comfort; practicing values rather than merely professing them.
- *Nonjudgment:* Having conversations without judgment; being honest and open about needs, thoughts, and feelings.
- *Generosity:* Interpreting the intentions, words, and actions of others with the utmost grace.

Brown also explains that trust develops as an accumulation over time of small instances of reciprocal vulnerability. Trust and vulnerability depend on each other and either grow together or fall together. This practice of trust requires ongoing support and renewal as everyone occasionally fails or disappoints. The resilience of this trust is about finding healthy ways to integrate disappointing, trust-damaging experiences into our lives—not merely enduring them or expecting to return to some reality that no longer exists, but instead establishing a direction for the future.[22] In the following paragraphs, I will explore how we develop resilient trust in Christ, in community, and in ourselves. Some of the challenges associated with this practice will also be exposed. The various elements listed above in Brown's BRAVING Inventory will help us identify some key empathic skills.

Integrity in Christ

In defining the Christian life, author and priest Brennan Manning wrote that "the supreme need in most of our lives is often the most overlooked—namely, the need for an uncompromising trust in the love of God."[23] A quick scan through the book of Psalms reveals the inescapable faithfulness of God, and his faithfulness makes him trustworthy. Christ, too, was faithful, so he is worthy of our trust (Hebrews 3:1–6). Our trust—our faith—is how we as receivers relate to God as the giver. Yale University professor and theologian Miroslav Volf refers to this faith as "empty hands held open for God to fill."[24] My faithfulness is imperfect, so I'm never wholly trustworthy in the way Christ is. My hope in Christ's redemption works together with my faith to shape my trust in God.

Some contemporary descriptions of trust suggest that people must be competent—sufficiently capable of handling whatever is entrusted to them—in order to be trusted. However, people are not fully competent in their faith and are nonetheless expected by God to be trustworthy. In spite of our personal failures and our uncertain situations, we can choose to behave in ways that develop trust. When I am honest about what I am going to do and I take responsibility for my mistakes and failures, then I am displaying reliability and accountability (the second and third terms in the BRAVING Inventory).

The times in which we live seem to be increasingly changeable, and we often face the question of how to trust the Lord despite our imperfect faith. As one who directs an educational program in the church, I often ponder how we Christians can show influential trust in Christ when our faith feels weak. I think the biblical answer involves "walking on the water" to Jesus when it seems irrational to do so. Everything in me cries out to get back in the boat, but Jesus just wants me to take a step. For example, I was preaching a series one time on the life of the patriarch Jacob, but when I came to the story of rape in Genesis 34, I didn't feel adequate for the task. I prayed for a way to bypass that chapter, but the answer I heard was to proceed. I prefaced the sermon by telling the congregation I was trusting the Holy Spirit to help me deliver this lesson. I knew I was not in a position to speak for Dinah, so I simply presented what I thought might be her perspective, since none of her words are recorded in the passage. As a result, the Spirit spoke mightily to the congregation about those who have no voice. Practicing resilient trust means letting the Holy Spirit demonstrate what he can do without us hijacking the outcome.

Does God trust us? Despite the fact that people aren't completely trustworthy, God has extended his favor and entrusted his message to people. Jesus told his disciples a parable about some slaves entrusted with the property of their master (Matthew 25:14–30). The slaves who were deemed trustworthy were the ones who did something with what they were given, but the amount of success they achieved was not the only factor. They did not all have the same capabilities or resources, and the only one who was found untrustworthy was the one who withdrew in fear, doing nothing with what the master invested in him. The master rewarded the slaves based on how they responded to being entrusted with something of value. God's resilient trust surpasses our transgressions, and that's our model for extending trust to others. King David knew that his meager attempts to trust God were met by God's love and forgiveness: "Steadfast love surrounds those who trust in the LORD" (Psalm 32:10).

Integrity in Community

Trustworthiness is modeled by welcoming, hearing, and respecting others as they express truth. Two specific individuals have modeled for me what a welcoming, trusting community looks like, and my spiritual walk has been an attempt to imitate their example. As I began my career in engineering,

I moved to New Jersey and looked for a church near my new home. I selected the first one I wanted to visit, and in the parking lot of the Whippany Church of Christ that Sunday, John Donelik greeted me and escorted me into the building. He took a particular interest in me and introduced me to everyone. By the time I left, I had signed up to serve the following Sunday and never had the opportunity to visit another church. My fiancée (now my wife) was perplexed that I had settled on a church without her input, but I connected with the group before I knew what had happened. They had entrusted me as a newcomer with responsibility I'd neither earned nor expected. That level of trust in strangers can create lasting bonds. We worshiped with that congregation for twenty-eight years, and we also embraced the same attitude of accepting guests as family.

The second model of confident, inspiring welcome that shaped my practices of faith was a gentleman I met under circumstances reminiscent of Mr. Donelik. My wife and I were considering a move from New Jersey to South Carolina, and as part of our search for a good location to live, we intended to visit several churches. The first one we visited in Greenville was Northeast Church of Christ (later to become Holland Park Church), and we were greeted and invited to lunch by Herb and Pat Smith. They were gracious hosts, and they were enthusiastic about the church. Herb joked with us that if we drank the local water, we would return and possibly move there. We were so enthralled with the beautiful area and the wonderful people that we decided to make the move. Herb wasn't at all surprised when he saw us again. We learned from Herb and Pat to trust the Lord to bring us into contact with people who are looking for spiritual family. We have now been with this same church family for over fifteen years.

A community of trust is built upon truthfulness (listed as *integrity* in the BRAVING Inventory). The apostle Paul encouraged the churches to "speak the truth to our neighbors, for we are members of one another" (Ephesians 4:25). The Holy Spirit is the one who guides us into truth, so a practice of resilient trust relies upon the Spirit to develop integrity in the community. Where relationships are built upon truthfulness, there's no need to express blame or shame because we do not conceal the truth about our own failures. As we practice trust and integrity, we demonstrate our love for the Lord and his impact on our lives.

Everyone who engages in the practice of resilient trust will encounter the tension between speaking truth and hearing truth. It's much easier to proclaim what you think is right than it is to listen attentively to the truth in what someone else is saying. With humility we learn that none of us has a monopoly on the truth—none of us should exercise leverage over another person.

Whenever a power dynamic is present, there's a tendency to try to control and manipulate people. However, respectful trust consists of exercising power and authority *with* other people rather than exerting dominance over them. Your authority is enhanced when you give it away to others. Also, when more people share authority, they are empowered together to greater things than one person can accomplish. We can share leadership by actively listening to others graciously and generously. A good listener helps others articulate their messages and gain clarity about their problems. Father Boyle says, "The essence of our credibility lies not in our rescuing or saving the poor but rather by humbly surrendering to their leadership and listening to them."[25] We can speak with integrity when we allow and welcome questions and critique from others as we seek to create a space where we accept and follow truth together.

One of the most significant aspects of building trust in a community is the first item in Brown's BRAVING Inventory: the recognition of boundaries. Whenever there are relationships, there are interactions between people that foster or diminish the cohesion of that group. Boundaries establish how the relationships are open to new people and ideas, and boundaries also close off particular directions and connections. Nouwen makes this point: "An intimate relationship between people not only asks for mutual openness but also for mutual respectful protection of each other's uniqueness."[26] The trusting environment guards each person's safety and privacy so that the challenges of being a member of the group are not overwhelming, embarrassing, or harmful.

An online community exercises resilient trust when the participants extend grace to each other and present themselves with respectfulness and integrity. I have observed by conducting videoconference sessions that most participants are respectful of everyone's boundaries, and the physical distancing makes it a little easier to discuss boundaries. Participants are usually considerate of each other's privacy and well-being, despite the security concerns associated with social media. However, there are some who abuse this trust by imposing their own agenda or disrupting a meeting with objectionable material. Therefore, online hosts of meetings, seminars, studies, and discussions must be vigilant in protecting community boundaries and holding people accountable (the third item in the BRAVING Inventory) while simultaneously welcoming mutual sharing and growth.

The ability of a group to change is limited by what the group is willing to discuss. There are norms and expectations that everyone shares explicitly, but there are also areas that are not addressed—assumptions, blind spots, and taboo subjects. The character of a group and its members is shaped both by what is acceptable to talk about and by what is agreed upon by the group to leave unsaid. For example, our larger society struggles with naming and discussing racism, sexism, ableism, ageism, and classism. In smaller settings, problems like managing money in a family or changing a church's worship style become topics of gossip because they are publicly dismissed. Discussing such topics requires people to trust God and each other. The practice of resilient trust opens up new spaces for dialogue, using truthfulness as a means to develop integrity.

Integrity in Oneself

After considering the importance of truthfulness for a community that practices mutual trust, we should reflect on the importance of individual truthfulness. When I'm not completely honest with myself about the reasons for my behavior, I usually end up justifying myself at all costs and creating a big blind spot. In order to avoid embarrassment, I must then blame someone else for the situation produced by my behavior, even though it was my own lack of truthfulness that started the mess. The path to integrity and influence is to recognize that blame can be a symptom of my attempt to avoid personal responsibility.[27] Practicing resilient trust eliminates an environment of blame.

The influential Christian is attentive to truth. Palmer maintains that we are to approach truthfulness with a heart of obedience, which means "to listen with a discerning ear and respond faithfully to the personal implications of what one has heard."[28] Obedience to truth presumes a relationship with the source of the truth. A key aspect of obedience is openness, which is a matter of removing our own barriers and clutter so that we can hear others without judgment. Just as God respects our "yes" and "no," we must respond to him and to each other with integrity (Matthew 5:37).

A trustworthy individual consistently treats personal matters with the utmost confidentiality (the *vault* in Brown's BRAVING Inventory). Respectful discretion is perhaps one of the most significant components of building trust, and it begins and ends with the individual. We must be transparent with our own lives and protect the privacy of others. We become trustworthy by valuing other people—especially when they choose to hold back parts of themselves.

Challenges to Resilient Trust

Trust can be developed, and it can be destroyed. The practice of resilient trust emphasizes the commitment to continue imitating Christ and to work toward building community despite the negative forces that diminish trust.

One of the challenges to sustaining this practice is the weakness of our own faith. Trust naturally deteriorates when we lack faith in God, in others, or in ourselves. Since community is built upon trusting relationships, it's our faith that prevents our withdrawal from the environment in which integrity is formed. Without faith, we are more likely to expect criticism and rejection, and faithless leaders who approach people with suspicion or fear often become self-defensive and self-protective rather than transparent and influential.

A second challenge arises when some of the people in a group are unable to trust others. Certain wounds, fears, and experiences of shame induce a persistent suspicion that no one can be trusted, deeply inhibiting personal expressions of vulnerability. People who cannot trust do not engage with others, even with those who might help lift them out of their condition. Instead, they may focus on either striving for self-sufficiency or withdrawing into their suffering. Nouwen suggests that helping people who are hurting requires connecting with them attentively in their specific situations. He says,

> No one can help anyone without becoming involved, without entering with his whole person into the painful situation, without taking the risk of becoming hurt, wounded or even destroyed in the process. The beginning and the end of all Christian leadership is to give your life for others.[29]

Nouwen recognizes that there is a risk of being hurt when one gets involved with another in a painful situation. In such cases, small steps of empathy and love may be the only path to building trust between individuals.

A third challenge originates in people's assumptions about their own capabilities. Most of us have a high opinion of our own integrity and would like others to trust us completely. I've encountered many individuals who presume that their position or credentials make them automatically trustworthy. Consequently, the need to actively build trust is ignored. In the gospel of Mark, there's an example of this obstacle when the disciples took for granted their own credibility and power to heal people. This may be a lesson about their need to trust Jesus, but it is also a lesson about becoming trustworthy in the eyes of the people. The disciples were unable to heal a young boy and were instead arguing with the scribes (Mark 9:14–29). The combativeness of the crowd indicates that they had lost trust in the disciples. Jesus resolved the problem, not by arguing with the crowd, but by persuading the child's father to trust him. Later, Jesus explained to the disciples that they were hindered by their lack of prayer. Prayer demonstrates trust in God. Their prayer would also have involved the crowd in asking God for the child's healing. By focusing on God, the disciples could have built trust with the people. Likewise, our dependence on the Lord puts us in a position to be considered trustworthy.

Each of these challenges comes as a result of automatically accepting certain assumptions, believing there's no alternative. Our responsibility is to move out of the fixed mindset that there's little we can do about creating trust and instead pursue the growth mindset that Christ helps us become trustworthy. Resilient trust is rewarding but not easy. Deep relationships require attention and effort.

When people come together and develop more than superficial relationships, the interactions are often unstable for a time while trust is developed within the group. As people discover their identities and roles relative to the group, their union becomes more fruitful than the sum of the individuals. However, the early stages of relationship can be a vulnerable time, when the members of the group either find ways to resolve their conflicts or they progress no further. It's a fallacy to hope that a group will not have to deal with differences and disagreements. Every thriving married couple knows that conflicts must be addressed rather than ignored. Relationships require a foundation of trust and a commitment to resilience.

The practice of resilient trust is our representation of how God trusts us. We are fully committed to both truthfulness and love. We demonstrate the characteristics of empathy by approaching people humbly and generously while respecting truth and confidentiality. We hold ourselves accountable for the benefit of others. In an educational environment, there is no partiality. In a professional situation, we follow through on our promises despite the cost. In a church setting, we choose courage over comfort. Every instance is different, but our reliability consistently honors Christ. As we increase our solidarity with people, the integrity of our character is developed in that community.

EMPATHIC SKILLS

The two practices described here—formative presence and resilient trust—come together to create a space for humility and generosity, qualities necessary for developing the engagement and respect needed to address systemic blind spots. One of the weaknesses in my own perspective is my assumption that others need my help rather than my encouragement. I would rather give advice or assistance than listen and encourage. A while ago I volunteered to help a local Support Circle, which is a program designed to encourage an individual to build up his or her capacity to make a life change.[30] The principle behind the circles is that intentional friendships enable people to have the strength to stay off of drugs, to pursue better employment, to find housing, to address an economic problem, or to deal with a bad relationship. Good influences and behaviors can improve a bad environment. Five of us were assigned to support a young woman who was struggling to avoid homelessness. Our role was to figure out how to be a positive influence without taking over her burdens. This was a challenge for all five of us. We had to learn to trust her to handle her own difficult circumstances with God's help. We prayed and we encouraged and we learned that presence is formative when it's offered for the other person's benefit. We could connect to her heart by listening to her and urging her to work through the difficulties. There were mistakes and false starts, but she reached some goals and made improvements. I witnessed firsthand that when we share our hearts with each other (without the usual buzz of activity to make something happen), people discover sources of strength. God works wonders when I stop trying to control the situation.

Love made truthfully plain is contagious. The story was told by Fred Rogers (of *Mister Rogers' Neighborhood*) that when Margaret McFarland, professor of child psychology at the University of Pittsburgh, wanted to introduce little children to the work of a sculptor, she told the artist, "I don't want you to teach sculpting. All I want you to do is to love clay in front of the children." As a result of the sculptor *loving* his clay in front of the children, they caught his enthusiasm for the art.[31] The greatest influence for love is someone who expresses it.

Windell Rodgers is an example of someone who demonstrates love. He pastors Greater Mount Calvary Baptist Church, located in a community that was once the home of the largest textile mill in Greenville County, South Carolina. Now the area has a diverse mix of ethnic groups and is experiencing an economic and cultural transformation due to gentrification. In the midst of this changing environment, Windell models the practices of formative presence and resilient trust. He stands in solidarity with the surrounding community and builds a sense of integrity by publicly recognizing the children's educational successes. He says his approach to reaching across social barriers is simple: Treat others as we like to be treated ourselves.

Windell values mutual respect and transparency between people. In order to grow together, we must make efforts to see each other and to allow people to see who we are. Windell suggests that we need to be willing to leave our own ideas behind in order to be afforded the opportunity to enter the world of others. People can help each other by faithfully stepping out of their comfort zones rather than fearfully retreating to a situation that is secure only for the dominant population. Windell notes that Black Christians are much more likely to attend a White church than White Christians are to attend or even visit a Black church. The diversity of cultures in our nation could have been the basis for creating a model of racial harmony, but we have instead allowed our differences to separate us. Windell says, "Here we have something that we have allowed to be a problem, and it should have been used as a solution." The church still has opportunities to be a presence that models resilient trust between cultures.

Our discussion in this chapter has been centered on developing two spiritual practices that emphasize identity and integrity, realizing that these qualities are formed in the Spirit, in community, and in oneself. Since the practices of formative presence and resilient trust were described in light of how empathy functions, the skills needed for both are similar. Both of them require cultivating an openness characterized by compassion, emotional safety, nonjudgment, and generosity. I will address this skill of cultivation in the next chapter using the term *reception*, which encompasses all the ways we express openness to each other. Another key proficiency common to both practices is a form of self-examination that's deeply observant and accountable to others, which I will refer to as *reflection*. The third skill translates our learning into practical, responsible action that respects interpersonal boundaries. I will call this last ability *response* because it's the culminating activity that builds on the previous two skills. These three skills—reception, reflection, and response—constitute the practices of formative presence and resilient trust. They are the practical, concrete skills any Christian can exercise in order to develop empathic influence.

QUESTIONS FOR GROUP DISCUSSION

The source of our influence is described in Ephesians 3:14–21. Encourage the members of your group to explore how to apply Paul's prayer. Also read Roman 12 in order to introduce the concept of spiritual practices. Discuss what Paul wanted his readers to do and why they should do it.

1. What are some methods for influencing people?
2. What is the best way you have found for you to learn from others?
3. How would you define spiritual growth? List some spiritual practices or disciplines that provide opportunities for personal and communal growth.
4. According to Paul (Ephesians 3:16–19), how does personal growth take place?
5. What part do you play in the church, the body of Christ? What roles do you have among other groups? How do these activities foster growth in yourself and in others?
6. How do you know when a person is fully present with you? How can you be a presence for other people in the way that God is present for you?
7. How is empathy a factor in being present with people? How do you show empathy?
8. How would you describe your identity? How has it been molded?
9. How does your sense of integrity or wholeness shape who you are?
10. How do struggles and adversities affect our identity and integrity?
11. How is trustworthiness developed? How do you help people trust you?
12. What does it take to fully engage and belong to a group or community? What are some examples of successful involvement?

THE LONG JOURNEY OF A
RELATIONSHIP HAS THE
MOST INFLUENCE

Dawn Dowden exemplifies the practices of formative presence and resilient trust. She and her family lived through some traumatic financial challenges that resulted in losing their housing. During a period of five years after her husband was diagnosed with a mental health condition, she depended on the support of their extended family. Yet she maintained hope that her situation would improve. Then in 2008 she accepted the help of Greenville's Interfaith Hospitality Network, which provides families with temporary housing in local church facilities. In less than a year, she was offered a job as an administrative assistant with Homes of Hope, and soon afterward she found housing for herself and her three children. Her job with Homes of Hope gave her opportunities to be a presence in the community, offering resources to people who were experiencing housing instability and homelessness. Today she considers herself a magnet for people's stories of hardship because she offers empathy for their struggles.

After serving Homes of Hope in a variety of roles for twelve years, Dawn is now the chief operations officer. This nonprofit business is a ministry-based housing developer that focuses primarily on the people it serves. Homes of Hope builds and owns houses that partner organizations offer as transitional and permanent affordable homes. The company also connects clients to local resources for jobs, GED preparation, financial education, objective-setting, and assistance with rent and utilities. In addition to offering houses, Homes of Hope gives a small number of men a free year of job training that provides construction skills needed by electrical contractors.

Dawn has learned a lot about trusting people. There are many circumstances in people's lives that cause trust to be broken, and different kinds of poverty affect people's ability to trust. Her own experience with temporary, situational poverty helps her relate to many people experiencing loss, yet her expectations during that period were different from the expectations of those who live in long-term, generational poverty. She had hope for the future because she trusted the people around her. Dawn's organization discusses expectations with the people they serve, and they make every effort to be considered trustworthy: "You can't make somebody trust you. . . . It's the long journey of a relationship that has the most influence."

Looking back on the struggles and uncertainty she has worked through, Dawn reflects, "There's this real sweet beauty in not knowing the next step and not having anything to cling to. I had to walk through that with open hands because I had nothing to bring." Her experience of trusting people during difficult times has helped her appreciate that the mission of the body of Christ is to love people well. Her presence with people gives them hope. She nurtures in them the very things she needed when life was most difficult for her.

4

EMPATHIC RECEPTION

The virtue of empathy drives the practices of formative presence and resilient trust. The skills necessary for these practices are interpersonal and interactive because empathic behavior is expressed in connection with God and other people. I have identified three areas of practical focus to be considered in depth—*reception*, *reflection*, and *response*. Each entails particular ways of thinking and of organizing our relationships. In this chapter, I will examine the skill of empathic reception, which is characterized by compassion, emotional safety, nonjudgment, and generosity. I will discuss some approaches to thinking openly and initiating apprenticeships that nurture connection with God and with people. Some of the crucial components to be explored are listening and dialogue. Listening is a form of grace, and dialogue is an effective vehicle for change. In later chapters, I will present the skill of reflection that includes thinking perceptively and developing relationships characterized by friendship, followed by the skill of response that incorporates elements of thinking socially and nurturing new bonds of kinship. Each of these chapters represents a further stage of character development that both deepens and broadens the range of relationships with people.

Reception is a delightful skill. For example, everyone loves a wedding reception. Celebration, food, and fun activities create a wonderful atmosphere. Although it's a solemn occasion to unite two people together, this couple wants to share the excitement and love with those who have supported and encouraged them—those who have *influenced* them. The festive gathering after the formal ceremony is called a reception because the couple receives society for the first time as a married couple. When my wife and I married in 1978, the tradition of wedding receptions involved the couple greeting guests with a receiving line. Every guest was individually welcomed by the couple. It can take a long time to receive a multitude of friends, so today a more popular practice is a grand entrance of the couple along with members of the wedding party. Wedding celebrations have now become more about society receiving the newly married couple. Whatever the custom, receptions are about welcoming people into community.

In order to understand what the term *reception* means, it will help to consider a New Testament example. The apostle Paul and his coworkers encountered a variety of responses to their ministry and their message, ranging from welcoming acceptance to violent rejection. After some Jews in Thessalonica jealously precipitated a riot, Paul left for another town where he received a warm welcome (Acts 17:10–12):

> That very night the believers sent Paul and Silas off to Beroea; and when they arrived, they went to the Jewish synagogue. These Jews were more receptive than those in Thessalonica, for they welcomed the message very eagerly and examined the scriptures every day to see whether these things were so. Many of them therefore believed, including not a few Greek women and men of high standing.

The welcome Paul received was different because the character of the Beroean Jews was more open-minded. Rather than creating a violent mob scene, they accepted the visitors and their message with goodwill, evidently predisposed to give Paul's proclamation a generous hearing.

The receptive behavior Paul encountered in Beroea included skills that he himself displayed on his next stop in Athens (Acts 17:16–34). After his arrival, the local philosophers took the apostle to the Areopagus (also called Mars Hill) to scrutinize his teaching. Paul exhibited his relational skills by first eliciting the questions and curiosities of his audience and then challenging them to consider an alternative conclusion. He addressed the subjects of God's identity and God's expectations together with his hearers and offered a path for them to critique and transcend their own understanding of supernatural immanence and moral truth. He observed their methods and listened to their explanations, and the Athenian philosophers responded with interest in further dialogue. By approaching his audience as equal discussion partners and thinking critically *with* them rather than against them, Paul managed to introduce them to the important questions of divine authority and truth. He began with the notion of a God they could comprehend, and he used his influence to walk them through the significance of having a relationship with God.

Paul chose to be open-minded like the Beroeans. He knew that learning is a mutual interaction, with both parties sharing responsibility for the learning. As Christians learn how to use empathic skills, they exhibit a greater openness to the wisdom available in their community. Open-minded thinking is exemplified in listening, questioning, communicating, and collaborating. In the manner that Jesus Christ walks alongside us as we trust him, so we also walk with others in a relationship that positions us more as fellow apprentices than as consumers and distributors of knowledge.

The next three sections examine the nature of reception, the contexts in which we should consider reception, and the way that apprenticeships encourage reception. As the figure illustrates, these are interlocking aspects of reception as a skill. Influential Christians learn how to accept others and hear their diverse voices. Open thinkers reach out to others in order to build new relationships.

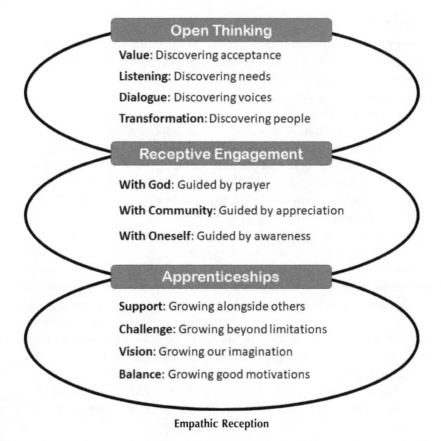

Empathic Reception

OPEN THINKING

The influential Christian is open to other people and to God. Empathic openness is characterized by expressions of compassion, a humble embrace of vulnerability in safe spaces, a generous pursuit of understanding, and collaboration rather than judgment. Influence becomes an act of reaching out to another person and connecting with that person's heart. Parker Palmer explains how we connect by knowing one another:

> The mind motivated by compassion reaches out to know as the heart reaches out to love. Here, the act of knowing *is* an act of love, the act of entering and embracing the reality of the other, of allowing the other to enter and embrace our own. In such knowing we know and are known as members of one community, and our knowing becomes a way of reweaving that community's bonds.[1]

Value

Genuine openness begins with regard for the value that other people have. Affirming the worth of every individual is an expression of acceptance for the humanity of other people. When we give our full attention to others, we communicate to them how much we value them and desire to be in relationship with them.

Palmer relates a story about a discussion among college faculty members in which they were criticizing their students for being unprepared for their classes. The dean told the professors they sounded like doctors in a hospital complaining about all the sick people and requesting healthier patients. Palmer summarizes, "The way we diagnose our students' condition will determine the kind of remedy we offer."[2] When we assume that the people we want to influence are inept, then our interaction with them will be ineffective and our influence will be negative. Mentoring expert Elena Aguilar says it more bluntly: "No one can learn from you if you think that they suck."[3] Disdain is a destructive element often present in discussions about partisan politics, racial differences, marital strife, and children's abilities. Appreciating every participant may be difficult, but it has the power to address some of the most significant motivational issues people have. We will be a positive influence only when we value all of the people around us.

The best preparation for thinking openly is to follow God's example: "God's reception of hostile humanity into divine communion is a model for how human beings should relate to the other."[4] Since God approaches humanity with love and respect for each individual, so we should also consider people as having intrinsic value and anticipate that each person has something to offer. God is generous with his presence, his gifts, and his delight in all of creation; therefore, we should be every bit as generous as he is. When people feel valued and respected, they know they will be safe and accepted, and they are more willing to be influenced. Such respect gives people the strength to listen despite differences. Influential Christians show they value people by modeling skills of listening and dialogue both inside and outside the church.

Stephen Covey had a friend with a rebellious child, and the father's attempts to build a relationship with the boy led to anger and failure.[5] After hearing about the benefits of being more open, the father decided to listen without evaluating or judging the boy's statements. Even this approach failed at first, because the boy was uncertain about the dad's sincerity. The father recognized his need to work on his own attitude so that he could accept his son unconditionally. When the father became capable of appreciating his son without attaching any stipulations regarding behavior, the father was able to be honest about his own feelings of anger and disappointment. When he allowed himself to become vulnerable to rejection for the sake of his son, he was able to connect with his son's feelings of vulnerability. The father was no longer trying to pry open the thoughts and feelings of his son, but instead he just focused on being present. The boy started to believe he was valued, and then he began to share his thoughts and feelings. Eventually the father and son had some meaningful conversations and began to build trust between them. We must learn, just as this father did, that we do not influence others by demanding that they change. We have to transform our own attitudes and behaviors in order to help others assess whether their change is worthwhile to them. Giving value to other people is risky because we relinquish total control of our relationships with them.

Listening

One of the most powerful activities that takes place between people is listening to one another. Writing about the nature of human understanding, the philosopher Hans-Georg Gadamer asserts that "anyone who listens is fundamentally open. Without such openness to one another there's no genuine human bond. Belonging together always also means being able to listen to one another."[6]

The best listening role model I have known was a humble gentleman who ably filled multiple vocations as preacher, elder, and mental health counselor. I met the late Carl Lancaster at the church my wife and I joined when we moved to South Carolina in 2006. His wife was beginning to experience symptoms of dementia, but he continued to include her on several mission trips and to carefully attend to her needs in every place. Carl was known around the world by many people whom he had helped. Once when I was in New Mexico visiting a small church, a couple whom we met knew Carl. He had performed the funeral service for their young child several decades earlier. Carl knew how to be an effective pastor, and he taught me some invaluable lessons about helping bereaved families during a period when I served as interim minister. For example, I followed him and studied his actions as he prepared for a funeral. He listened to the grief, empathized with the pain, and encouraged families in their despair. He drew out their concerns and needs without imposing his own views or preferences. Later, when I was called upon to perform funeral services myself, I realized that Carl had modeled Christian influence in my presence. I learned from him not only how to perform a funeral, but also how to listen attentively and how to be fully present with people. Carl freely opened himself to others and pointed them to Christ by listening to and truly hearing their thoughts and feelings.

Jesus was also concerned about the manner in which we hear—how receptive we are to truth and how willing we are to act upon that message. He admonished the people, "Let anyone with ears to hear listen!" and "Pay attention to what you hear" (Mark 4:9, 23–24). The first skill expressed in the practices of formative presence and resilient trust consists of developing ears that hear and eyes that see the stories of individuals and the activity of God. Jesus encouraged this skill with several people, including Nicodemus (John 3:1–15) and the Samaritan woman (John 4:5–30). He met them where they were in their understanding and piqued their curiosity before addressing their spiritual needs. Jesus's attentiveness to them prompted their listening to him.

Unfortunately, attentive listening is not a commonplace activity in our noisy, boisterous society, even though most people long to be deeply heard and understood. Michael Nichols, family therapist, author, and professor of psychology, describes one of the difficulties of listening:

> Genuine listening involves a brief suspension of self. You won't always
> notice this because it's reflexive and taken for granted and because
> in most conversations we take turns. But you might catch yourself

rehearsing what you're going to say next when the other person is talking. Simply holding your tongue while the other person speaks isn't the
same thing as listening. To really listen you have to suspend your own
agenda, forget about what you might say next, and concentrate on being
a receptive vehicle for the other person.[7]

In a world preoccupied with talking, listening offers grace. Attentive listening is ultimately the way to truth, especially when there are diverse viewpoints calling for a response from us. Effective listening requires focusing on
what is going on in someone's life, and this kind of receptivity begins with
genuine interest or curiosity. It's like the close reading of a poem, causing
us to enter empathically into the context behind the words. It's also similar
to letting a piece of music envelop us so that we sense the composer's emotions. Listening often requires a slowing of the pace of the conversation so
that reflection on the message is possible.

For those of us who influence others through teaching, an emphasis
on listening reminds us that we are called to lead *people* rather than *lessons*.
Author and Orthodox Catholic pastor Dominic Ashkar points out the
importance of thinking about the individuals in a class rather than regarding the group as an impersonal collection of people. Addressing individuals
"requires insight into the special needs, weaknesses, [and] aptitudes of each
member; it also requires special preparation of the lesson so as to apply it
to each member, awakening each one's aptitude, overcoming each weakness, [and] meeting each need."[8] Such preparation may seem daunting, but
the goal of influence is to increase everyone's awareness of and connection
with each other, not to resolve everyone's issues. Those who lead discussion with listening skills have a clearer idea of who or what is controlling
the conversation, and they can more easily identify which voices are *not*
being heard. Finally, everyone who listens to different perspectives can
sharpen their own thoughts in comparison with others. I avoid a bubble
of like-minded thinking (the echo chamber effect) by valuing and trusting
someone else's critical assessment of my statements, with the result that I
can clarify my own views.

Dialogue

When there's mutual listening, there's the possibility of meaningful dialogue. Reuel L. Howe, who was instrumental in the development of
clinical pastoral education, defined *dialogue* as "that address and response
between persons in which there is a flow of meaning between them in

spite of all the obstacles that normally would block the relationship."[9] The Greek term from which the word *dialogue* is derived, διαλέγομαι (*dialégo-mai*), is used in the New Testament to describe several of Paul's interactions with people. His debates in both the synagogue and the marketplace (Acts 17:2, 17), as well as his discourse in the church at Troas (Acts 20:7–12), are referred to as *dialoguing* rather than *preaching*. Paul's opening statements often led to questions and discussion about concrete situations, followed by deeper dialogue about God's plan. It may be surprising to realize that Paul was as apt to listen as he was to speak, but one of his gifts was an ability to create diverse communities built upon shared interests. Love for Christ and for humanity motivates the apostle and us to reach across differences in order to connect with rather than exploit each other. We support other people's growth through active listening, engaged questioning, open dialogue, and appreciative responses.

The Support Circles program I mentioned at the end of the previous chapter offered me a valuable opportunity to learn how to listen and encourage dialogue. I found that it's a benefit to others when I suspend my desire to *speak truth* and instead train myself to *listen to truth*. An environment created to help someone address personal challenges must support that person in expressing his or her own voice. In order to do that, the supporters have to defer any judgment or advice until it's sincerely and constructively requested. I had to shut down my analytical way of thinking and learn how to be present for the other person rather than for myself. For me, this is a difficult transformation—one that causes me to reconsider how I assess my own value and the value of other people.

In a discussion about team dynamics, Brené Brown explains that the problems inhibiting effective interactions often include making inappropriate judgments, giving unsolicited advice, interrupting the one who's speaking, and undermining confidentiality. Then she says, "The behaviors that people need from their team or group almost always include listening, staying curious, being honest, and keeping confidence."[10] These latter actions are central to effective dialogue because they are ways to establish trust.

Transformation

Active listening often brings about change, so we should expect some kind of transformation. In order to become listeners, we have to allow ourselves the opportunity to entertain different perspectives, which means that vulnerability, risk, and change are not only possible, but likely. However, people in Western culture often avoid interactions in which they might appear vulnerable, so it's not surprising that listening often seems impossible. Developing listening as a skill requires two unintuitive but practical actions: We have to relinquish control, temporarily letting go of our own narrative and objectives. We also have to respectfully protect each other's identity. If we are receptive, we accept other people's worldviews on their terms, not our own, while also respecting how they set boundaries on their perspectives.

Mac Arnold is an example of a receptive person. He is a well-known blues musician, having played with top musicians around the country, including B.B. King, John Lee Hooker, and Muddy Waters. After living in Chicago and Los Angeles and working in both music and television, Mac returned to his hometown of Greenville in 1990. He established the I Can Do Anything Foundation, supporting music education and several local festivals, including the annual Cornbread and Collard Greens Festival. Mac says he wants to be an influence by "just being myself and doing what I love to do." He respects people, and he lets God navigate his life.

Mac regularly visits the local schools in Greenville County with his Blues in the Schools program, which is designed to encourage children's interest in music. He plays for the students, answers their questions, and then invites some of the students onstage to play. Most of them have not experienced live blues music, and Mac has witnessed music's effect on them—he can see the transformation from disinterest to engagement in their faces as the music starts up. As a result of this interchange between Mac and the students, a few of them decide in each session that they want to be musicians. He provides young people with a means to consider their dreams and bring them to light. Mac collects instruments to donate to the schools so that students have an opportunity to have their own instrument. He likes to point out that music changes people. Blues music is about sharing an experience—both the good and the bad: "Blues tells you where you're going, and it reminds you where you've been, and it warns you to keep your eyes open for what may happen down the road."

When we join in a constructive conversation with others, we give them a stake—a responsibility—in creating a worthwhile outcome. We are also more likely to understand and address the things that are *not* being said—what's presumed, what's desired, what's feared, and what's taboo. Several years ago, there was a significant shift in workplace environments from separate offices to sectionalized cubicles and then to mobile, collaborative spaces. Many executives perceived the active, creative atmosphere as energizing, but large numbers of employees found it invasive and overwhelming. In many cases, employees were not consulted about their needs for productivity, and the result for many corporations was an increased level of employee fatigue and burnout. What may seem like a good idea can fail when there's a lack of listening to real needs. In this case, dialogue with the employees—the stakeholders in the work environment—could have identified changes that would improve the environment.

RECEPTIVE ENGAGEMENT

Listening and dialogue are vital elements within the practices of formative presence and resilient trust. They are receptive skills that build communities of integrity. In this section, I will examine how these skills function in relation to God, our community, and ourselves.

Receptive to God

One of the most important Old Testament texts for Jews and Christians alike is God's admonition to be receptive to him. It's called the Shema, which in Hebrew means "hear" (Deuteronomy 6:4–5):

> Hear, O Israel: The LORD is our God, the LORD alone. You shall love the LORD your God with all your heart, and with all your soul, and with all your might.

The Shema restates the first of the ten commandments in a positive way (Deuteronomy 5:6–7). It's a proclamation of affirmation that calls Israel to love God with their heart (the will, mind, and emotions), their soul (the entire being or self), and their might (their whole strength). The Shema was recited by faithful Jews weekly in the synagogue and also daily during morning and evening prayers. Its importance is far greater than knowing what God says; in Hebrew, the notion of hearing has a broad range of meaning that includes listening, understanding, discernment, and obedience. The Shema presumes that God will speak and that his people will follow only him.

Jesus Christ, the shepherd of God's flock, also speaks with an intent to be heard: "My sheep hear my voice. I know them, and they follow me" (John 10:27). Many of Jesus's healing miracles provided sight or hearing to people, enabling them to see and hear him. Similarly, we are enabled by the Holy Spirit to hear God (John 16:13). Saint Augustine of Hippo, the fourth-century theologian and philosopher, declared that when we approach the biblical text to inquire after God, we discover that God is searching for us.[11] As we seek to interpret and apply Scripture to our lives, we find that Scripture is interpreting us, revealing what our lives mean to God. The voice of God is most often heard in conjunction with either the text of the Bible or the words of a person. American philosopher Dallas Willard explains that recognizing God's voice takes practice:

> Those who want to live under God's guidance and who by proper teaching or God's other special provision become convinced that he will speak and perhaps *is* speaking to them can learn through experience the particular quality, spirit and content of God's voice. They will then distinguish and understand the voice of God; their discernment will not be infallible, but they will discern his voice as clearly and with as much accuracy as they discern the voice of any other person with whom they are on intimate terms.[12]

Thinking openly about God is a matter of observing his activity in the world, listening for his direction, discerning his call and message, and seeking to faithfully engage in his work of reconciliation.

Jesus pointed to little children as models for spiritual growth: "Truly I tell you, unless you change and become like children, you will never enter the kingdom of heaven" (Matthew 18:3). Jesus pointed out that children have a way of being receptive that many adults have lost. The innocent child is dependent upon someone greater. Our birth into God's kingdom is a dying to our own self-rule. In order to receive the life God intends for us, we must give up the life we fashion for ourselves: "Those who try to make their life secure will lose it, but those who lose their life will keep it" (Luke 17:33). At the heart of this change is accepting that our true identity is bound together with Christ.

Prayer is a dialogue with God. As we pray from the heart, God hears our heart and responds to our heart. This dialogue is possible because God's Spirit dwells within us and sustains the prayer of our hearts (Romans 8:12–27). Pastor, theologian, and author Tim Keller offers a succinct definition: "Prayer is continuing a conversation that God has started through his Word and his grace, which eventually becomes a full encounter with him."[13] This prayerful encounter with God changes us into the image of his Son. There are many kinds of prayer—petition, adoration, confession, intercession, thanksgiving—and they are all about relationship. Prayer is communication between creature and Creator, and in a broader sense, prayer is about being in a place where the Holy Spirit transforms us. Listening to anyone requires us to allow ourselves to be changed in some way; dialogue engages that process of change. In our relationship with God, we seek opportunities for change in ourselves as well as in the world around us. The influential Christian knows that God responds to our prayers in conjunction with our other practices, disciplines, and activities—like worship, meditation, and reading Scripture. The result is that believers "stand mature and fully assured in everything that God wills" (Colossians 4:12).

Receptive to Community

Nichols summarizes the primary steps in hearing another person: "Effective listening requires *attention, appreciation,* and *affirmation.*"[14] The process begins with attention, a difficult behavior in our culture of distraction. We must remove all barriers and tune in exclusively to the other person. Most of us know what it feels like to be on the receiving end of another's full attention, but we often neglect the skill ourselves.

Secondly, the good listener is appreciative and encourages the speaker to direct the discussion. Active support is evidenced by showing genuine interest, with all of the associated clues like eye contact, posture, smiles, other facial expressions, voice tone, and supportive responses. Some leaders fear that intentional listening will bring issues to the surface that they are not prepared to handle, but the act of listening itself brings healing to a multitude of problems. The connection between people elicits a joy that cannot be achieved by merely giving advice.

Finally, the listener affirms the other person's discernment in personal matters, allowing both people to learn together. We may assume beforehand that we are in disagreement, but until there is listening, there is no foundation for speaking an opinion into that relationship. It's by understanding and validating people's doubts, fears, and anxieties, as well as their motivations and aspirations, that we become capable of speaking into their situations. In this sense, listening becomes an act of specialized discovery centered entirely on another person's own experience and character.

Our connections extend across cultural, geographical, and technological boundaries, and we are apt to make false assumptions about groups we do not understand. Different world cultures express messages differently, so we must always be careful to avoid reading our own perspective into another culture's situation. Edward T. Hall, a well-known anthropologist, suggested that some cultures have inherent differences in the way they communicate.[15] High-context groups, such as some Eastern cultures, share many assumptions, traditions, and norms. Their collective patterns of thinking and behavior allow them to leave their intentions and reasoning unstated, but there is no lack of understanding or clarity within the group. A close-knit family is an example of a high-context group that develops its implicit patterns of behavior over a long period of time and has clear ideas about insiders and outsiders. Low-context people, such as in some Western cultures, express meaning explicitly, verbally, and cognitively. Relationships within a low-context group usually have a shorter duration and are secondary to the tasks being accomplished. A school's Parent-Teacher Association is an example of a low-context group that is easy to know how to join, how to contribute, and who is in charge. Effective communication is a significant component of influence, and every group has a context in which its methods of communicating are meaningful.

Listening for commonalities between people is as important as hearing the differences. Psychologist and professor Martin Hoffman explains,

> [There are] emotional commonalities that exist across groups despite the differences in social structure, culture, and physical appearance. These emotional commonalities include similar fears, anxieties, and life goals. They include similar emotional responses to being applauded, criticized, and treated unfairly, and similar emotional responses to universal life crises and significant events such as attachment, separation, loss, and aging.[16]

When the dialogue is an empathic engagement aimed at the discovery of group harmonies, we can learn how others handle the same situations we experience. These commonalities present us with natural points of connection that are opportunities for building relationships and becoming influential.

Some voices are heard more than others. Near my house is a neighborhood swimming pool that offers swimming classes. One of the instructors has a voice that can be easily heard several blocks away. He has a natural ability to capture attention. Of course, loudness is not the only quality that enables a voice to be noticed. There are some people who are heard more often because they talk more frequently. There are also policies and structures that elevate some voices by giving them the support of an institution or a population. A person's hierarchical position, wide acclaim, or successful accomplishments may boost his or her voice above others. Unfortunately, the people who are not being heard may possess the greatest wisdom in certain situations—especially in situations of inequity between groups of people. The challenge is to hear everyone's voice without partiality.

The biblical writer James emphasizes the practical nature of hearing each other: "You must understand this, my beloved: let everyone be quick to listen, slow to speak, slow to anger" (James 1:19). Genuine dialogue between dominant and subordinated groups often requires members of the dominant culture to intentionally *talk less*, so that the conversation is used for supporting people rather than suppressing them. Dialogue can liberate oppressed voices, but it can also be used to suppress or subordinate particular voices. Therefore, some first steps toward becoming receptive to community should include observing which people are not being heard and appreciating how those voices can and should be heard with equal authority. Another helpful step is to pray—initiating dialogue with God—about the need to dialogue with people. God's Spirit will inevitably respond by presenting opportunities for valuable, but not necessarily comfortable, connections.

We can give priority to listening by asking questions that enable others to speak. Curious questions draw people into each other's thoughts and into the challenges of the subject to be discussed. Jane Vella, an authority in education and teaching, says, "An open question invites critical reflection, analysis, review, and personal perceptions."[17] She defines an *open question* as one that does not have a predetermined response and that allows a sharing of influence within a group. The goal of using open questions is to encourage participants to compose their own thoughts and responses rather than merely reciting someone else's thoughts. There are several types of open-ended questions that are helpful for launching fruitful discussions:[18]

- *Explorative questions* lead to new insights ("What do you think about . . . ?")
- *Affective questions* invite the sharing of feelings ("How do you feel about . . . ?")
- *Reflective questions* encourage elaboration ("What might be at the root of . . . ?")
- *Probing questions* invite thinking ("Would you explain . . . ?")
- *Fresh questions* challenge assumptions ("Why must it be that way?")
- *Connection questions* elicit new perspectives ("What are some other ways?")
- *Analytical questions* examine causes ("Why has this happened?")
- *Clarifying questions* remove ambiguity ("How does that follow from . . . ?")

The gospels reveal that Jesus himself asked many of these types of questions as he taught his disciples and ministered to the people he encountered. For example, he asked his disciples exploratory questions about his identity (Matthew 16:13–15), reflective questions about the power of Satan

(Matthew 12:26–29), probing questions about their blind spots (Matthew 7:3), connection questions about King David's relationship with the Messiah (Matthew 22:41–46), and analytical questions about the nature of sin and repentance (Luke 13:1–5).

Receptive to Oneself

We often joke about the craziness of talking to ourselves, but we usually think it's wise to listen to ourselves. We need to develop a receptive spirit toward ourselves, because the ability to access one's own inner, emotional life affects the skills of empathy that one exhibits toward others. A sense of self-awareness is necessary in order to accept the truth about oneself, and that truth is fundamental for sharing oneself with others. Earlier we saw the importance of recognizing that others have intrinsic value; now we must examine the significance of our own core values. Our ability to grow is often limited by negative values—such as a fixed mindset or narcissism or self-contempt—that we refuse to relinquish. However, values that are linked to growth (such as devotion to Christ) enable us to thrive.

One of the negative values I had as a young adult was that my success depended only on my own capabilities. Early in my engineering career, I was promoted from being an individual product designer to being a supervisor over other engineers. I assumed that since my individual skills had gotten me that far, they would continue to be the ticket to further success. I considered myself as still being a team member, though I behaved like I had superior insider knowledge. Eventually, one of the people in the group startled me with the assertion that becoming a manager meant I was no longer like the rest of them. I realized then that I had not been listening for what the group needed from me in my new role. I thought nothing had changed except that I had taken on more authority. It was a learning process for me to discover that I was no longer a star player; now I had to develop star players. To my delight, I observed that the team was ready to share responsibility when I gave them the opportunity. My authority was not mine to hold on to, but instead something to be shared.

The primary barrier to personal change and self-receptivity is erected by the fears, uncertainties, and hostilities that we have about ourselves and our relationships. Nouwen explains how we often build walls around ourselves to prevent change:

> We indeed have become very preoccupied people, afraid of unnamable emptiness and silent solitude. In fact, our preoccupations prevent our

having new experiences and keep us hanging on to the familiar ways. Preoccupations are our fearful ways of keeping things the same, and it often seems that we prefer a bad certainty to a good uncertainty. Our preoccupations help us to maintain the personal world we have created over the years and block the way to revolutionary change. Our fears, uncertainties and hostilities make us fill our inner world with ideas, opinions, judgments and values to which we cling as to a precious property. Instead of facing the challenge of new worlds opening themselves for us, and struggling in the open field, we hide behind the walls of our concerns holding on to the familiar life items we have collected in the past.[19]

Although fear inhibits our ability to engage in open, receptive, loving relationships, acts of love diminish fear (1 John 4:18). Our devotion to Christ enables us to overcome fear and genuinely accept ourselves in light of our relationship with Christ. He gives us such newness and hope that our changes no longer weigh heavily upon ourselves. We depend on him.

The self-receptive person realizes that change in the world does not come about by controlling other people's behavior, but by changing oneself. This perspective, together with the convicting influence of the Holy Spirit, enables one to start listening beyond differences and biases in order to understand how our place within society and our behavior within our groups of influence affect the ability of others outside that group to flourish. One of the key steps to listening to our community is to accept how we as individuals are complicit in the social forces that perpetuate oppression of certain peoples. The problems of exclusion and exploitation are not just occurring *out there* but are also present in each person's subconscious assessments of other people. Our obligation as receptive influencers is to understand when and how our customary behaviors harm ourselves and others. What are my hidden assumptions? What story am I telling myself? How does my story compare with the narrative of suffering that some people experience? Listening to ourselves is the beginning of truly listening to others. The popular theologian Frederick Buechner once commented,

> If I were called upon to state in a few words the essence of everything I was trying to say both as a novelist and as a preacher, it would be something like this: Listen to your life. See it for the fathomless mystery that it is. In the boredom and pain of it no less than in the excitement and gladness: touch, taste, smell your way to the holy and hidden heart of it because in the last analysis, all moments are key moments, and life itself is grace.[20]

APPRENTICESHIPS

The skill of reception provides an entry into empathic practices so that we can develop genuine openness in our relationships. We need to create opportunities for listening and dialogue, especially if we are accustomed to doing most of the talking. For most of us, becoming better listeners requires changes in how we approach relationships in order for us to benefit from others telling us about our behavior. We need involvement with others—maybe even their intervention—in order to confront our persistent denial of unhealthy behaviors. The practices of formative presence and resilient trust can help us grow in our ability to see and influence others, but to implement those practices, we need help. Evan B. Howard, an expert on spiritual formation, suggests that the help we need is available in special relationships: "We need people who will guide us through the appropriate practices into an authentic spiritual life."[21] They help us learn to see ourselves, the world, and the Lord.

I refer to this special relationship as *apprenticing* because the primary perspective of interest here is that of the person who desires to improve. Other terms that can apply to the same affiliation are *protégé, mentee, trainee, directee,* and *disciple.* There are some peculiarities about each of these identifiers, but the differences are minor for this discussion. Understanding how to be the learner is a prerequisite for discovering how to become a mentor/coach, and the effective mentor continues the lifelong process of learning. My objective in this section is to outline some key aspects of being the protégé as well as being the coach.

Support

Laurent A. Daloz, a widely published teacher of adult education, says that a mentoring relationship offers support, challenge, and vision and that these components must remain in balance.[22] These characteristics form the framework used here in the context of apprenticeships to discuss how influence is developed. From the perspective of the apprentice, to be supported is to gain affirmation of the boundaries and norms that the mentor and mentee establish for their relationship. Both the mentor and the mentee thrive in an empathetic environment because each is being celebrated where they are in their own growth. When they encounter limitations or barriers, they walk together to discover new approaches.

Apprentices want guides who will provide some scaffolding for growth and then gently step away as the apprentice takes on more responsibility.

The mentor and the mentee together create an environment in which the experienced practitioner encourages the learner to watch, listen, ask questions, and practice specific skills. Although the relationship is often pictured as a master and a single student, experts have observed that more learning occurs among a group of people who are apprenticing together.[23] This is why cohort models in education work well. The participants learn from each other, and the key to their growth is the opening of themselves to fully appreciate others. Unfortunately, becoming an apprentice is often difficult for those who already occupy leadership positions. Among those who find it very difficult to relinquish their authority are pastors, teachers, executives, managers, professors, physicians, organizers, coaches, and even parents.

A good way for a leader to encourage apprenticing within a group is to give people positive leadership experiences in which the help they need is easily accessible. These leadership experiences are often tasks like teaching, organizing, facilitating, or visiting. Motivated volunteers who are looking for apprenticeships are innovative and optimistic, and they usually seek out assistance for the task from people in the group whom they respect. I've observed in my congregation that more people are willing to lead in an environment that encourages everyone to learn from each other. Those who feel like they have influence are more motivated to volunteer for leadership. Teachers who approach their role as an apprentice learn from other teachers and from their students.

There are many ways to develop apprenticeships—some are long-term experiences to develop a particular proficiency, while others are brief visits to increase one's awareness in an unfamiliar territory. I love to learn from people who are experts in their craft, so I enjoy exploring new areas with a capable guide. During the time my wife and I were serving a small church in New Mexico, we marveled at artistry and skills that were very different from our East Coast world. One of our church leaders was a renowned saddler, and he showed us how he was using a mixture of old techniques and new technologies to create the necessary gear for ranchers and rodeos. Another church member was a veterinarian who worked with both large and small animals. He took us with him on multiple trips to tag herds of buffalo and to examine an adolescent camel named Stanley. We toured a factory where New Mexico chile peppers were dried and ground into chile powder. We also found out that pecan orchards are prepared for irrigation by laser-leveling the ground across which a sheet of water will gently flow. Learning from others can be a delightful venture for a novice apprentice.

Christian apprentices, like their mentors, learn to pay attention to what God is doing in people's lives and how God communicates with his servants. One of the ways that Jesus modeled the practice of formative presence was by sending the Holy Spirit to be present alongside his disciples as their advocate (John 14:15–26). We imitate the Holy Spirit when we position ourselves as mediator, intercessor, or helper in support of another person. We all need others who will walk alongside us; fundamentally, apprenticing and mentoring are both about walking with others. This partnership turns out to be a three-sided relationship between the apprentice, the human advocate, and the Holy Spirit as heavenly advocate. Therefore, the significance of Christ's role and the position of the Spirit in our lives is maintained even in our reliance upon one another.

Challenge

In addition to support, the apprentice needs to be challenged in order to push through some of the barriers to developing influence. Support builds trust in the relationship, and challenge develops a sense of personal agency—the ability to contribute to one's own growth. The first challenge for the apprentice is learning to follow someone who has a different viewpoint. Finding value in another perspective allows us to go beyond the comfort of our own current thinking. A mentor can offer fresh insights or point us toward a model to follow. Jesus mentors his disciples to see the world as he does, encompassing both the struggles and the blessings of life. Jesus's perspective opens our eyes to the gap between the world's condition and God's intentions for his creation. Seeing things in a new way challenges us by disrupting our environment as we knew it. The apprentice and mentor together learn what leadership may look like by focusing their attention on specific issues created by that disruption in our perspective.

The second major challenge for the apprentice is to do what is called *adaptive work*.[24] As apprentices, we examine the gap between the current situation or perspective and the outcome we desire (motivated by our knowledge of God's plan for the world). The challenge is to establish a route from where we are to where we want to be. The objective is to move in a constructive, responsible direction without causing excessive distress for ourselves or for others. This is the kind of work that doctors help their patients do when coping with a life-threatening diagnosis. The challenge for the patient—the apprentice learning about health—is to learn to move forward and take appropriate responsibility for the situation.

I encounter similar challenges while developing teachers in an educational environment. I try to cultivate potential teachers by offering a variety of opportunities and guidance. One such man whom I've encouraged is a gifted speaker who struggles with regular Bible study. Rather than feed him with generalized techniques, I took time to value his perspectives and give him space to be creative in articulating his relationship with Jesus Christ. Together we searched for and identified ways that he could sustain his engagement with God's Word, and he has since led numerous classes and ministries. In this manner, the apprentice learns to handle problems successfully and manage the stress of change. The role of the mentor is to make sure that the tension of the challenge continues but that it does not become overwhelming.

Jesus established an example of mentoring in his training of the disciples, and the disciples exemplify how apprentices should meet the challenges they face. Unlike the Jewish rabbis who expected their disciples to serve them, Jesus ministered to his followers and taught them to serve one another (Luke 22:26–27). He nurtured them and provided them a relatively safe environment in which to grow. He showed them how to face temptation and adversity, how to pray, how to live righteously, how to express love to the Father, and how to love difficult people. Because Jesus invested himself in the lives of his apprentices, they experienced firsthand the development of character and community. The apostle Paul also learned from Jesus how to share his life with his fellow Christians and to embody the truth he proclaimed. Paul explained to the Thessalonian church how his approach to mentoring worked: "You became imitators of us and of the Lord" (1 Thessalonians 1:6). His protégé, Timothy, was in turn a model for others, showing how learners become teachers and followers become leaders.

Vision

A vision or perspective of a future outcome drives the apprentice's response to the challenges to be faced. Developing a vision for an activity or a project is difficult for someone with little experience, so the mentor helps the apprentice assess and plan the journey. Together they imagine where the leaps and crossings are possible. The concept of Support Circles can also be applied to situations that call for vision. One time I was participating in a group that was helping someone with interviewing for a new job, and we created a role-playing environment that helped her envision a successful interview. The practice sessions turned out to be valuable to all members of the group as we became mentors and apprentices for each other. A few of the supporting members began to envision a successful job interview as their own personal goal, and they asked the group for additional help for themselves. Sometimes we can catch a vision of an outcome by supporting each other through practices of growth.

A big barrier for apprenticing is that many of us are not accustomed to letting others lead. Our typical vision of authority is hierarchical, and apprenticeships represent a reversal of that perspective. Jesus flipped the way we are to see leadership: "Whoever wishes to be great among you must be your servant" (Matthew 20:26). Instead of studying successful people as role models, Jesus recommended that his disciples—his apprentices—learn from the very people the world normally regards as weak or worthless. In the Sermon on the Mount, Jesus first declares that his followers should learn about God's blessings from the poor and those who mourn (Matthew 5:3–4). His statement is much more than simply an appeal to remedy social needs; Jesus wants us to be *taught* by those who are poor, oppressed, and suffering. Their experience is a blessing from God upon the apprentices who will learn from their adversity.

Unless we appreciate the significance of first learning to be apprentices, our charity is likely to become paternalism and our mentoring may become a form of colonizing. Especially among those who represent the domineering side of American culture, there's an urgent need for apprenticeships that rely upon diverse, multiethnic, multigender leadership. Our vision for influencing people must be based on receiving and appreciating what people offer rather than simply giving what we want to give. Nouwen suggests that our own salvation depends on our willingness to receive from others:

> I am increasingly convinced that one of the greatest missionary tasks is to receive the fruits of the lives of the poor, the oppressed, and the suffering as gifts offered for the salvation of the rich. We who live in the illusion of control and self-sufficiency must learn true joy, peace, forgiveness, and love from our poor brothers and sisters. As long as we only want to give, we remain in the house of fear—so much giving can be a way of staying in control.[25]

Those who appear to be powerless are empowered by God, and they are often the ones who should be sought as mentors. Revolutionary change comes about by trusting the people who have been oppressed. Diversity in leadership can occur when the dominant culture not only shares their authority with others, but also seeks leadership from those who have been denied roles of leadership. A first step toward that goal is to seek mentors and coaches who are culturally different from us.

Balance

Apprenticing is difficult, and both the apprentice and the mentor will probably be tempted to have an imbalanced view of their roles. When viewed from the perspective of the apprentice, some typical temptations include impulsive behaviors like envy, self-reliance, overconfidence, and entitlement.[26] The first temptation is our envious desire to imitate those whom we admire and to convince people to like us. An unscrupulous mentor can exploit envy by manipulating an apprentice. The second temptation, self-reliance, is caused by the pressure we feel in our society to be independent and not to be open to learning from others. The mentor has an important role in modeling the pursuit of wisdom as a never-ending adventure; the mentee's goal is to become a capable, influential learner. The third temptation is that apprentices can become overconfident regarding what they know and are able to accomplish. Mentors who are primarily problem-solvers may suggest to mentees that all problems have to be fixed, and the objective becomes expertise instead of spirituality. This temptation—focusing primarily on achievement and competence—is one I've struggled with as an engineer. Finally, a sense of privilege can lead to feelings of entitlement for the apprentice. One of the important topics of discussion between mentor and mentee is an examination of their assumptions, expectations, and motivations regarding their future opportunities. Apprentices can learn to be influential by exploring how others have overcome obstacles and stereotypes in their development.

In summary, anyone who wishes to develop empathic skills can learn from experiences that emphasize listening and dialogue. Positive interactions are built upon an appreciation for other people and a humble respect for their willingness to engage. No one should be made to feel obligated to educate any of us. An apprenticeship can be initiated by expressing humble appreciation for another person's example and simply requesting a dialogue with them. Some examples of possible apprenticing initiatives include the following:[27]

- Cultivating unlikely friendships to stimulate new learning
- Learning to encourage and listen to people in poverty
- Receiving counsel from people who live sacrificially
- Engaging in the lives of people with disabilities
- Standing in solidarity with people who have been victims of crimes or abuse
- Showing hospitality to immigrants

- Supporting underrepresented groups like women in leadership positions
- Seeking to be mentored for leadership by persons of color

These relationships develop trust and transparency so that we can uncover our own blind spots and broaden our perspectives. A fruitful apprentice/mentor relationship helps both parties comprehend what controls, restrains, and motivates their behaviors.

RECEPTION AND CHRISTIAN INFLUENCE

The most important step in applying empathic practices and skills is getting started. Brené Brown says, "If you're expecting someone to operate from a place of receptivity, then you had better show up open, curious, vulnerable, and full of questions. You have to model the behavior."[28] Church leaders can kick-start an atmosphere of receptivity by engaging people in the local congregation and welcoming them into ministry responsibilities as quickly as possible. Many churches are reluctant to empower people without adequate training, but people get motivated to learn when they are entrusted with a role that requires learning. Building a receptive environment in which Christians learn from each other will help generate a contagious, communal equipping of the church body.

Church assemblies, educational programs, and professional gatherings must create space for cultivating relationships and encouraging diverse dialogue. The people who are invited into these activities should include as broad a spectrum as possible, so that new leaders can emerge out of the work they are doing. This approach is not about embedded leaders *allowing* diverse people to have responsibilities that perpetuate the dominant culture's status quo. Dialogue is used here as an opportunity for new leadership to emerge rather than as a tool for suppressing diverse participation. The process begins when the recognized leaders seek to hear and learn from God and each other. The process can then be assessed by monitoring the *persistence* of the participants in ministry. For example, we can look for people who are asking questions, are seeking challenges, are broadening perspectives, and are excited to recognize and contribute to the activities they witness God performing.

Practical Exercises

Imagine that you have an appointment in fifteen minutes with someone who requested an opportunity to talk with you.[29] This person is someone whom you do *not* want to see at this time. Picture in your mind the person who will be coming. Try to feel deeply what you are sensing about this person and about the prospect of listening to him or her for the next hour. In detail, envision the person who arrives for the appointment. How old? What gender? What features of appearance or manner stand out? Why did he or she come? What about this person are you reluctant to see or hear? After taking a few minutes to process that image, I want you to picture another scene. You have another appointment in fifteen minutes with someone who wants to discuss a problem. This time, however, the person is someone whom you are eager and happy to listen to. What do you envision about this person? How old? What gender? What sort of attitudes and behavior are noticeable? Why did he or she come? Why is this person someone you want to see and hear? Now, if you were able to imagine these two people, how would you compare and contrast them? Did you recognize that you instinctively prefer some kinds of problems and certain types of people?

Finally, I want you to imagine a third appointment. This time *you* are the person who wants to discuss a serious concern. Envision the person whom you wish to have as your listener. How old? What gender? What features of appearance or manner stand out? Can you see any connection between the listening you desired and the way you imagined listening to others? How might the person listening to you feel about that experience? Did he or she want to hear you? *What would it be like to listen to you?* The purpose of this exercise is to give you insight into the kinds of people and behaviors that you find (un)comfortable. There were probably differences in the characteristics of the people you envisioned. Discussing these differences with someone you trust might reveal some aspects of your character that you hadn't previously recognized. These differences could also point toward a person or group of people whom you might approach to help you grow as an apprentice.

Becoming receptive is also a challenge for communities. I recommend two group exercises for your growth and for the benefit of your community. First, relative to the discussion of the Sermon on the Mount, churches can learn about the suffering, poverty, and powerlessness that exists nearby. Find some group projects that work *together* with people who are hurting rather than merely on their behalf. People who are in shelters, detention/

prisons, and nursing/hospice facilities want to be heard, and there are community services that will encourage churches to connect with people.

Another exercise is to engage in forums that promote learning from other cultures, traditions, socioeconomic classes, or backgrounds. Churches have opportunities to lead in celebrating diversity by planning events to hear, understand, and engage people in learning from each other. Rather than creating new programs, it may be more productive to look for existing projects in which you can follow rather than lead. Just as teachers are often the best learners, the converse is also true: Sometimes our interest in learning from the community affords our greatest opportunities to be an influence. Making an inquiry to learn from a distinctive group about its history, traditions, music, and literature can open doors to fruitful discussion and learning. Author, professor, and social activist bell hooks emphasizes the importance of hearing each other's stories:

> Stories help us to connect to a world beyond the self. In telling our stories we make connections with other stories. Journeying to countries where we may not speak the native tongue, most of us communicate by creating a story, one we may tell without words. We may show by gesture what we mean. What becomes evident is that in the global community life is sustained by stories. A powerful way we connect with a diverse world is by listening to the different stories we are told. These stories are a way of knowing. Therefore, they contain both power and the art of possibility. We need more stories.[30]

There's healing in the telling of stories, and everyone has a need to be heard. The sharing of stories connects us with each other. Being heard has a significant healing effect because listening creates and restores relationships. As Christians, we can provide a safe place in which pain can be expressed and new life can be discovered. My specific recommendation for church leaders is to find ways to become more curious, open, and honest with the surrounding community, admitting that the church needs the community as much as the community needs the church. When the church listens, God's grace is evident, and the community is offered reconciliation.

QUESTIONS FOR GROUP DISCUSSION

You can get a better understanding of empathic reception by reading Acts 17. Discuss the various kinds of reception Paul received and how he exhibited it himself. Also read John 4:1–30 and discuss how Jesus treated the Samaritan woman.

1. According to Acts 17:10–12, what does it mean to receive people in a welcoming manner?
2. Why did Jesus select children as an example for spiritual growth? (Matthew 18:2–4).
3. What does it mean for a Christian to be open toward other people?
4. What might be some ways to determine how much you value specific groups of people?
5. What are some behaviors you exhibit when you listen attentively? How do these behaviors affect the person who is speaking?
6. Describe the qualities of a dialogue that you find engaging and stimulating.
7. Why do you think we are often so reluctant to change ourselves?
8. How do you go about hearing God?
9. What can you do to improve communication with people who are different from you?
10. Describe a relationship in which you were effectively mentored or coached by someone.
11. What sort of support do you need from other people?
12. Who are some individuals and groups that are not usually regarded as resources for learning? How might you take an initiative to learn something from them?

IT TAKES COURAGE TO STEP
OUT INTO THE DARKNESS

Beth Messick has a passion for working with women who are living through unfortunate circumstances, such as prostitution, drug addiction, unwanted pregnancy, and physical abuse. She helps them consider what they can do about their situations and what God is doing as part of his bigger plan for them. Recognizing that their pain is similar to her experience in dealing with sexual abuse as a youth, Beth encourages them to discover their self-worth. She tells them about the God who loves us and grieves with us. "I don't believe that God sent me out to the margins to change the margins, or the streets to change the streets. He sent me out there for me to be changed." She demonstrates that when we embrace our own brokenness, we touch other people's lives: "It takes courage to step out into the darkness."

After studying psychology and trauma at Furman University, Beth began working with pregnant teens. She first observed human trafficking in Greenville during the 1990s, when she came into contact with a preteen girl whose father was allowing men to abuse her for money. Since then, Beth has worked with the Greenville County Detention Center and Triune Mercy Center to help women break the vicious cycle of homelessness, drug addiction, prostitution, and incarceration. She goes into the areas where prostitutes work and talks with women whom no one else notices nor cares about. She understands that these women feel trapped by their circumstances and invisible to the community. "God began to take those broken pieces of my life and build them into a way for me to actually help other people," she says. A few years ago, Beth was invited to a meeting to discuss human trafficking in Greenville, and she was the only person in the meeting who actually knew the women on the streets.

Beth helped develop the concept of Jasmine Road, a residential program based on a housing-first model—providing safe housing rent-free for two years as the starting point for women to restore their dignity and value. One house currently supports five women in recovery, and Jasmine Road has plans for additional houses in the future. Several community partners provide the women with access to available services—health care, financial literacy, GED completion, outpatient addiction treatment, and trauma counseling. Jasmine Road also provides the women with meaningful employment and a lifelong community of support as they are reintegrated into the community in a healthy, sustainable way.

Beth influences by example. She is certain that God puts people in our path for a reason, and he helps us step out on their behalf. We are not called to fix other people's problems—our part is to listen to God's guidance and to listen to other people's perspectives. Beth finds that simply being curious and interested in people's lives helps them open up to possible changes. She explains that it can take years of interaction with people to become credible and to demonstrate that we genuinely care about their well-being. She listens intentionally to the difficult stories that women tell her, knowing that empathy drives connection. God is doing a holy work that bridges gaps between people—one small step at a time.

5

EMPATHIC REFLECTION

As important as receptive skills are, they alone are not sufficient to develop influence. In order to fashion a heart prepared for empathic forms of leadership, there must also be reflective consideration and application of that which has been received. You've listened to a person's story, and now you can learn together. For example, there's a young man in my congregation who exemplifies reflective influence. Derek Williams teaches college English classes and occasionally leads a Bible study on Sunday mornings. He's thoughtful about everything he shares with his class, and he connects with class members by describing his own experiences, learnings, and mistakes. When there are comments in class, Derek listens with his whole posture, making eye contact and physically leaning toward the speaker. Then he visibly ponders the remark, after which he affirms the comment and offers some dialogue to further the contemplation of the idea. If the speaker's assumptions are evident, Derek will often say something to gently uncover the significance of those underlying suppositions. He pours out support and encouragement in every class session, incorporating humor but not judgment. The mood is contemplative and respectful. The members of the group have opportunities to voice their realizations, and the empathic interaction influences their growth in both knowledge and character. This is what it looks like to welcome new perspectives and then to process what that perspective means for oneself and for the group.

This chapter will explore how empathic reflection builds upon receptivity in order to deepen one's understanding of what was received and to strengthen one's commitment to finding significance in both people and learning. Peter Senge, an expert in complex social systems and learning organizations, asserts that learning occurs as a result of both effective listening and reflection on the received information. Specifically, Senge points out two different types of openness—participative and reflective. The first consists of stating one's view, and the second is a matter of questioning one's own assumptions.[1] Senge states, "Skills of reflection concern slowing down our own thinking processes so that we can become more aware of how we form our mental models and the ways they influence our actions."[2]

Reflection is a method of thinking perceptively in order to reveal underlying assumptions and to find significance in events, statements, or experiences. The assumptions may pertain to historical knowledge about an event, cultural expectations about behavior and intent, religious attachments to specific doctrines, personal access to financial and educational resources, or entitlement to human services. Reflective thought carefully considers any knowledge or belief with regard to whatever arguments or suppositions are available to support it. In other words, does the supposition hold true in all cases, or does it apply to specific people and circumstances? The skill of empathic reflection helps a person clarify the significance of assumptions so that he or she develops a better understanding of the various factors contributing to personal character and influence on others.

Jesus provided an example for his disciples to imitate. He showed the disciples how to learn through reflection by temporarily withdrawing from the crowds and considering their experiences before taking the next step in their ministry. He assigned them more responsibilities as they became more capable of analyzing their assumptions in meaningful ways. Jesus asked his followers many questions, and I believe his reason for asking was to help them consider their own thoughts. After all, he certainly didn't need their insights or advice! Jesus's questions were often aimed at developing their skill of reflection. For example, consider what Jesus wanted to achieve by asking the following:

- "Why are you afraid?" (Mark 4:40)
- "But who do you say that I am?" (Matthew 16:15)
- "Why do you call me 'Lord, Lord' and do not do what I tell you?" (Luke 6:46)
- "For who is greater, the one who is at the table or the one who serves?" (Luke 22:27)
- "Do you want to be made well?" (John 5:6)

Like Jesus, the apostle Paul was an advocate of personal reflection. He encouraged the churches to reflect on their identity in Christ and to give careful thought to those things that contribute to godliness. He wrote to the church in Philippians 4:8,

Finally, beloved, whatever is true, whatever is honorable, whatever is just, whatever is pure, whatever is pleasing, whatever is commendable, if there is any excellence and if there is anything worthy of praise, think about these things.

Reflection is a vital component of spiritual formation, and it encompasses much more than merely looking back on past deeds. Paul suggests that in reflecting on Jesus's character, we become like him and *reflect him* to the world (Philippians 2:1–11).

Already we can observe a variety of connotations in the term *reflection*, and Paul affirms our use of all of them. Our reflection might be an act of *perceiving* how we actually think, feel, or behave. In this way, it's a recognition of ourselves and our situation. Reflection can also be an *imagining* of how our thoughts, feelings, or actions could be understood in different settings. This kind of reflection reaches outside our current situation to broaden the scope of possible contexts and corresponding behaviors. Finally, reflection can be a *mirroring* of a person, an object, or an idea. In this sense, it occurs when we connect with something so strongly that we imitate it, whether consciously or unconsciously. In summary, reflection can refer to awareness of something, contemplation about something, or replication of something.

All of these meanings of reflection play some role in how it is developed and applied as a skill. Reflection is a process that consists of contemplating information, experiences, and events, interpreting the meaning relative to past experiences, and building the necessary connections for fresh perspectives. The reflection process is realization, pondering, and mirroring; as a result, we adopt an identity or image of that which we think about most. As we think about (reflect on) the people, events, and experiences from which we learn, we become like (reflect) those people, events, and experiences. For example, I, like many other students, have become an imitator of the professors I appreciated the most in college and seminary. I didn't set out to copy their style, but as I learned the subject material from them, I also learned their way of articulating and relating to the content. The implication here is that we are all students of the people who have guided us, and we have learned not only some ways to think but also some models to imitate.

The next three sections examine the nature of reflection, the contexts in which we should consider reflection, and the way that friendships encourage reflection. As the figure illustrates, these are interlocking aspects of reflection as a skill. Influential Christians uncover assumptions—their

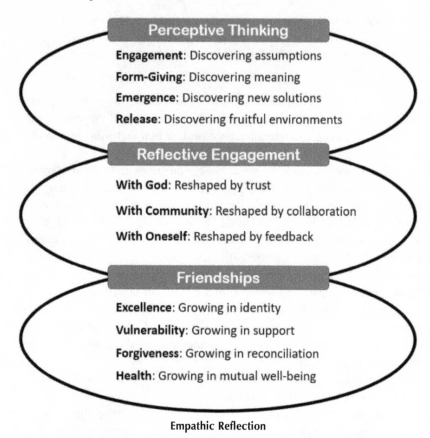

Empathic Reflection

own beliefs and their suppositions about others—and make sense of their encounters with people, subjects, and experiences.

PERCEPTIVE THINKING

Maria Harris, an author, speaker, and advocate for religious education, described learning as an artful process of imaginative reflection. The steps in the process of learning are (1) contemplation, (2) engagement, (3) form-giving, (4) emergence, and (5) release.[3] Although she presented them as a general paradigm to help teachers, I'm adopting these categories specifically for the purpose of distinguishing the functions of reflection. *Contemplation* is an openness to learning from an encounter that stimulates dialogue and thought. This stage of thinking openly was discussed in the previous chapter and consists of observation, remembrance, and replay of the information

or experience. *Engagement* is the first step in what I will refer to as perceptive thinking, and it involves analytical interaction with other people, the
world, and a range of texts and issues. *Form-giving* represents the initial
move toward reflective meaning-making and includes personal and communal expressions of significance about the subject(s) being reflected upon.
Emergence is the stage at which the reflective person or group promotes or
develops new ideas, solutions, and methodologies that imaginatively address
the original issue or event. *Release* is the stage at which actions or solutions
are distributed or publicized.

Learning consists of more than receiving and storing information.
Knowledge is not simply a commodity to be passed from one person to
another. Learning involves modes of thinking that engage the individual
and the community in processing, comprehending, and synthesizing various experiences. The sort of thinking that enables learning begins with
the basic act of valuing experience. In most cases, people's experiences are
communicated and appreciated through storytelling. As discussed in the
previous chapter, the skill of empathic reception is the first step toward
hearing and seeing the stories around us. Whether or not the story is our
own, the beginning of learning is reflection on the story.

Engagement

The process of engagement occurs when people follow a path of discovery
that exposes their own thoughts, feelings, and convictions to analysis and
comparison with other perspectives. This form of deep reflection is often
labeled as critical thinking, critical reflection, or critical pedagogy. Daniel
Willingham, professor of psychology at the University of Virginia, explains,

> Critical thinking consists of seeing both sides of an issue, being open
> to new evidence that disconfirms your ideas, reasoning dispassionately,
> demanding that claims be backed by evidence, deducing and inferring
> conclusions from available facts, solving problems, and so forth.[4]

In this context, *critical* does not always imply an unappreciative or negative
critique. It's an expression of curiosity and interest. The focus of reflection
is on the discovery of underlying assumptions, opinions, rules, and interpretations. Perceptive engagement includes both a reflection on past experiences and a mindful awareness of present and even future experiences.

My wife grew up in a home where alternate perspectives were
encouraged. Simply by using the phrase "on the other hand," her family

members could voice an opposite point of view without seeming argumentative. Often when a strong statement was made, the automatic rejoinder was a consideration of a contrasting view. The result was a broadening of their perspectives in the context of a casual conversation. It took me a while after I met her to begin to understand this behavior. I initially perceived her responses as refutation, not realizing the constructive background in which she learned it. She helped me learn that the purpose of perceptive engagement is to have a bigger vision.

A prime example of a *lack* of critical thinking can be observed in the way that people often respond to social media comments. If we surround ourselves with only like-minded voices, many of our online conversations become characterized by an arrogance of presumed uniformity and a vehement disregard for other perspectives. Many of us assume that all of the *good* people believe the same way we do, without an examination of their own underlying assumptions.

Fred Korthagen, an expert in teacher development, offers a good summary of the layers of reflection that people consider when engaging with their environment. Beginning with the most observable elements and moving toward deeper aspects, the layers of reflection include our environment (the situations we encounter), our behavior (what we do), our competencies (how we are able), our beliefs (what we commit to), our identity (who we are), and our mission (what drives us to do what we do).[5] To illustrate the function of reflection within these different layers, consider the case of a student teacher trying to be reflective in a new environment. The teacher observes the classroom, the students, and his or her own behavior in that space. Competencies and beliefs are still in the formative stage, and the teacher reflects on them in various training sessions with the help of administrators, mentors, and the children's parents. Yet most teachers have already established an idea of their personal identity and mission—they already envision who they are and why they are teachers. As the middle layers of reflection evolve with training and experience, the teacher may neglect further reflection on identity and mission. The teacher's commitments can then become disconnected from personal identity, possibly resulting in discouragement and fatigue. Thoughtful deliberation on all of the layers with respect to specific experiences can keep people motivated and directed toward meaningful problem-solving in their environment.

During my engineering career, I participated in many self-improvement workshops, and my favorite was one held by the Goldratt Institute. Based upon a book titled *The Goal* by Eliyahu Goldratt, the course introduced a new way of thinking about how the elements of a process work together.

Every decision point among a group of people carries with it a set of assumptions, and major disagreements occur in decision-making when there are conflicting assumptions. We often treat conflicts as endemic and irreconcilable, but when we uncover and examine assumptions that produce those conflicts, most conflicts disappear. Some difficult political and ideological examples were discussed during the workshop, and for each one we determined that the conflicted parties had similar values but saw different ways to address the matter, consistent with their own assumptions. For example, the two main U.S. political parties appear to have very different platforms, but the desires and objectives of most Americans are very similar—popularly framed as life, liberty, and the pursuit of happiness. The differences exist because there are different assumptions and preferences about how to achieve those goals. When the skill of empathic reflection is used, we can begin to understand how we are all more similar to one another than we realize.

There are assumptions underlying all of our decisions, actions, and judgments, and these assumptions operate in different ways. We hold some things as facts without questioning their truthfulness. We also make assumptions that cause us to believe certain things ought to happen, and these are often driven by moral judgments. For example, if we assume certain groups of people are more likely to break the law, then we will likely believe that people in those groups should receive more severe prison sentences. Also, if we assume all unemployed people are lazy or dishonest, we will likely believe that jobless people should receive fewer benefits and services than those who are employed. We make assumptions about how the world operates (or should operate), so we expect certain patterns, sequences, and logical outcomes. Our influence on people often depends on the similarity of our assumptions, and conflicts can occur when suppositions about truth differ. Perceptive people examine their assumptions for truthfulness. They also seek authenticity by scrutinizing whether they are being honest with themselves and with others about their emotions and thoughts.

We usually limit our reflective engagement to those things we regard as relevant, with a normal disregard for a large range of our sensory experience. As part of our community's socialization, which is different across cultures, we learn what's appropriate to ignore, with the result that reflection requires looking for what we cannot easily see. Robert Kegan and Lisa Laskow Lahey, experts in adult learning at Harvard Graduate School, suggest that our most problematic assumptions "are not so much the assumptions we have as they are the assumptions *that have us.*"[6] Therefore, when we observe an unexpected or incoherent outcome from a decision or course of action, we should reflect on what assumptions previously seemed obvious to all who were involved. The hiddenness of our assumptions may be the reason why revolutions in thought are rarely prompted by new data. What's needed is a new perspective—a new way of looking at the same reality. Big discoveries are often the result of seeing the familiar in a different light or from another angle. Using the lens of empathy to view Christian influence is a new way of reflecting on how to develop influence, so it may uncover some assumptions we haven't considered.

A variety of methods might help us become more reflective, offering the prospect of enlightening, surprising, or disturbing us with an "Aha!" moment.[7] These methods involve exploration and creative expression using techniques such as writing, mapping, art, role-playing, and exploring an unfamiliar culture. Reflective activities have the potential to provide a better understanding of what we and others think and believe, with appreciation for alternative views and explanations. Reflection does not in itself improve the accuracy of our beliefs, but the activity may clarify our thinking and uncover some overlooked aspects of our beliefs.

Form-Giving

The form-giving step in reflection consists of making sense and meaning of a particular subject or experience. It's a process of trying on various structures or narratives in order to find a good fit between sense and experience. The nature of meaning and meaning-making is important because learning is about connecting events, information, and people to a narrative that offers suitable explanations and hope. For example, we encounter a persistent barrier at work and wonder what it means, or we scrutinize a particular work of art for its meaning. In order to understand the meaning of something, we view it in relation to other things we know. As we examine our assumptions and accept new insights, we can connect our new understanding with other areas of our knowledge. Connections are what give purpose and meaning to the experiences, objects, ideas, people, and activities in our lives. We make meaning at every level and aspect of our lives—from individual words and sentences to the purposes we share with our community—and these expressions of meaning contribute to the stories we live by. We instinctively pull together the most significant events and characters of our lives into meaningful stories. People bind themselves into shared narratives in order to affirm their identity, and if there's no story readily available to supply a meaningful explanation, we will often *make one up*. We have a basic need to move toward something significant.

We construct meaning by associating one thing with another. When we look for meaning, we are typically examining something in order to understand the significance of what it represents.[8] We look for connections between things we want to understand, and our assumptions behind those things affect the connections between them. At the most basic level of meaning, we may be interested in what a word or event stands for in its context. For example, the popular debate about the term *Xmas* demonstrates that some people interpret the *X* as *Christ* being omitted from *Christmas*. However, others consider the letter to symbolize the presence of Christ since the Greek letter *chi* (X) is the first letter of the New Testament word Χριστός (*Christós*), translated *Christ*. Still others have considered the *X* as a symbol of the cross of Christ because its appearance is like a tilted cross. The way you understand the *X* yourself may change how you perceive the debate.

Another layer of meaning involves the relationships that exist when multiple things combine together. For example, a sports team uses certain maneuvers or sequences (plays) to coordinate the roles of the players on the field, irrespective of their individual identities as people. The meaning of a specific play is a matter of how it helps the entire team, rather than the individuals, compete against another team. A third layer of meaning is constructed socially according to the conventions of how a group commonly uses certain terms. The same object or event may be perceived differently by someone in another culture, making the context a significant factor for understanding the intent behind the preferred sense. For example, the meaning attributed to a campfire is very different in the context of a group of young White Christians comfortably engaging in mutual camaraderie than in the context of shipwreck survivors urgently trying to stay alive. Social meanings rely upon the possibility of many people, or a small number of people repeatedly, sharing patterns of experience and associating those patterns with symbols that can be used to communicate such experience.

Once a person is invested in a particular story (whether or not it has been proven to be true), shifting to another narrative is difficult. Most of us have been puzzled by people describing an image quite differently from how we see it, and we notice that shifting to another perspective is not easy.[9] The very connections and recognitions that open certain areas of meaning also close other avenues, making it necessary to "jump" perspectives in order to understand more than we currently see. Our willingness to make this jump is important in the context of cultural differences because one group's approach to reception and reflection may be misunderstood by another social group. People construct meanings differently from each other due to differences in their perceptions of reality. For example, a person whose perspective is that of a dominant group will likely assess the power dynamic in a given situation quite differently from people who feel subordinate to that group. Our reflections are limited by the assumptions lying beneath our perspectives, so it's difficult for one set of people to view a situation the same as another set of people.

Our construction of meaning affects our behavior, so our behavior is difficult to change without reconstructing the assumptions that drive what's meaningful to us. Conflict is often a necessary catalyst for change and learning because it prompts people to reflect upon the current situation and consider alternative possibilities. Getting out of our comfort zone can provide new opportunities for expanding our awareness of how we are giving form to our assumptions. However, without the skill of reflection, conflict is more likely to hinder change. A commitment to working through messy problems is necessary for formulating innovative solutions.

Emergence

Reflective emergence involves new ways of thinking that produce new kinds of solutions. The old ways of thinking will most likely reproduce the old results. One of the ways to constructively disrupt our thinking is to use the lens of empathy, which focuses attention on affective as well as cognitive perspectives. Spiritual reflection on the use of social power, mutual trust, and the persistence of our own biases can stimulate greater change in our perspective than continuing to merely perpetuate the status quo. For example, the choices that seem pivotal to many Christian leaders—choices regarding conservative versus liberal, mega- versus small, clergy-led versus lay-led, or traditional versus contemporary—may turn out to be less important than choices regarding lordship versus popular idols or risk versus comfort.

Our guiding narrative can either broaden our vision or restrict it. Our attachment to our own viewpoint can be so strong that we are blind to alternative perspectives. The sort of engagement I described earlier with the phrase "on the other hand" can lead to bigger solutions than were possible with a limited point of view. Reflection on alternate approaches and explanations—even some that initially appear wrong or futile—can help us better understand the direction we have chosen. Jennifer Riel and Roger Martin, management experts at the University of Toronto, recommend exploring the core values of *opposing alternatives* with the goal of creating a great, new choice, for "it is in the tension between competing ideas that we come to understand the true nature of a problem and start to see possibilities for a creative answer."[10] This tension is the catalyst for contemplating new solutions. If we broaden our vision, we may discover that the apparent social polarities consuming our attention do not represent the actual forces working to pull people apart. The problem of our disconnectedness requires new kinds of approaches that reach into our hearts for alternative solutions.

Release

The release stage involves sharing solutions and evaluating the results. The ideas that emerged in the previous stage are released into the community that will benefit from the reflection. Empathic reflection, operating through perceptive thinking, often results in change in the ones who engaged in reflection as well as in the situation reflected upon. When there is too little reflection or not enough different perspectives to enhance the reflection, a group of people will seek to maintain their current direction and identity, looking for new experiences merely as a means to validate the group's existence. However, a learning environment that uses reflection in its practices has the potential to dramatically improve both the motivation among its participants and the quality of the mutual experience.

Empathic reflection can improve influence in at least four distinctive ways.[11] First, there is greater inclusion expressed among people who collaborate in their scrutiny of assumptions, as they draw on more perspectives. The influence within this group is increased because the process of thinking deeply together binds the participants to each other—even if they haven't learned any new truths from the experience. The second improvement is that participants in reflection may develop a positive attitude as a result of their mutual effort to increase their understanding of a situation. They benefit from an affirmation of both their identity and their ability to discern a direction for the future. The third improvement in influence is a shared sense of enhanced meaning regarding the significance of the subject they have been considering. Having been through a challenging, thoughtful learning experience together, they are more connected with each other's perspectives and with the value of the subject itself. Finally, those who have reflected together realize they have developed an increased competence in that subject and in working together. Their confidence in their ability to influence one another is usually greater than it was before they began the process of reflection. These results come about through an awareness that everyone is connected and accepted, and that their interests, values, ideas, and histories are appreciated.

The benefits of reflection are well-known among experienced project managers. When I worked in such a role, my team was charged with developing and producing new products on relatively short schedules. There are many uncertainties in moving a new product from design to manufacture, and the traditional tracking procedures actually slowed the development process by allowing every stage of activity to assume a maximum interval for completion. I arranged for my team members to *engage* with the lead designers and with some process experts to find out what everyone really needed for success. We recognized that everyone in the sequence of activities is most energized as a team when the critically urgent items receive the greatest attention. The *form-giving* significance of this realization was that fewer items had to be tracked—as long as the team members kept each other current on which items were most critical. The *emergent* solution was to reorganize some existing process components to streamline the project's reporting effort. The new approach was easier to *release* to the product team than most process changes because there was a noticeable decrease in the amount of extraneous information to be reported. The team members were allowed to focus on the parts of their jobs they enjoyed rather than the extra documentation they disliked. As a result, they were more motivated and enjoyed a greater team spirit, confident they were doing excellent work.

REFLECTIVE ENGAGEMENT

In this section, we will explore how reflection operates in various contexts. We will see how reflection is important for our heavenly relationship, our community relationships, and our relationship with ourselves.

Reflective with God

God is in love with his creation, and "he is mindful of his covenant forever" (Psalm 105:8). God reflectively thinks about us, and he has made our reflection on him possible by revealing himself to us. Author and theologian N. T. Wright explains, "Being in God's image is *both* about reflecting God into the world (the purpose) *and* about receiving and returning the divine love (the relationship)."[12] While our human attempts to reflect upon God are inadequate as a means to comprehend God, we are able to reflect upon God because he made himself accessible through the presence of his Spirit, the inspiration of Scripture, and the illumination of those who read and hear the Word. The Holy Spirit penetrates our hearts and persuades us regarding God's will.

We depend on the Spirit, and we also seek God in his Word. Since God's in control, we might be surprised by what we discover when we read and reflect on the Word. Swiss theologian Karl Barth explained that the Bible "offers us not at all what we first seek in it. . . . It is not the right human thoughts about God which form the content of the Bible, but the right divine thoughts about men. The Bible tells us not how we should talk with God but what he says to us; not how we find the way to him, but how he has sought and found the way to us."[13] The questions we earnestly bring to the Bible are all redirected toward the one who's at its center: Christ the Word. The self-revealing God of Scripture makes it possible for us to participate in the humanly impossible endeavor of knowing the Word of God. I've found in my work with church teachers that regular Scripture reading and reflection are helpful practices for allowing the Holy Spirit to be our guide.

Prayer is also vital for a reflective relationship with God. We need to reflect on our own lives and the situations of other people, and we also need to engage the Lord in that conversation. The apostle Paul admonished the Ephesian church to pray *in the Spirit* as a way to reflect on God in the context of defending one's faith and persevering on behalf of other Christians (Ephesians 6:18). In prayer we express our willingness to be reshaped by the Word of God in our decisions and actions, despite the temptations we encounter. Beyond the reception of God's Word examined in the previous chapter, reflection on God in both prayer and the Word connects us to his will in ways that guide and empower our steps to serve and imitate Christ in the world.

In an educational ministry, there are many opportunities to reflect with God on his will. Once, an experienced teacher expressed to me a strong desire to lead a Sunday-morning adult study series on the subject of self-defense, especially relating to personal safety. Due to people's strong emotions surrounding gun laws, the subject could potentially become divisive and stimulate a variety of personal disputes. I prayed for wisdom and guidance, and I searched Scripture for help. I learned that God expects us to trust him and exhibit wisdom in our actions. The Bible is clear that we should let God avenge all wrongs, but there's ambiguity in how to live that out in various circumstances. I decided I needed more advice than usual because my personal views on this subject are not the same as everyone in this congregation. I enlisted the help of several leaders in the congregation, who prayerfully discussed the situation and discerned—despite having a variety of views on this subject themselves—that such a class would not promote peace or unity at that time.

When I responded to the teacher that we preferred to focus on subjects promoting peace in the body of Christ, he was unexpectedly belligerent; he felt driven to lead a class on this subject and felt stymied by the leadership's decision. As a result, he declined the opportunity to teach a class on a different topic. This reaction confirmed for us that the decision we had made was truly in the best interest of the church and that a prudent discussion about violence and self-protection must be handled in a balanced fashion. Reflection upon the possible alternatives revealed that a more constructive class topic could emphasize what God is doing for his people and what it means to wait upon the Lord.

Reflective with Community

In spite of our cultural tendency toward individualism in the Western world, most of our learning is accomplished in collaboration with other people. It takes place in some form of community that influences our perceptions and interpretations of life. Educational scholars Stephen Preskill and Stephen D. Brookfield point out, "We cannot learn to be critically reflective, analyze experience, question ourselves, practice democracy, sustain hope, or create community without the necessary involvement of others."[14] Much of our thinking is a participation in what others before us and those presently around us have thought. Our common experiences suggest that people share certain *mental structures* that influence our perceptions.[15] Much of what we notice and remember is shaped by our communities of interpretation—those friendships, families, traditions, and organizations that contribute to our faculties of attention and reflection. The manner and context in which we approach learning affects what knowledge we obtain.

As a young adult recently out of college and newly married, I was deeply influenced by Curtis Stamps, who began his preaching tenure in New Jersey shortly after my wife and I moved there. The church often enjoyed having a potluck meal on the church grounds, followed by an outdoor devotional in the shade of the tall trees. I vividly recall one of the first devotionals Curtis delivered, in which he asked everyone to gather in a circle. He pulled out a ball of yarn and tossed it to someone across the circle, while holding on to the end of the string. He asked that person to do the same and throw the ball to someone else, while holding on to the string. After several repetitions of this activity, the ball of yarn was expended and the string crisscrossed the group many times. Then Curtis asked one of the people to tug on the string. The result was that it pulled at everyone in the group. We were all connected together, and the movement of any one of us affected everyone else. Influence in a community is about moving together with the "tugs" of the individual participants.

Another example of reflective cooperation is found in the disciples' discussion after seeing Jesus on the road to Emmaus (Luke 24:13–35). Confused by the recent events surrounding Jesus's death and the report of his resurrection, they welcomed an explanation from their unexpected companion. After recognizing Jesus, they sought out the eleven apostles, who were also grappling with the resurrection, and they all shared their experiences and interpretations with each other. Their reflection with one another confirmed their experience of walking with Jesus.

People generally feel a need to belong to a group and be part of a larger whole. A community provides meaning through belonging. In downtown Greenville, SC, Triune Mercy Center reaches out to people who are homeless and disadvantaged. Its previous pastor, Deb Richardson-Moore, observed that the members of the community who were being served by the church would often linger to help with various chores. They also appreciated being included as readers, singers, and liturgists in the worship. There was a longing for more than being served—there was a desire to belong as servants. People were regularly overheard to say, "This is our church."

The narrative that attracts the group together also defines who is outside the group. The reality is that our identity is shaped by discovering the people with whom we are connected and also by pulling back from those who dwell outside our social boundaries. The presence of these boundaries has both positive and negative implications. The integrity of both the group and the individual depends on the possibility of thoughtful, critical reflection on how the margins of the group's social identity are constituted. Thinking about the people on the edges of the group who are cautiously accepted or intentionally rejected can help us understand how our boundaries affect our identity—and how our identity is perceived by those outside our group. I understood this kind of reflection better after I moved away from my hometown to a more populated area. I grew up in a small town in Tennessee where the community was relatively homogenous, so when I moved to New Jersey after college, I was amazed at the diversity in the population. Then as I traveled with my work, I visited other parts of the world and my perceptions of people broadened immensely. I consciously reflected on how community diversity—racial, economic, and religious— offers the benefits of social collaboration and also presents the challenges of understanding people's intentions. As the boundaries of my social world have expanded, I have come to prefer and expect greater diversity than I ever considered as a youth.

Western society is facing a serious issue with the polarization and hardening of ideological viewpoints. The tendency of people to surround themselves with like-minded voices and pursuits has created cultural environments both offline and online characterized by arrogance and disdain toward those who might think differently. Specific ideologies that appeal to groups of Christians become guiding principles that are promoted as representing God's will. When dogmas are no longer open for critical reflection, then they become objects of devotion, idols of our own making. This phenomenon is like *groupthink*, a concept based on George Orwell's novel *Nineteen Eighty-Four*. It's a way of conformity in which group values are viewed as more than merely practical—they're regarded as the standard for what is right and good.[16] Of course, not all ideologies are idolatrous; the problem occurs when people (including Christians) refuse to hear alternate voices and stories that represent different—and truthful—perspectives. The parties in opposition—whether political, religious, or aligned with specific social issues—behave like fervent team supporters who will do anything, regardless of the moral cost, in order for their team to win. This form of group narcissism is particularly noticeable online, where many people prefer to remove from their news feed any ideas that differ from their own. Jesus modeled the solution to groupthink by prayerfully and empathetically respecting those who were outcasts and marginalized. Tolerance alone is not enough; the remedy is a loving engagement with those who feel like outsiders. If we, like Jesus, make it our mission to bring release to those who are oppressed, then we will be living in God's story rather than one of our own making.

As I mentioned earlier in this chapter, reflection requires examining hidden assumptions. Applying perceptive thinking to practices of reflection requires more than just questioning assumptions: It is a social process, accomplished within a collaborative group. It's concerned with power relations and the effects of maintaining or disturbing the status quo. It aims at emancipation of those who are oppressed and transformation of those who contribute to oppression. Critical reflection and social change are closely connected; both the powerful and the marginalized are easily deceived by existing power structures. Theologian Miroslav Volf explains that critical reflection includes the voices of others:

> We enlarge our thinking by letting the voices and perspectives of others, especially those with whom we may be in conflict, resonate within

ourselves, by allowing them to help us see them, as well as ourselves, from *their* perspective, and if needed, readjust our perspectives as we take into account their perspectives. Nothing can guarantee in advance that the perspectives will ultimately merge and agreement be reached. We may find that we must reject the perspective of the other. Yet we should seek to see things from their perspective in the hope that competing justices may become converging justices and eventually issue in agreement.[17]

This sort of reflection on the diverse voices in our community (especially including those who are otherwise unheard) is aimed at revealing the underlying structural causes that can be addressed by collective action. Such collaborative reflection is important for our discussion about formulating responses in the next chapter.

Influential practices like formative presence and resilient trust call upon us to reflect accurately on our purposes and behaviors. Our spiritual formation requires the presence of trusted colleagues who will observe our behaviors and provide us with feedback. Otherwise, we cannot see ourselves as others see us and we will not develop influence. Others can often identify our assumptions better than we can. As we hear others in community describe their experiences, we can improve our own practices.

Reflective with Oneself

Randy Pausch, the late professor of computer science at Carnegie Mellon University, made a fundamental observation: "The only way any of us can improve . . . is if we develop a real ability to assess ourselves. If we can't accurately do that, how can we tell if we're getting better or worse?"[18] We need to think perceptively about our own lives. We are responsible for considering our own behavior; nevertheless, reflection requires our diligent attention to feedback from others. In speaking about the bad behaviors we cannot see in ourselves, priest and theologian Barbara Brown Taylor says,

> Our shadows are often behind us, where others can see them better than we can. If we want to hear and see more—even the parts that expose our scornfulness—we need partners from outside our in-groups to keep telling us how we sound. Some of them get tired of doing this, I know, since those of us in the mainstream are not particularly fast learners. The people who stick with us seem to understand that they can benefit as much as we do, since one of the best ways to learn more about your

faith is to engage people who do not share it. The more we mix it up with others, the more we find out about who we really are.[19]

The development of a reflective community begins with individuals listening to diverse voices (including self) and constantly identifying and checking assumptions. We need to know ourselves and that requires more input than merely from ourselves.

When I worked as a telecom engineer, my goal was to move to higher positions in the company. I had some successes and promotions, and I thought I was doing well. However, at one point I looked around at the managers above me, reflecting on what I might become by following in their footsteps. I was shocked; all of them, as far as I could tell, were either divorced or in troubled marriages as a result of their higher positions in the company. That was *not* how I defined success, and I realized through reflection what I truly valued. I decided I did not want that result, and it changed my focus to be more oriented toward the people around me. I knew that my wife meant more to me than my position, and I learned that my friends meant more to me than my advancement. The narrative I choose for my life must be one that challenges me to become the person of integrity I desire to be.

The self-reflective individual is not only aware of his or her role in situational encounters, but also considers how he or she has contributed to the situation. However, our tendency is to replicate methods and traditions that affirm our own status. Our biases are connected to the underlying narratives we have believed. In addition to the assumptions we already acknowledge, there are hidden influences hindering our ability to work well with those who are different from us. Privileged behaviors such as racism, sexism, ableism, ageism, and classism are perpetuated by refusing to acknowledge and confront our values and prejudices. In other words, one of the features of privilege is not having to think about privilege. An approach to becoming more open about our contributions to various social, economic, and political inequities is to consider our assumptions and biases as *emotional investments* that we are actively supporting as protection against threats to our status quo.[20] Our passive neglect of inequities may in reality be an active compliance with dominant norms. A hesitancy to reflect on our assumptions may represent a fear of confronting our idols, and we must be willing to relinquish our idols of privilege in order to develop influence beyond our own social circles.

Critical reflection is risky and it can potentially increase anxiety. Today's quick-fix mentality is uncomfortable with the enormity of the problems in our society and has the potential to short-circuit reflective efforts. Nevertheless, Jesus said, "Do not let your hearts be troubled.

Believe in God, believe also in me" (John 14:1). When we trust God and his solutions, our identity and integrity no longer depend solely upon the world's judgment. We can bring our brokenness to God and to our friends or family in order to see ourselves as we truly are, rather than as targets of blame and shame. Connecting hearts with people and with God requires our own heart to be firmly joined with Christ. Our primary strength is not in ourselves, but in God's Spirit.

The irony of personal reflection is that we are not capable of making accurate assessments of ourselves by ourselves. We need community in order for our perception to develop a healthy wholeness. Friendships that bridge our social barriers are vital for developing character in ourselves, in relationship with our community, and in connection with God. Friends are companions in life who seek benefits for each other, often requiring significant investment. The next section examines the nature of friendships and how they help us develop influence.

FRIENDSHIPS

In the context of empathic reflection, relationships based on friendship offer a supportive, constructive environment for learning about ourselves, other perspectives, and influential practices. The change in ourselves necessary for wholeness is facilitated by friendships that offer a shared love for that wholeness. Long before my wife, Beth, and I were married—and ever since then—we have been close friends. We have shared mutual joys and mutual dislikes: We both enjoy hiking and traveling, but neither of us likes late-night studying or early-morning appointments. We have weathered emotional storms together, and we have scaled some amazing peaks. Some keys to our relationship have been empathic reception and mutual reflection. Early on we discovered that significant decisions like jobs, moves, and big purchases required both of our hearts focused together. We wanted it to be good for both of us, not a compromise. Minor decisions—such as setting schedules and making small purchases—allowed for individual freedom of expression. Reflecting together on goals, fears, hurts, and responsibilities has helped us know each other and to support each other. Therefore, big changes like my going to seminary or her launching an art business were easier because we trust and value each other's perspective. We love our relationship and want it to flourish.

Excellence

During the Classical Period of Greece, the philosopher Aristotle described three types of motivation for having friends—a utilitarian usefulness, a desire for pleasure, and a pursuit of excellence. Aristotle said the latter form is most virtuous because it consists of giving affection rather than receiving it.[21] Thomas Aquinas, a Dominican friar in the thirteenth century, understood friendship as a gift from God; in fact, the blessing of God's friendship gives meaning to our lives. Friendship provides an encounter with another who is distinct from ourselves and can draw us out of ourselves into a new identity. Jesus regarded himself as a friend of his disciples because he offered himself to them and for them, asking in return that they follow his directions (John 15:12–15).

Friends draw us into various forms of connection and intimacy that build mutual identity and integrity. Father Boyle suggests that this unity strengthens our conception of both God and each other. He explains that a Spanish way of speaking about a close friend is "like the fingernail and the dirt under it."[22] We accept and love each other even with the dirt—our baggage—that we all bring with us. This kind of relationship reaches for the best that each person can become while acknowledging that we all have constraints and weaknesses.

Vulnerability

Everyone needs relationships in which they can risk vulnerability. In particular, we desire friendships in which we can offer healthy challenges to one another, knowing we can lower our defenses in each other's presence. Proverbs 27:17 asserts that "iron sharpens iron," and the discomfort of the sharpening is less when applied by people we trust. We need the painful sharpening, and we need friends who are careful that the sharpening doesn't overwhelm us. Each of us must also be the kind of friend who allows only a level of discomfort that's beneficial for the other person. The relationship between the apostle Paul and his friend Timothy is a good example of a vulnerable friendship. Paul needed Timothy as much as Timothy needed Paul (1 Corinthians 4:17), even though their roles were different. When Paul was hurting and near despair, he expressed his weakness to Timothy and asked him to come help (2 Timothy 4:9–18). Our friends are a source of strength during times of testing or significant changes. Friends not only challenge each other, but also acknowledge the distress and provide relief when the sharpening of our hearts is painful.

The best friends are the ones who can see the parts of our character that need changing and help us to see it with them. Helping a friend become vulnerable and open to necessary criticism requires gentleness and empathy. Greg Jones, previously dean of the Divinity School at Duke University and now president of Belmont University, describes this relationship as a holy friendship. He explains, "Holy friends challenge the sins we have come to love, affirm the gifts we are afraid to claim and help us dream dreams we otherwise would not dream."[23] There are sins we justify to ourselves, and only someone close can reach past our denial to make us better. Friends can also see the gifts we are neglecting because we fear change. Even our own aspirations can remain hidden due to our self-image or past experiences. Holy friends lift us up to greater heights than we imagine for ourselves. They are truly God's agents in our lives to "to accomplish abundantly far more than all we can ask or imagine" (Ephesians 3:20).

Several years ago, my congregation was constructing a new building, and we used our own members to perform some of the unskilled jobs and thereby reduce costs. My wife and I organized several teams of members to work at the construction site on weekends. The tasks included sweeping and picking up construction debris around the work site, recycling cardboard, unloading and stacking materials, laying out the lawn irrigation system, and eventually installing windows and ceiling tiles. Each team had two co-leaders who watched over the work of their team, and we tried to select pairs of co-leaders who would work well together. One pair of co-leaders in particular developed a close friendship in spite of some big differences in their lives. Brett and Sam learned to respect and trust each other to such an extent that they could freely express frustration and disagreement while continuing to feel supported. After the construction was completed, Brett had a health crisis and went through several torturous surgeries. Sam was fully present, emotionally connected, and mutually reflective during every procedure along the way. Each could confide in the other, and they both drew strength from their friendship—an inner strength that was one of the biggest factors in Brett's physical healing.

Opening ourselves to others is especially important in friendships that cross cultures or social categories because the risk of hurting one another is greater. One person interprets a word or a gesture according to certain norms, and another individual may use the same word or gesture with an entirely different meaning. I went to seminary at a school with a different denominational background than my own, and I learned through some awkward exchanges that groups often use the same terms to mean different things. We also use dissimilar terms to mean the same thing, so there's hope if we will pay attention. One of the most common sources of miscommunication is the assumption that everyone uses (or should use) language the same way. Friends who reflect together on their own communication increase trust. Try initiating friendships with people who are not like you, and you will find that opening yourself to them will broaden and deepen your world. Together we learn that differences can enrich the language we develop as friends.

Forgiveness

One of the most vital, restorative aspects of the relationship between friends is forgiveness. Proverbs 17:9 indicates that forgiveness is a means of pursuing friendship. Dr. Jones links forgiveness to God's plan for reconciliation:

> In the face of human sin and evil, God's love moves toward reconciliation by means of costly forgiveness. In response, human beings are called to become holy by embodying that forgiveness through specific habits and practices that seek to remember the past truthfully, to repair the brokenness, to heal divisions, and to reconcile and renew relationships.[24]

These four aspects of embodying forgiveness provide an excellent road map for developing reflective friendships. Together people can *remember the past truthfully* because they trust one another, and this mutual vulnerability enables them to love through the pain they know and share. Forgiveness helps friends *repair the brokenness* in themselves and in others. There is evil and sin inside us that causes us to hurt one another, and we become enemies because we seek our own selfish gain at the expense of others. Forgiveness is what changes exclusion into embrace.[25] It breaks down hostility to *heal divisions* and to mend the wound of exclusion, and it comes at a cost to the one who forgives. The price that God paid to restore us was to cover our sin himself—requiring Christ's death (1 Peter 2:24; 3:18). Therefore, imitating our Lord means covering the cost of what others do against us. The enemy is no longer considered an enemy. The call to holy friendships is an appeal to *reconcile and renew relationships* between people who are different and broken. Friends who find ways to embody forgiveness are formative in their presence with each other because both parties change. Moreover, friends develop resilience in the trust they extend to one another as they persist in moving toward reconciliation and breaking down the barriers that identify people as *us* and *them*. Martin

Luther King Jr. explains, "Forgiveness means reconciliation, a coming together again. Without this, no man can love his enemies. The degree to which we are able to forgive determines the degree to which we are able to love our enemies."[26] Christians model reconciliation by demonstrating attitudes of love and forgiveness.

Forgiveness is cultivated in friendships through many small acts of reconciliation. Big acts of forgiveness get a lot of attention, but seemingly insignificant demonstrations of mercy strengthen relationships to handle adversity. Developing a forgiving heart is like building trust, which I described earlier as an accumulation of small acts of reciprocal vulnerability. The ability to forgive is an element of trustworthiness. It certainly contributes to the resilience needed in the practice of resilient trust. One of my pet peeves is to be ignored or forgotten, as when someone misses an appointment with me. My initial reaction is often to malign their intent. If that person is a friend, however, I'm more likely to extend grace and assume a reasonable explanation. Having built trust over time, the relationship is better positioned to be forgiving.

Health

In order to maintain a friendship that encourages both accountability and responsibility, the individuals must exercise self-control and self-regulation in such a way that they do not enable or perpetuate unhealthy outcomes. Edwin Friedman, a noted family therapist and leadership consultant, calls this behavior *self-differentiation*, while psychologists Henry Cloud and John Townsend describe it as maintaining healthy personal boundaries.[27] According to Friedman, there's a natural tendency in a relationship to form an emotional triangle—a relationship in which two people cannot resolve a conflict with each other, so they draw in a third party who relieves some of the tension by taking sides and receiving some of the blame. A triangle creates an illusion of intimacy in order to satisfy the well-being of one person at the expense of another. Leaders are often drawn into destructive relationships because people want to exploit the leader's power. Therefore, the leader must take responsibility for his or her own character and behavior, which often requires difficult actions to avoid manipulation even while remaining open to other people. In a healthy relationship, each person thinks perceptively about the relationship and how individual behavior contributes—positively or negatively—to the welfare of others.

Healthy friendships consist of people who are vulnerable enough with each other to expose their inner thoughts and feelings while also being separate enough to bring the strengths of their own individuality to the relationship. Genuine mutuality requires both the attachment of being connected and the detachment of maintaining independence so that neither party abuses the other. In Support Circles groups, there are often opportunities to substantially help the person who's making a life change. The group of supporters wants to enable a successful transition, so there's a strong temptation to overwhelm the individual with gifts. Instead of helping the person become independently capable of meeting life's challenges, we can—while meaning well—give so much that we create dependence rather than self-reliance. We must learn to reflect on our relationships, and spiritual disciplines can help. Praying together, combined with honest confession to each other, helps us avoid unhealthy tendencies.

Friends are often the primary catalyst for perceptive reflection and making sense of our lives. When I was diagnosed with prostate cancer in 2016, I knew I needed the support of a few friends who understood my situation. Multiple biopsy procedures had earlier returned negative results, but those experiences had prompted me to assemble a group of knowledgeable, empathetic friends along the way. When doctors eventually determined that I had a fairly aggressive form of cancer, I knew that it had been detected early and that fervent prayers were being offered on my behalf. The diagnosis was nevertheless a shock, and the encouragement I received from my friends helped me focus on God's abilities rather than mine. Donovan Norris influenced my decisions significantly because he had experienced the same condition and the same procedure. He reflected with me on my prognosis, and he demonstrated compassion without criticism. With his help, I was able to make sense of my options and decide how to move forward. The recommended surgery was a success, and I learned through these circumstances that God often uses friendships to provide strength during our suffering. Since then I have had opportunities to influence and support other men who have dealt with prostate cancer.

A true friend wants what is best for the other person, and that means each friend supports the flourishing of that person's own gifts and talents. God's loving care for us in Christ models the nature of friendship, and together with friends we fulfill God's design for us. Friends support and encourage each other to reach beyond brokenness to achieve God's calling. They also challenge us to face our behaviors and attitudes that obstruct God's purposes. Close friendships demonstrate the power of influence to develop one's inner character.

REFLECTION AND CHRISTIAN INFLUENCE

Reflection is an often overlooked skill. We live in a "get 'er done" culture in which we feel an urgency to move quickly from the issue to the solution. We may take time to listen attentively and appreciatively, but there's often little time spent considering the meaning of the event and entertaining the value of alternative solutions. Sometimes our reflection should focus on the time we spend with others rather than a particular problem or solution. However, the pressure to produce a result is usually strong. We tend to launch toward an outcome before collecting input. A better way to be an influence is to engage with multiple perspectives earlier and include all interested parties in the reflection. Then the response is shared by everyone who cares about the outcome.

Teachers can help students reflect by expressing their passion for the subject and emphasizing the value of learning. Students usually appreciate their teachers' enthusiasm, and sometimes it's contagious. While I was in engineering graduate school, I took some classes at a school of preaching in Oakland, California, long before I ever had an urge to preach or teach. I was drawn to those classes by the vibrant love of the biblical text demonstrated by one man: Kenwood Devore. Over forty years later, I still hang on to my notes from those classes. Passionate, influential educators can introduce a topic or a study as though they were introducing a close friend—a friend whose complexity and mystery are fully appreciated by the teacher:

> The teacher who loves a subject must not try to force that love upon the students. The teacher, like any lover, must be capable of having a lover's quarrel with the subject, stretching and testing the loved one and the relationship. In this way students are invited into the negation as well as affirmation, into argument as well as assent, within the secure context of friendship and hospitality.[28]

Modeling reflective practice—entertaining alternate, opposing viewpoints—convinces learners that reflection is useful. Reflection and feedback can be used in classrooms, meetings, and even informal gatherings as a way to cultivate curiosity and encourage dialogue between all of the participants—both leaders and followers—as they learn how to address difficult problems and situations.

Leaders can model reflective practice by questioning their own ideas and assumptions in the presence of the group. In my experience, this behavior is rare among teachers and leaders because no one wants to risk being wrong or appearing weak in public. However, questioning oneself is not the same as doubting or berating oneself. The strength of humility is maintaining confidence while putting authority in the hands of others. Meekness is controlled strength. In such an environment, a leader demonstrates—and influences others by example—that risk and change are valued. Students, employees, volunteers, and other learners will become open to new ways of thinking as reflection is modeled for them in their environment. Failure is not an embarrassment when the focus is on learning rather than succeeding. By reflecting perceptively on failures as well as successes, new alternatives and modifications become possible. Organizations that conceal failures and silence any discussion about sensitive issues cannot learn how some problems are connected to others. Consequently, systemic disorders often don't get addressed.

How can we assess whether we are reflective? One way to evaluate ourselves is to observe whether we try new things. I know of a person who was served a dish of an unfamiliar food, and unwilling to try it, she simply replied, "I like enough things." She missed an opportunity to taste and learn something new. She also failed to benefit from reflection on her range of preferences. Becoming more reflective will result in finding more things we like and don't like. In order to take that step, we need people who will nudge us forward—friends who will provide constructive feedback and reflect with us on how to improve our interactions. Years ago while on a tour in China, our group was served a buffet for breakfast. Rather than reflect on the culinary experience, an American objected to the unfamiliar appearance of the food and complained, "Who eats this for breakfast?" A quick-witted iconoclast countered, "Several million Chinese people." We all occasionally need a nudge to be open to the ways of others and reflect on how our customs are different.

How well do you explore questions, display enthusiasm, and build relationships? All of these are reflective behaviors, and they are difficult to assess in ourselves. Most of us receive feedback, but not all of us pay attention to it. If you are in a position of power or authority, you may have more freedom to ignore feedback than those who depend on others. Regardless of your position, your influence depends on reflection, and you need reflective relationships in order to help you become more influential. In order to get started, initiate a conversation with a few of your peers and discuss how each of you likes to work. Invite someone into your workspace or offer to visit them. If you are self-employed or you are a stay-at-home parent, reach out to some people in a similar vocation or situation. Find out what motivates them and what resources they find useful. If you work in a service industry or a volunteer organization, find out more about who depends on your activities. Ask about your church's activities and offer to help. If you are retired, find out who might like a visit. Build some new relationships with a variety of people outside your neighborhood, company, church, and community. Reflect with people on what each of you value and listen for their heart.

Exercises in reflective thinking can help us be aware of our effectiveness. The following sample exercises provide an opportunity for you to experiment with reflective thought. The intent of these activities is to demonstrate the impact of empathic reflection. The next chapter draws upon the discussions about receptivity and reflection in order to make practical application in the social networks of our lives. Our responsibilities to others—as both leaders and learners—become clear as we determine how we will implement practices of formative presence and resilient trust in the context of our communities and our commitments.

Practical Exercises

In order to understand what sort of influence you have on people, you can reflect on how and when they approach you. Do others come to you with problems to be solved, or do they want to spend time chatting with you? Do they entrust you with sensitive matters and new ideas? Do people want you on their team, and if so, in what capacity? If you seldom receive such requests, you may need to focus on the receptive skills discussed in the previous chapter. The more encounters you have with people, the more opportunities you have to reflect on what they perceive about your presence and your trustworthiness.

Another exercise is to ask yourself a series of questions to guide your reflection.[29] Please write your answers so you can read them afterward. The objective is for you to think about what you have learned and how it has changed you.

- What is something—anything—you can now explain to someone that you could not have a year ago?
- What's the most important thing you have learned about yourself in the past year?
- Which of your assumptions about influence and learning have been most challenged during the past year?
- How much of your learning is primarily intellectual (cognitive) versus emotional (affective)?

- How much of your learning during the past year has been in an entirely new area? How much has been a refinement, rethinking, or adaptation of something familiar?
- Who has encouraged and challenged you in new ways to be a leader?
- What events or experiences have been most significant or transformative for you?

After reading your responses, reflect on how you learn and how you influence others. Write down these reflections. As a result, you should have a sense of how you have been changing.

This final exercise is aimed at developing a reflective frame of mind over a period of time. Start keeping a log or journal of events, situations, and perceptions you encounter. Try to spend a little time regularly in reflection, with at least one entry each week. Include the details of events that you remember vividly. The following questions can help you think about what to write:

- What was a moment this week when you felt most connected, engaged, or affirmed in your own purposes and mission?
- What was a moment this week when you felt most disconnected, disengaged, or bored with your direction and activities?
- What was a situation that caused you anxiety or distress—something that kept replaying in your mind?
- What was an event that took you by surprise, shook you up, gave you a jolt, or made you unexpectedly happy?
- What worked well for you this week, and how might you do more of it?
- What didn't work well, and how could it be better?
- Who was a significant encourager for you this week?
- Whom did you accompany on their path, and for whom did you sacrifice?

Schedule some time each month to read your entries, observing any patterns in your responses. You may begin to see that particular situations give you pleasure or pain. Then you can consider how your energy might be redirected toward better engagement and collaboration with people. Consider suggesting this exercise to some of your peers or colleagues and then sharing your responses with each other. Your friends can help identify patterns and assumptions that you might otherwise ignore.

QUESTIONS FOR GROUP DISCUSSION

A good example of reflection is found in Luke 24. What did the disciples reflect upon while traveling with Jesus to Emmaus? Also read 2 Timothy 4:9–18 and discuss what Paul reflected on near the end of his life.

1. What does it mean to reflect on an idea or event?
2. List some characteristics of perceptive people.
3. What are some things that are worthwhile to ponder? (see Philippians 4:8).
4. What are some ways to become more curious about people and topics?
5. How do our assumptions create conflicts?
6. What are the big stories that give direction to your life?
7. How can we reflect on God?
8. How do the groups and organizations to which we belong contribute to our perceptions?
9. What does it take to build a great friendship?
10. How do close friends help each other? Explain how "iron sharpens iron" (Proverbs 27:17).
11. How is forgiveness an important component of personal influence?
12. How can we determine whether we are reflective?

IF YOU DON'T REFLECT,
IT DIDN'T HAPPEN

Glenis Redmond is a poet and teaching artist. Her main objective is to help youth develop a sense of agency for themselves. She creates safe spaces for kids to ignite their artistic passion and pursue their dreams. She says, "I want to be a living example of what an artist and what a community advocate can be in the world." She helps students learn to connect with an audience and to express themselves on stage as well as in their writing. She teaches them to look for stories that are relevant to their lives and also to tell their own stories. She asks questions and challenges her students to go on a quest for deep reflection. The students explore "their own personal plummeting down deep to the past, to the unknown, and whatever they brought back up, it was relevant [to them]. This relevancy creates an authenticity." Glenis emphasizes the need to spend time in reflection, saying, "If you don't reflect, it didn't happen." Then she urges her students to express their discoveries in some creative fashion.

Glenis first began writing in the 1990s as a way to nourish her own health. She initially volunteered for poetic events in the Greenville area, and the South Carolina Arts Commission acknowledged her vocation by establishing her as a statewide teaching artist. She began partnering with the Peace Center in Greenville in 2003, designing and leading workshops in creative writing for all ages and abilities. About the same time, she was also invited by the Kennedy Center's Partnership in Education Program in Washington, D.C., to lead workshops as a teaching artist across the country. In 2011, she became the Peace Center's first artist-in-residence. She has initiated several programs such as Peace Voices, which is dedicated to poetic outreach and engagement in the community. She also created Poetic Conversations as an opportunity to lift up other poets and other communities of experience to have a platform to speak about who they are.

Glenis approaches people with a profound sense of humility and respect for the experiences they bring to her writing workshops. She doesn't begin with telling, but rather with an openness to hear what people are saying. Her own personal experiences with poverty, disability, and racial issues have affected her empathy for others. She realizes that "everyone has something they're dealing with," and she suggests that we can relate to each other better by respecting what everyone is going through. She develops close relationships with youth and adults as they share their perspectives. Her poetry speaks to people and encourages them to express their own voices.

6

EMPATHIC RESPONSE

A Christian's inner character is shaped and grounded in a particular identity formed in and by a community of Christians. Moreover, a Christian's integrity—the wholeness that glues together the various components of identity—is sustained through relationships that nurture resilient trust. This formation of character results from what we receive and reflect upon, but the process does not end with individual reflection. When we act upon our environment in a constructive manner consistent with our reflection, then our growth comes to life in specific activities. The third empathic skill—response—is developed and evaluated in the community where the action takes place.

All of us respond in both private and public contexts. We have personal interactions that call for dealing with problems or taking care of people. For example, a neighbor or a child gets in trouble and we offer help. Sometimes very little reflection is required, but attentive listening is always important before taking action. At other times, more contemplation and connection are necessary. I noticed in a hospital recently how deliberate the nurses were with each patient, weighing the consequences of every action. Understanding the significance of our responses to every situation affects the influence we have in a public context. Our responses to other people have social implications. The influence we have in relatively minor settings can make a substantial difference in the lives of the network of people with whom we are connected.

Three interrelated terms are important for our discussion—*response*, *responsiveness*, and *responsibility*. H. Richard Niebuhr, a prominent Christian theological ethicist, made the assertion that all action is a response to a prior action. Any judgment of morality regarding that response depends on how the prior action was interpreted.[1] People exhibit a *response* as a result of how they are affected by some event. An active transformation in the individuals' lives incites the response, whether great or small. The response is a matter of living out the learning stimulated by the event.

The next term, *responsiveness*, introduces the dynamic of interpersonal and intercultural relationships. Everyone in a group has assumptions about how they should relate to one another. The manner in which the parties interpret these relational assumptions establishes a range of opportunities for the parties to move closer together or further apart. The environment is usually structured in such a way that the participants function according to their positions in the network of people. The most effective personal responses are often empathetic, taking into account the other person's relational assumptions. The participants are influenced not only by their thoughts, but also by their emotions, connections, prior baggage, cultural norms, fundamental beliefs, future expectations, and current state of well-being.

The notion of *responsibility* furthers the consideration of a person's relationships to include society and culture. Responsiveness precedes responsibility. In order to develop responsibility, people must learn to be responsive *to* someone. Our responses form an unspoken, metaphorical dialogue with others as we react to their behavior and anticipate how they will react to us. Since we have expectations for how the interaction will proceed, we attempt to hold each other accountable for the appropriateness of their responses.

The early church grappled with the paradox of *what is* versus *what ought to be* in their lives. They saw themselves as pilgrims journeying through the present struggles of pain and sorrow toward the glory and joy of a future that has not yet been completely fulfilled. They described themselves as *resident aliens* (1 Peter 2:11)—people who live within the structures of the world without being limited by them. That's how Christians stand apart with a heavenly perspective. The Epistle to Diognetus, a defense of Christianity written in the second century, expressed the belief that Christians are in the world for the benefit of society: "What the soul is to the body, Christians are to the world."[2] We are a responsible, formative presence in society for the sake of others. Such a balanced attitude of responsibility is exemplified in the way that the Samaritan traveler in Jesus's parable assessed the situation and responded to the need of the wounded victim (Luke 10:29–37). The Samaritan's response was different from the other people on the road because he understood his responsibilities differently. The religious leaders who passed by the injured man were probably most concerned about their own safety and plans. They did not see themselves as culpable, but the Samaritan acted as a neighbor by exhibiting responsibility toward someone in need.

The response of a person or group contributes to an ongoing dialogue, looking backward in order to evaluate the significance of an event and also looking forward with a view to agency. This duality of perspectives regarding the past and the future causes some confusion about the purpose and scope of responsibility. The late professor and political theorist Iris Marion Young explained that a *liability model*, which emphasizes retribution for past faults, dominates much of Western culture's legal and moral discourse. By focusing blame for culpability on specific individuals, all others are absolved and the majority of people remain unaccountable for their participation in detrimental social processes.[3] An example of this model of responsibility operating in our society is the tendency of the dominant, White culture to blame racial terrorism on a few bad individuals rather than on a larger institution or social perspective. Focusing on a few individuals comfortably absolves the larger population from culpability. A *social connection model* provides a better balance than the liability model between looking backward and looking forward and is not as likely to get stuck in the past. It emphasizes agency rather than fault and promotes a shared responsibility for the future among all who contribute by their actions to the propagation of collective structural problems. Young offered an example of a context in which to understand our responsibility for structural issues:

> A sensible understanding of the sources of *any* person's situation, whether poor or not, should refer *both* to the structural constraints and opportunities he or she faces, *and* to his or her choices and actions in relation to them. Those of us who are not poor—or not poor right now—participate in the same structures of privilege and disadvantage, constraint and enablement, as those who fall below the poverty line at some point. We need to assess *our* responsibility in relation to these structures.[4]

A responsible agent—contrasted with passive fault-finders—first recognizes the options available to everyone involved in the situation. The person who is constrained by the need to care for family members, the encumbrances of a disability, the limitations imposed by a past incarceration, or the lack of job training has significantly fewer prospects for prosperity than someone who has the privilege of wealth, health, education, and social position. The responsible person then reflects upon these options to some extent before acting, which results in choices that show concern rather than blame for how the consequences of those actions may affect others.

Tony McDade is someone whom I have observed demonstrating responsibility to his community. He has exercised leadership in South Carolina by ministering alongside churches, volunteering to support people, initiating new ministries, and directing United Ministries, a nonprofit organization that empowers individuals to achieve self-sufficiency. A tireless advocate for disadvantaged families and those experiencing homelessness, Tony helped create a program—Interfaith Hospitality Network—that engages several churches together in using their facilities to provide temporary housing. While he hasn't experienced homelessness himself, he is a compassionate listener. He knows he doesn't automatically have influence, but instead "you have to earn your voice." He enjoys working with people individually to get to know them and their struggles. He says most people are seeking something bigger than themselves, and they are willing to collaborate in an environment that offers respect and trust. The influential Christian speaks truth in love while bearing in mind what is at stake and who might be affected.

Responsibility is about working together to influence a better future for everyone. As the influential person helps people progress together, there are inevitable conflicts and tensions requiring attention. People have different perspectives and opinions about the future that are difficult to reconcile between people. Pastor and theologian Dietrich Bonhoeffer recognized this when he said, "Responsibility implies tension between obedience and freedom."[5] People desire the freedom to express themselves, yet they also choose to follow the directions associated with particular groups, ideals, or traditions. The balance between personal freedom and personal obedience, as well as the specific way that each of the two is understood and pursued, varies among people.

We act responsibly toward people by respecting their ability to make choices and engaging in dialogue with them about those choices. If we think a person cannot make wise decisions—as in the case of young children or impaired adults—then we cautiously provide direction for how they should proceed. Otherwise, we are not acting responsibly toward others when we limit their freedom and obedience by imposing our will upon them. We act responsibly when we honor others' responsibility. One of the reasons for the intense, partisan animosity in our society is that we have lost much of what it means to act responsibly toward one another. Like children who selfishly demand their own way, we want to dictate rules to others rather than create relationships with others. For example, White people prescribe to people of color how to conform to White culture. People on both sides of the abortion debate insist on their own ways to preserve life. Capitalists and social reformers both declare how the economy should bring benefits to people. There is too much telling and not enough listening and reflection. Effective influence is based on dialogue and trust rather than legal or religious coercion. Our responses to people and situations should be based on empathy and should embody our responsibility to each other.

The way empathic response works is illustrated in one of the methods Starbucks uses to train its employees. While serving customers, baristas face many occasions for unpleasant experiences, and the popular purveyor of coffee has specific procedures for handling complaints. The managers at Starbucks refer to one of their procedures as the *LATTE* method: "We *Listen* to the customer, *Acknowledge* their complaint, *Take action* by solving the problem, *Thank* them, and then *Explain* why the problem occurred."[6] Listening and acknowledgement correspond to the skills of reception and reflection discussed in the previous two chapters. The *response* to the situation consists of immediately taking action on behalf of the customer. Thanking the person is a way of being *responsive* by engaging and establishing a relationship of appreciation and trust. Finally, the employee demonstrates *responsibility* by offering an expectation of accountability. The explanation is not so much a justification of the action as it is a recognition of how the company's processes affect the consumer and might be altered or continued in the future. When influential Christians encounter dissatisfaction with their own actions or with the behavior of the church, they can employ a response like the *LATTE* method to acknowledge and resolve problems.

Jesus demonstrated that he was a responsible agent of both grace and truth. When the people who heard and saw him wanted to know whether he was the Messiah whom they were expecting, he told them to look for the answer in what he was doing: People were cured, evil spirits were sent away, the unclean were cleansed, and the poor had good news brought to them (Luke 7:18–23). Jesus shared God's grace with people by touching them and responding to their most immediate needs. He also upheld God's integrity by being responsive to those who desired God's mercy—whether they were Jewish or not. Jesus's responses took him in directions that many of the Jews did not expect because they did not understand what it meant to exercise responsibility *to* God and *for* creation. What responsibilities do Christians have? Do Christian influencers carry greater responsibility than others? Like Jesus, everyone can be a visible agent of grace and truth, connecting one's own responsibility to an identity given by God and to a sense of integrity nurtured in God's community.

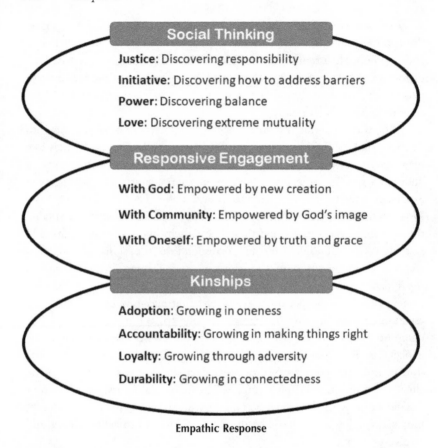

Empathic Response

The next three sections examine the nature of social responsibility, the contexts in which we respond, and the way kinships shape our responses. As the figure illustrates, these are interlocking aspects of responsiveness as a skill. Influential Christians learn how to address barriers between people and work toward balanced social structures. Motivated by our sense of God's presence, we develop kinships to nurture an ongoing cycle of connectedness.

SOCIAL THINKING

The pursuit of justice—which I define in a Christian context as supporting and empowering people to behave in accord with biblical norms of what is right—is an important concern for people who want to exhibit godly character. "To do righteousness and justice is more acceptable to the LORD than sacrifice" (Proverbs 21:3). The Hebrew term for *righteousness* refers to the right conduct of people toward one another, and *justice* usually carries a legal connotation. Both are expected to be characteristic of our behavior and to be applied in positive ways to social contexts. The prophet Amos proclaimed God's instruction to "let justice roll down like waters, and righteousness like an ever-flowing stream" (Amos 5:24). Just as Jesus gave hope to people who were downtrodden by society (Matthew 12:17–21), his followers are called to pursue social justice (Matthew 23:23; compare Micah 6:8). Influential Christians have a responsibility to demonstrate and elicit responses that connect with the righteous work God is doing in the world.

Our motivation—the condition of our heart—is one of the most important elements in responding with righteousness. Assistance should always be offered in a way that allows people to retain dignity and independence. There's always a danger that a person will provide "help" in a way that emphasizes superior social position and constrains the other person to long-term dependency. Even tough love—stern treatment initiated to help someone take responsibility for their actions—can be detrimental when one person exerts the power of coercion over another.

In most group settings, the actions and expectations of the members reinforce the definition of responsibility adopted by the group. Most Christians understand responsibility in light of the biblical teachings about the church. The distinctiveness of living the Christian narrative implies a specific emphasis on *being the church* rather than assimilating with the world,[7] while at the same time, the Spirit of God is using Christians to break down factional barriers that divide people into classes or hierarchies. Christians are supposed to remain separate from worldly behaviors but still maintain connections with people outside the church. Jesus's Sermon on the Mount (Matthew 5–7) is a tremendous example of teaching people to move beyond the typical interpersonal barriers associated with wealth, power, violence, legalism, justice, faithfulness, truthfulness, piety, security, loyalty, and judgment.

Justice

Justice is a key outcome of effective responsibility. The influential political philosopher John Rawls stated that social justice consists of "the way in which the major social institutions distribute fundamental rights and duties and determine the division of advantages from social cooperation."[8] The most basic perspectives on justice highlight the roles of individuals and the roles of institutions. The responsibilities of individuals concern how people are treated when they are encountered directly. Many people view justice solely in this respect as a private matter regarding their personal culpability for harming other people. The second perspective considers how people contribute to collective, structural processes that make certain people more vulnerable than others. Some people blame institutions to such an extent that they absolve themselves of accountability for injustice. Neither of these perspectives alone is sufficient because personal responsibility cannot be separated from the social context.

Justice was personified in ancient Roman culture as a woman carrying a set of balancing scales and a sword. The scales represent the weighing of evidence for the support or opposition of a particular case. The sword depicts the authority of the court. Since the sixteenth century, a blindfold has often been added to the popular figure, representing her impartiality. The goal of blind justice is that it should be applied without regard for wealth, power, or status. However, we are all accountable to each other to notice when power and wealth upset the scales. God expects us to have our eyes wide open to distortions of justice so that people are not exploited for monetary gain or left defenseless for lack of financial means (Deuteronomy 16:19).

Our responsibility originates in our commitment to Christ, the church, and society, all of which embody systems of interdependent processes that rely upon our cooperation. When the group's processes produce unjust outcomes, the members of the group bear responsibility, even though they may not be individually culpable. Each of us can reproduce structural injustice even while following the accepted societal norms. A simple example of how this often works is the phenomenon known as *gridlock*— all the drivers are trying to reach their destinations while obeying traffic laws, but a congested collection of drivers who refuse to yield can prevent everyone from making progress. Church leaders have a specific responsibility to appraise their church's contributions to oppressive conditions and formulate a response aligned with biblical directives regarding justice for the oppressed. The Lord instructed his people to exercise justice and righteousness by helping people who have been wronged and oppressed, regardless of whether they were part of God's kingdom (Jeremiah 22:3). We should be able to identify with those who have little hope because we have experienced God's rescue ourselves.

Initiative

There are many types of barriers that divide people today, and they all function to buttress the self-interest of some at the expense of others. For example, there are social barriers that categorize people by race, class, age, and sexual identity. There are economic barriers that hold people in poverty and gender barriers that limit advancement. There are barriers that inhibit access and participation by differently abled individuals. These hurdles create social classes when they are used to exploit or disenfranchise groups of people. The actions that perpetuate these classes may not be intentional, and that is why we must examine our responses in light of our responsibility.

Martin Luther King Jr. offers us a model for empathic response. His "Letter from Birmingham City Jail" is particularly relevant as a perspective articulated in adverse circumstances. The movement led by King was one of many initiatives among Black organizations during the civil rights era to move beyond the barriers that had been erected by the dominance of White culture. King saw that racism had distorted the character of the White population and that Black people could deliver both White people and themselves from destruction by demonstrating God's love in the face of mass hatred.

After leading a march in Birmingham, King and several others were arrested on April 12, 1963, and he was placed in solitary confinement. Someone secretly brought him a Birmingham newspaper that had published "A Call for Unity" by eight White clergymen in Alabama. King was incensed that these men repudiated his campaign as "unwise and untimely," motivating him to respond with an open letter of his own. The "Letter from Birmingham City Jail" was widely published and later anthologized in several books.[9] Its contents demonstrate how Christian responses might be formulated. King addresses the necessary responsibility for justice and injustice, methods of nonviolent response, obedience to law, the disappointing failure of White churches, and a challenge to break through the status quo. Perhaps the most significant feature is that King's desire for reconciliation is paramount throughout the letter. His quotations and references in the letter indicate he was listening to both his critics and his supporters, and his past reflection on their viewpoints brought him to a point where he could articulately address the situation.

Early in the letter, King explained how he was being responsive to his supporters as well as to the opposition who viewed his allies as outsiders trying to stir up trouble. Specifically, he said his reason for being in Birmingham was that injustice was there. Like the apostle Paul, he was compelled to bring help to those who were calling out (see Acts 16:9–10). Although King's operations were based in Atlanta, he proclaimed in his letter, "Injustice anywhere is a threat to justice everywhere." The authorities in Birmingham had not been responsive to the underlying causes of oppression and distress, so he clearly identified the steps that he and his organization were pursuing—fact-gathering, negotiation, self-purification, and direct action. The segregation and brutality in Birmingham were widely acknowledged, and the Black population had tried unsuccessfully to engage in good-faith negotiations with those in authority. Despite their deep disappointment, the oppressed people took the initiative to learn about nonviolent procedures and to reflect upon their own integrity and readiness to proceed with such action. They reminded themselves that justice must be demanded by the those who are oppressed and that laws can be unjust when they degrade humanity.

Power

Dr. King explained that the problem of segregation was perpetuated by a legally enforced imbalance of power. His letter includes a litany of indignities resulting from the subordinating power exercised by privileged White people, and he pointed out that groups with power seldom yield their advantage voluntarily. For this reason, King saw the campaign's actions as a way to create an opportunity for negotiation. The objective was to call upon all parties to accept responsibility for the structures that have produced unjust outcomes. Both the beneficiaries of such institutions and those who were marginalized by them are obligated to work on transforming those structures so that the injustices do not continue. King encouraged the church to become a *thermostat* rather than a *thermometer*—transforming society rather than merely reflecting popular opinion.[10]

Christians today have opportunities to initiate a restructuring of power because our influence in one-on-one encounters and in community gatherings is an important exercise of power. Responding with empathy is not a demonstration of weakness; it's a way to connect with a different perspective and engage in a dialogue about justice. Our calling is not to fix the other person, but to stand with that person as a co-recipient of God's grace and reflect on how we are together affected by our institutions. Dialogue and reflection, empowered by God's Spirit, have the ability to diminish and redirect the dominance of unjust authority. The strength of working together is greater than either party operating alone, and the result is a richer set of possible responses.

Before Deb Richardson-Moore retired from her role as pastor and director of Triune Mercy Center, I spoke with her about the challenges of leadership. She began her ministry at Triune in 2005 with food and clothing pantries, along with providing meals and counseling. However, Deb realized that the immediate needs being served didn't address the underlying problems. There needed to be more attention to the addictions and mental illness that prevented people from escaping homelessness and poverty. The structures that keep people in poverty include not only discriminatory public policies but also a lack of opportunities for people with disadvantages to engage with everyone in the community. Therefore, in addition to the counseling services and case management support provided by their capable staff members, Triune offers literacy training, bike repair, vegetable gardening, a music room, painting, computer usage, drama programs, various support groups, beauty/portrait events, and much more. Privileged, middle-class people work beside displaced and disadvantaged individuals, and they all believe this is what the kingdom of God looks like. Other churches and human services organizations partner with Triune, offering volunteers, health services, and other forms of support. Deb suggested to me that churches can collaborate further by examining how they use their budget, time, and other resources. How does our attention to society's marginalized population compare with our responsiveness to the established, privileged members of the church? Everyone can have an impact on rebalancing the prevailing power structures that affect how we connect with people.

Love

Dr. King called for love as the middle way between the extremes of complacency and bitter hatred. Responding to accusations of being an extremist himself, King pointed out that Jesus was an extremist for love when he told us to love our enemies (Luke 6:27–28). King understood that mending the divide between races requires acts of love for enemies. Jews and Gentiles hated each other but were called instead to reconcile in love (Ephesians 2:13–18). Similarly, White people and people of color are called to reconcile in love. King knew this would be difficult because so many White Christians desire to maintain the status quo of cultural dominance, and they see any gain by Black people as a loss for themselves.

Regardless of our own individual culpability, we are collectively accountable for fostering a just and loving society. In the parable Jesus told about a Samaritan helping a wounded man (Luke 10:29–37), Jesus praised the Samaritan neighbor for risking his own safety and covering a significant cost for the sake of someone who was unlikely to gratefully reciprocate. The person who asked Jesus to define *neighbor* was a prominent Jew who was unlikely to ever consider a Samaritan worthy of providing help; in fact, he had difficulty admitting to Jesus that the Samaritan was the one who had helped. The hated Samaritan is the one who offers restoration and healing! In a sermon on this parable, King spoke to the challenge of being that neighbor:

> The ultimate measure of a man is not where he stands in moments of comfort and convenience, but where he stands at times of challenge and controversy. The true neighbor will risk his position, his prestige, and even his life for the welfare of others. In dangerous valleys and hazardous pathways, he will lift some bruised and beaten brother to a higher and more noble life.[11]

The risk King describes goes beyond creating simple diversity. It's an extreme form of love. It requires a fundamental transformation in how people encounter one another and do things together.

RESPONSIVE ENGAGEMENT

Developing responsible character is a process of reconciliation. This process focuses on restoring broken relationships and systems through ongoing attention to repentance, forgiveness, and justice. Reconciliation requires dealing with the past so that the future is not held hostage to invalid, archaic norms. Dr. King gazed through his disappointment in the failure of White church leadership toward a larger vision of the hope of future reconciliation. He looked forward to a time when heroes of reconciliation would be recognized and applauded by the public. In the meantime, our love for our enemies must drive our responses, and our responses move us toward reconciliation between people. In other words, the hope of reconciliation is grounded in responsiveness to God, community, and oneself.

Responsive to God

God acts responsibly toward his creation. He is the Creator, and he is not dependent on our actions. He is the one who says, "I am the first and I am the last" (Isaiah 44:6; compare Revelation 22:13). The reason for the presence of justice in the world is that the Just One who created the world is present in it and desires that all creation reflect his nature. How wonderful it is that the one who fashioned the heavens and earth has not abandoned that creation to its own devices! This is the Lord who "will not fail you or forsake you" (Deuteronomy 31:6). He is the one "whose kindness has not forsaken the living or the dead!" (Ruth 2:20).

This kindness is the foundation of God's loving presence that was mentioned earlier with respect to the practice of formative presence. As the late Rabbi Lord Jonathan Sacks pointed out, covenant love (*hessed* in Hebrew) finds expression in responsible action.

> *Hessed* is the love that is loyalty, and the loyalty that is love. It is born in the generosity of faithfulness, the love that means being ever-present for the other, in hard times as well as good; love that grows stronger, not weaker, over time. It is love moralized into small gestures of help and understanding, support and friendship: the poetry of everyday life written in the language of simple deeds. Those who know it experience the world differently from those who do not. It is not for them a threatening and dangerous place. It is one where trust is rewarded precisely because it does not seek reward. *Hessed* is the gift of love that begets love.[12]

This sort of love creates a bond that surpasses the relationship between friends and the fellowship between mentors and apprentices. As I will discuss later in this chapter, the connection is best described as *kinship,* and the Father models it for us in the covenantal sacrifices he makes on behalf of humanity.

Jesus is our example for understanding how we are to respond to the Father. Before Jesus engaged in ministry, he looked for what his Father was already doing. "The Son can do nothing on his own, but only what he sees the Father doing; for whatever the Father does, the Son does likewise" (John 5:19). God is already working, and he guides his followers in discerning how to participate.

In the context of following God's direction, faith is best understood as both a response to God and a responsibility to God. It's not an obligation for particular works on our part, but a grateful response to him. The ministry of reconciliation has been given to the church, but that ministry does not begin with the church. It begins with God. As Paul explained to the Corinthian church, reconciliation with God is possible only because of God's gift of new creation. The Christian's role is to be an ambassador for the one who makes everything new (2 Corinthians 5:17–21).

Responsive to Community

Those who are ambassadors of reconciliation work within community. In his letter from a jail cell, King emphasized that the work of justice is a community endeavor, and he was disappointed that most of the White churches refused to support it. There was an opportunity for Christian leaders to demonstrate how to work toward recognizing and reconciling differences between people. When the Christian community exhibits resilient trust—in people as well as in God—an otherwise chaotic world witnesses the value derived from confidence in Christ's lordship. This point is easily missed because many Christians have not fully grasped the meaning of professing Christ as Lord—the deep commitment to serve him in every aspect of our lives. He's the one who establishes our identity, direction, and behavior. Just as Christ demonstrated that he is responsive and restorative to all people, so should his followers be to all people.

Churches haven't always been responsive to the cross-cultural needs of society. Christians often follow the patterns of the dominant secular culture that tend to alienate and oppress people at the margins of the culture. Churches that are responsible to their communities initiate various forms of equitable engagement with as much of the population as possible, celebrating rather than controlling diversity. The community of reconciliation recognizes the differences between our neighbors and ourselves not as a threat but as essential for our life in Christ. Just as different body parts are necessary for the body to function properly, the diversity of people in the church is a factor in its healthy operation (1 Corinthians 12:12–26). Sacks astutely directed religious leaders to pay attention to the outsiders: "The challenge to the religious imagination is to see God's image in one who is not in our image."[13]

Our responsiveness leads to reconciliation among people when we are fully present—as a formative presence—with the world in its differences, attuned to the needs of those whose faith and behaviors are not like ours. King made the point that our lives are all interrelated: "We are inevitably our brother's keeper because we are our brother's brother."[14] Christians are the incarnation of Jesus Christ—he dwells in his people—for the purpose of reconciling all people to him. When we forget that we influence others with our presence, our responses will not reconcile people.

Several years ago, I witnessed an example of a response failing to reconcile people. My wife and I were visiting Japan and used the high-speed train system to travel between cities. At the time, the ticket machines were not labeled in English, so we stood back from the crowd and observed how other people purchased tickets. An American couple approached the machines and were completely disoriented. Out of frustration, the man began yelling at his wife. He seemed incapable of reflecting on his situation and responding to it with loving patience. He didn't appear to comprehend that he and his wife were in this situation together and that his behavior affected them both. He could have made a responsible choice to acknowledge his wife's anxiety and encourage her. Instead, he blamed her for his anxiety and made the situation worse. Our responses in the midst of adverse circumstances demonstrate whether our inner character has a secure foundation built on Christ's presence.

Jesus explained in his Sermon on the Mount how his followers should be responsive to the demands made of them and to the difficult situations they encounter. Toward the end of the sermon, Jesus describes some responsive actions that reconcile rather than divide people. First, Jesus says it's better to examine yourself than to advise the other person (or to yell at your wife in a train station): "You hypocrite, first take the log out of your own eye, and then you will see clearly to take the speck out of your neighbor's eye" (Matthew 7:5). Then Jesus tells his disciples, "Ask, and it will be given you" (7:7). Simply asking God for help is often difficult, and Jesus says the Father is just waiting to pour out blessings on those who will ask. God will also help his people find the way—"the narrow gate"—to the path that is challenging but leads to life (7:13–14). Jesus ends his series of mini-lessons with some actions that bring people together—seeking and encouraging good fruit from people (7:15–20) and pursuing actions and behaviors that are securely grounded (7:21–27). Our responsibility to God motivates us to become the kind of constructive influence that reconciles people with one another and with Christ.

Responsive to Oneself

Despite his disappointment with White church leaders and the dominant religious structures, King commended the real heroes who have "carved a tunnel of hope through the dark mountain of disappointment."[15] These people, like King himself, examined their own motives and preparedness for being responsible to both themselves and to the community. Taking responsibility for ourselves requires acknowledging our own situations, our own history, and the ways that our lives have intersected with others. We have affected other people and they have affected us. In order to be responsive to them, we must accept that we have been resistant as well as receptive toward them. Tensions arise in all of our relationships, and we must address those difficulties in order to be honest with ourselves and responsive to ourselves.

H. Richard Niebuhr, a theological ethicist, defined responsibility in terms of how people interpret actions and respond to those actions. The way we interpret people's actions takes into account our personal ideals, the prevailing norms or laws, and what we expect from our community. Niebuhr suggests that these three contexts of interpretation highlight three aspects of the self. There is the person who seeks what seems good, the person who seeks what is right, and the person who seeks dialogue with others. The first two perspectives, which represent the traditional understandings of personal responsibility, emphasize what God and people have already done. The third suggests God is also currently active and human actions are in conversation with him as well as with other people. The responsible self organizes its actions around more than God's plan and God's laws; it also considers the participation of people in God's current workings.[16] This definition of responsibility relative to the self emphasizes the responsiveness of the individual to God and to the world. The way personal responsibility operates in a collective environment becomes a matter of choice. I am morally responsible for the character, attitude, and behavior I choose for myself. In order to understand my life, I must become aware of the decisions I make about who I am.

Psychologist and professor Carol Gilligan has shown that men and women tend to emphasize different aspects of their moral character. Whereas men typically focus on an ethic of justice, fairness, and rights, women more often pursue an ethic of care and nonviolence. All of these aspects affect our ability to influence people, and learning to balance both justice and care promotes a healthy responsiveness toward one's own wholeness.[17] Empathic responsiveness is evident when a person's behavior includes both respect and compassion—both integrity and love. This equilibrium is best demonstrated when we, like Jesus, are visible agents of both truth and grace. The journey toward developing this balanced moral character requires relationships that are more substantial than apprenticeships and friendships. The following section will describe a kind of kinship that's not limited to our biological family.

KINSHIPS

We need mentors and friends. Even more than those, we also need kinships to develop influence based on empathy. A kinship is a long-term relationship characterized by responsibility *to* each other, not simply *for* each other. It's also a mutual commitment to a shared mission. Kinships bind a group of people for an extended period of time and have the capacity to produce social changes that require deep commitment.

Jonathan Sacks suggests that the notion of *family* is a stronger connection than the contractual relationships found in many economic and political contexts. Describing what the Bible calls *covenantal* relationships, Sacks explains that they are based on "certain fundamental concepts—love, loyalty, responsibility, authority, obedience, fairness and compassion. These are the filaments holding the family members together."[18] Such intimate and sacrificial relationships are based on the bond created by *hessed,* the covenant love modeled by God.

Kinship is created when we feel like we belong to one another. Kinship seeks and celebrates both joy and justice for every member of the family that shares this bond, whether or not they are blood relatives. Kinship is more than serving each other; it's a relationship in which we become one with others—similar to the way that Jesus is an incarnate presence with us. It has also been called solidarity, a relationship among people who are different and yet decide to stand together in a union that is deeper than most friendships. Dr. King referred to this kind of communal relationship as the *beloved community*, a brotherhood that surpasses the character of any specific neighborhood.[19] Our kin are those whose "love is strong as death" (Song of Solomon 8:6).

Adoption

The family or kinship relationship that binds us together is available because God adopts people. He provides an inheritance through Christ's redeeming sacrifice and by means of the indwelling of the Holy Spirit (Ephesians 1:3–14). The God of heaven, who is supreme in all the world, summons the world to establish its hope in him (Deuteronomy 10:17–20):

> For the LORD your God is God of gods and Lord of lords, the great God, mighty and awesome, who is not partial and takes no bribe, who executes justice for the orphan and the widow, and who loves the strangers, providing them food and clothing. You shall also love the stranger, for you were strangers in the land of Egypt. You shall fear the LORD your God; him alone you shall worship; to him you shall hold fast, and by his name you shall swear.

In the world of the early church, Christians regarded other believers as sisters and brothers with an intensity that non-Christians restricted to blood relatives. Their attachment to Jesus, not their natural lineage, made them family. The theologian Tertullian, writing in the early third century, marveled at Christians' love for each other: "How they love one another

. . . how they are ready even to die for each other."[20] How influential the church would be if more Christians bonded with one another this way!

There are some friends whom we choose to regard as family. My mother-in-law considered one of her closest friends a "sister by another mother" and framed a certificate of their mutual adoption. The longevity or the intensity of the relationship makes these friends stand apart from others. My wife and I have some friends from college who have been family with us for decades. We adopted Patty and Tom Bowers as much more than friends. They have been counselors, confidantes, and coconspirators. Somewhere along the way, we became participants in their potluck Thanksgiving dinner, and we began a tradition of *family by choice*. We are fellow spiritual sojourners with them and godparents to their children. We share favorite books, personal victories, unfulfilled aspirations, delicious recipes, and new adventures. Each of us has endured frightening health situations, and our kinship has been a source of strength, calm, and healing during these times. We may not consciously think about influencing each other, but our lives reflect the presence of each other. We are who we are because they have been integral to our lives.

Accountability

Kinships are built on responsibility to specific people. The well-known author Wendell Berry has written about people being bound to each other and to the land. He uses the term *membership* to represent a submission of one's entire self—identity, interests, and ambitions—to the needs of those who share that bond.[21] The Bible refers to membership in a similar way, using the human body to describe the relationship between Christians. Familial love is possible beyond our own households because we have been adopted in God's Spirit through Jesus Christ. As part of God's family, we are accountable to our relationships, which Christ has extended across many different types of people (Galatians 3:27–29).

Kinship can foster inclusion by connecting with lives that are very different from our own. Kinship is an opportunity to become God's new creation in all of its diversity. A key test of our ability to create kinships is whether we can see God's presence in the strangers we encounter each day. Otherwise, kinship has the potential for becoming exclusive and lacking accountability to people outside the narrow ways that we often define ourselves.

In May 1961, the first Freedom Riders arrived in Rock Hill, South Carolina. This racially diverse collection of men and women was traveling through the South on Greyhound buses so that the federal government would have to enforce its recent law banning segregation on interstate travel. After John Lewis and others exited the bus in Rock Hill, they were attacked and beaten by a group of young White men. Almost forty-eight years after that event, one of the attackers, Elwin Wilson, arranged to meet with Lewis again. This time it was in Lewis's Washington, D.C., congressional office, and Wilson explained that he was one of the people who had beaten him that day in Rock Hill. He looked Lewis in the eye and said, "I am sorry about what I did that day. Will you forgive me?" Lewis immediately accepted the apology, viewing it as proof that love can overcome hatred. A new kinship was formed through forgiveness. Lewis had endured more than forty arrests and multiple beatings, but this was the only time someone apologized for hurting him.[22]

The motivation behind an apology is what makes it genuine. Elwin Wilson offered the type of apology that expresses accountability. He admitted what he did and that it was wrong. He felt remorse for the hurt he had caused and desired to make it better. Today we often hear public figures making wrongly motivated semi-apologies that are not fully accountable. For example, the statement may express doubt whether harm was done: "I'm sorry if I hurt you" or "I'm sorry you feel hurt by what I did." Also, the apology falls short when it originates solely out of a need to appease one's own guilt, to gain approval, or to coerce a reciprocal apology. A sincere apology is a genuine sign of accountability, and accountability is a key characteristic of kinships.

Loyalty

Dr. King's letter emphasizes the solidarity which he felt with others across the country: "We are caught in an inescapable network of mutuality, tied in a single garment of destiny. Whatever affects one directly affects all indirectly."[23] The kinship he shared with the oppressed Black population enabled him to engage in all of their suffering and to speak out against their oppression as offenses he felt personally. King described the humiliation and despair felt by young daughters and sons who were deprived of opportunities and distorted by bitterness. He spoke of the disrespect and fears endured by honest people at the hands of vicious mobs and hateful officials. When he described waiting for more than 340 years to receive constitutional and God-given rights, he was uniting himself with the hopes and dreams of his people. This family relationship is naturally cultivated in groups that are suffering together. It's also a solidarity that Christians are called to create with everyone who follows Christ as Lord.

Influential Christians are most effective standing together with people through all sorts of situations and appreciating the embodied expressions of grace that are evident when people are united despite their differences in wealth, race, age, ability, education, gender, identity, or social status. Loyalty to others provides space for both grace and truth. By grace God heals and raises the fallen. In truth we learn about God, ourselves, and each other. Emmanuel Katongole and Chris Rice, cofounders of the Center for Reconciliation at Duke University Divinity School, observe that in the presence of suffering, "our call is not first to 'make a difference' but to allow the pain of that encounter to disturb us."[24] Loyalty in a relationship means being present and connected with those who are in pain. Nevertheless, the bond of kinship does make a difference. Social change becomes possible when people who would otherwise remain strangers reach beyond themselves to offer formative presence and create resilient trust. Christian influence breaks down barriers of difference by refusing to regard anyone as an outsider to God's grace. The environment becomes one in which those who have been marginalized become the leaders in changing everyone's attitudes. No longer are we *us* and *them*—now we share our lives and build new inclusive structures together.

Durability

Developing kinship with a diverse spectrum of people is not commonplace because it's not easy. We have a tendency to associate with people like ourselves—particularly those with whom we already have some connection. However, it's possible to create deep and lasting relationships if we develop receptive and reflective skills and also desire the closeness of kinship connections. As we begin to change our behavior, we also think differently about ourselves. As our identity develops, it will reinforce our new behavior. This positive cycle of growth makes our relationships durable.

Family members and close friends often describe their reunions as "picking up where they left off." They are such a part of each other's lives that they don't really separate when they are apart. This kinship demonstrates the unity Christ wants for all humanity. We are one household, and we are called to think socially—to reach beyond the structures that constrain us and to discover how to remain in each other's lives. It's no coincidence that kinship is often renewed in our homes, for Jesus desires to make his home with us (John 14:23). It's not surprising that kinship is strengthened around meals, for Jesus offers to be our nourishment (John 6:48–58). The first step in building durable relationships is to allow Christ to be our bread, our wine, our light, and our life. He is our bread today and our life tomorrow. When Christ is our vine and we are his branches (John 15:1–8), we will experience with him what it's like to "pick up where we left off." Our kinship with the Lord connects us with the rest of our spiritual family.

RESPONSIVENESS AND CHRISTIAN INFLUENCE

We face a conundrum in this chapter. In earlier chapters, I emphasized the importance of inner character or heart. I suggested that the development of character has been a missing element in Christian influence. Now I have shifted more toward *doing* than *being*, emphasizing response as a form of active expression. However, the action described here is an expression of one's *being* because responsibility is attached to identity and integrity. This action contributes to the completion and validation of our faith (James 2:14–26). Empathic responses are demonstrations of the power of God in his people, for as Paul declared, "the kingdom of God depends not on talk but on power" (1 Corinthians 4:20). Therefore, using empathy as a lens on Christian practices results in a recognition that our responsiveness is not a matter of gaining righteousness by works, but rather it's a matter of faithful action. Paul's desire for the church was that "Christ may dwell in your hearts through faith, as you are being rooted and grounded in love" (Ephesians 3:17). Jesus is the one who's at work developing our character and directing our behavior.

Christian responses communicate what a congregation believes. Regardless of what we claim, our doctrine is evaluated by how our actions are perceived outside the church walls. Are we cognizant of the message that we in the church are communicating? Does that message match the intentions of the church leaders and align with the church's responsibility to Christ? Churches communicate their character through worship and prayers, through service and generosity to the community, and through love and truthfulness. Learning to think and communicate openly, perceptively, and socially increases the engagement between church and community. Broadening the range of people involved in the communication can have a significant effect on developing accountability and building trust with the community.

We influence others by passing what's important on to them and by receiving what they offer to us. The handoff occurs in the engagement and connection between people. This is how Israel was taught to propagate its truth, and Christians have the same commission. People become responsible as they are entrusted with responsibilities. The influential Christian is responsible for the welfare of others and shares that responsibility with people who represent a diversity of cognitive perceptions, physical abilities and appearance, emotional temperaments, historical narratives, socialization, and experience. Valuing people in their differences requires that we look for ways to connect people together and help them grow.

My dad likes to farm the few acres where he lives in Tennessee. In order to handle the amount of work to be done, he hires some workers, including teenagers in high school. He has always been a no-nonsense manager, expecting all of his workers to be diligent and responsible. Quite a few young people have learned a lot about farming from him, and some have gained a little wisdom. Several years ago, a teenage boy's father visited my dad and thanked him. The father had not been able to persuade the boy to go to college or pursue a career, but because of some respectful conversations between the boy and my dad, the boy chose to enter college. My dad didn't even remember the discussions, but out of his character, integrity, and love for education, he had been a positive influence on a young man's life. Most of us, like this teenager, learn responsibility by seeing it modeled.

How might we prepare ourselves and others to create an environment that's responsive to the needs of a broad range of people? First, we have to be intentional about building a diverse learning community. There are plenty of examples of groups inviting a range of different types of people and then expecting them to conform and assimilate. In order to be socially responsible, we must break with that mindset and begin to appreciate both the joy and the discomfort of respecting every voice. Second, we must create an environment that fosters dialogue and reflection. In order to become an influence, we must be willing to be influenced by the lives of other people.

Community development specialists Steve Corbett and Brian Fikkert observe that people exhibit a range of attitudes toward change and influence. In order to help others handle change, our responsibility is to walk alongside them, "listening well to their fears, working to build trust, and demonstrating to them that change is possible."[25] Most people desire to be encouraged and supported, and with someone beside them, they can make the necessary decisions to advance their personal growth. We can help by creating safe spaces in which others can express emotions, doubts, and dilemmas. Our attachment to truth and transparency enhances our credibility and develops relationships of trust. We can be a responsible presence and a formative influence. We can be responsively trustworthy and help others develop resilience. The practices of formative presence and resilient trust embody the empathic skills that develop influence among people.

James, the author of the New Testament book bearing his name, makes the startling assessment that not many should become teachers because "we who teach will be judged with greater strictness" (James 3:1). The reason for the caution is that our responses are seldom perfect, and the manner in which we represent Jesus Christ affects the community in which we live. Therefore, our response must be offered as an embodiment of love. As we learn how to navigate ways of becoming responsive and responsible in society, our guiding star is the God of love.

Practical Exercises

The church's responses are assessed both by God and by the watching world. The broader community notices how we represent God's truth and grace, how we recognize patterns of inequity, how we encourage inclusive behaviors, how we build trust through empowerment, how we adapt constructively to the complexities of change, and how we graciously confront fears and conflicts.[26] Each of the following paragraphs approaches one of these specific areas and asks you to observe your responses. The questions are not specific to any designated congregational role because every member contributes to the influence of the church. Please answer each question as an individual Christian and as a representative of the church.

Representing God's truth and grace. We are responsible to God when our actions are consistent with the obedience he desires. The following questions are aimed at examining your relationship with the Lord.

- What are the standards you rely upon for obedience to God?
- What are some ways that God's Holy Spirit operates in your life?
- How does prayer affect your actions?

Recognizing patterns of inequity. Becoming responsible to a community requires an understanding of the experiences of its members in terms of both historical inequities and current challenges. As you answer the following questions, the character of your environment—as seen by those who have been ignored—should become clearer.

- What sort of prejudices or biases have you heard mentioned in your community—even if you have not personally observed biased behavior?

- How do you respond when you recognize that a negative assumption, such as a denigrating stereotype or false attribution, is being made?
- In what ways do you contribute as an individual or as part of a group to oppressive conditions for some people?

Encourage inclusive behaviors. Inclusion does not happen without focused effort. It's not enough to assume the community is fully represented at meetings and at voting events. Since the most vulnerable people in the community are often invisible to dominant groups, their voices are not engaged in much of the local activity. The following questions are aimed at determining who's absent when church and community discussions take place.

- What are some ways in which certain people are vulnerable within their own communities?
- How do you know when a comment or action is offensive to someone other than yourself?
- How might you be responsive to someone who is offended or injured without diminishing that person's sense of dignity?
- What opportunities are there for you to belong to a group that's culturally different from you?

Building trust through empowerment. Those who share their authority and power are the ones who truly possess it. Effective leaders observe how people are working together, and they draw upon those resources rather than impose their own methods. The influential person looks for the diverse gifts and assets within the population, including those whom some might regard as "the least." The questions here probe for your perception of your responsibility and how you might welcome the responses of other people.

- List some people and/or things that you are responsible *to.*
- What does it mean to you to be responsible *for* someone or something?
- Within your group (church, organization, corporation, etc.), who is in charge? In what ways do the leaders—including yourself—differ from the followers?
- How do you identify other people's giftedness? How do you help them see those gifts and support them in using those gifts?
- How do you feel when your help is not needed?
- What does it mean to practice resilient trust?

Adapting constructively to the complexities of change. Most people resist difficult changes, so we must be careful in navigating the changes with them. There are often complex emotions to acknowledge and uncertain challenges to face. We can lead change by fostering trust and transparency. The questions below consider how the presence and contributions of every person strengthen the group and provide opportunities for transformation.

- What are some ways the community ought to change in order to treat everyone more equitably?
- What are some changes you are going through that are equipping you to serve Christ?
- Who are some people who desire improvements in their living conditions? What can you do to help them be in a position to lead those community changes?
- What does it mean to practice formative presence?

Graciously confronting fears and conflicts. People who have difficulty facing their fears often prefer to avoid conflict with other people. However, avoiding conflict often leads to other conflicts. Differences should be discussed so that they can be navigated and employed as strengths, and such a dialogue is fruitful when the participants can disagree constructively. This final set of questions explores how you deal with discord that arises from differences.

- Who are the groups of people that have recently been disparaged in your presence?
- What attributes would you need to develop in order to be able to speak up when someone makes an offensive or disparaging remark?
- What are some possible ways to respond to injurious comments while remaining responsible to all of the parties in the conversation?
- Dr. King explained that our responses should move us toward reconciliation between people. How are you being reconciled to people with whom you have differences?

Our guiding narrative provides the map for our journey of learning and development. Part of our responsibility to others is to understand our current situation in relation to our community's ultimate goals, identifying the gaps that necessitate change. The complexities of human growth, along with the immensity of God's promises, make this journey both frustrating and exciting. The process of reception, reflection, and response is often chaotic and circuitous. For every answer, there's a new question, and for every vision of the destination, there are more mountains to climb. The descriptions of empathic skills given in these few chapters have introduced some methods that can help us become both leaders and followers on this journey. In the final chapter, I will apply these skills—and the practices that include them—more specifically to the development of influence.

QUESTIONS FOR GROUP DISCUSSION

Encourage the group to explore what responsibility means. Read the parable of the good Samaritan in Luke 10:25–37 and discuss how Jesus's perspective differed from the behaviors of most people. Also read Matthew 5:14–48 in order to understand what our responses to one another should look like.

1. What does it mean to have responsibility? How is responsibility *to* someone different from responsibility *for* someone?
2. What does it mean to be responsible for justice? Is it a private or collective matter?
3. How is God the supreme example of righteousness and justice?
4. What are some of the barriers to justice that people experience today?
5. To what extent are Christians responsible for the collective sins of our nation?
6. How does the hope of reconciliation help us develop responsible character?
7. What are some ways that Jesus's example helps us understand how we should respond to God the Father?
8. What can you as an individual do to overcome the church's lack of responsiveness to the cross-cultural needs of society?
9. What are some qualities that hold families together despite obstacles?
10. Why might you consider someone as part of your extended, adopted family?
11. What does it mean to be accountable? Why do you need to be accountable to people?
12. How is it possible to create kinship among very different individuals?

OUR COMMUNITY CAN
RISE TOGETHER

Sean Dogan has been the pastor of Long Branch Baptist Church in Greenville, South Carolina, for twenty-three years. He is also CEO and interim president of the Urban League of the Upstate, a nonprofit organization dedicated to civil rights and economic equality for African Americans. Sean has volunteered for several community projects and board memberships during the past twelve years, providing a voice for people of color in South Carolina. He enjoys meeting people where they are, and he responds to many requests for help from other community leaders. The requests address issues of providing opportunities for educational advancement, economic empowerment, and interracial dialogue. In order to determine how to help, Sean gathers input from people who understand the problems, and then he recommends to the community leaders some appropriate people or resources to address the issues. A significant part of his work is listening closely to people's stories so that they have a voice in the community solutions.

Sean says the people who influence him most are those who demonstrate that they are accountable to others and provide opportunities for a variety of people to express their thoughts and feelings. Two pastors modeled effective leadership for Sean, demonstrating to him how to stand up for people and how to negotiate public policies. Today he ministers in the Greater Sullivan community of Greenville, which is undergoing gentrification and experiencing the displacement of families. His church reaches out to the community with food distribution, financial assistance, and spiritual encouragement.

He relates a story about his church providing meals to disadvantaged seniors and discovering that the driveway to one individual's home was obstructed by a huge pothole. His church group took the initiative to repair the driveway with gravel. Now he encourages his staff members to *be* bags of gravel for people in need. People have a variety of potholes in their lives, and we can all help by laying a firm foundation, enabling them to move forward.

Sean wants his own influence to be like that of a coach and a mentor—assisting others in recognizing and verbalizing where they are, where they want to be, and how they want to get there. He has found that his influence is strongest when he listens and shows compassion. He tries to understand how people are affected by their circumstances and uncover what is inhibiting progress toward their goals. Sean says we should never make decisions for people, but rather empower them to make a decision and work in that direction. He declares, "I think our community can rise together."

Influence also carries a weighty responsibility. "Influence really puts a target on you," Sean says, pointing out that Jesus Christ was the greatest influencer of all time, and he was killed. We must be careful with the responsibility, or else in our pride and arrogance, we will become self-serving and not influence many people. Sean suggests we surround ourselves with people who will give us honest feedback and keep us grounded.

7

INFLUENCE AND ITS IMPLICATIONS

The most valuable kind of influence reaches deep into people's hearts and makes long-lasting changes in their lives. The influence most of us desire to receive is the kind that makes us who we are for the rest of our lives, and we also want to exhibit influence that affects and improves other individuals' lives. Those who lead sacrificial lives, like many teachers, doctors, soldiers, pastors, parents, and close friends, offer themselves for others and provide examples of how to live a purposeful life. Sometimes people have the ability to create radical change for others, as with organ donations, large monetary grants, and acts of deliverance or rescue. Other people model a characteristic or ideal that others want to imitate or join, such as charisma, selflessness, or insight. People can also make short-term influential impressions on one another by acting in purposeful ways—such as showing compassion, offering a gift, sharing recipes and health ideas, correcting a behavior, explaining a new concept, and providing assistance with mobility or a difficult task. In big ways and in small ways, all of us influence somebody because we are continually interacting with people.

We need the influence of others because we're not capable of handling every subject and every situation ourselves. I need the presence of people in my life who help me become the best person I can be. Moreover, my own growth depends in part on my willingness to participate with others in mutual learning and to be the influence they require. God provides spiritual gifts to build up his people (Ephesians 4:11–12), and the gifts we have received are meant to be shared. The reason we should seek to be an influence is that people need us as much as we need them.

Our influence is a representation of who we are, what we value, and how we put those qualities into action. People notice our character and decide whether that's what they want for themselves. Therefore, we

165

need to understand our own identity, how others understand themselves differently, and how the sharing of truth is possible between us. We have a tendency to try to change other people and groups, even though most individuals and organizations resist attempts to change them. The people who have been most successful in producing change in my life are the ones I wanted to imitate, not the ones who imposed or coerced changes upon me. The significance of their influence was more than solely their actions. Most behaviors are manifestations of the inner character, or heart—inner thoughts, emotions, beliefs, and desires. Jesus said, "The good person out of the good treasure of the heart produces good" (Luke 6:45), and a person's influential heart can change us.

The treasure of the heart that produces influence is formed in several ways. First, God changes hearts—he provides a new identity and a new purpose. Accepting God's initiative forms each of us into a new person. The second way to contribute to this treasure is to actively fill our hearts with good things. King David cherished God's Word as a bulwark against sin, a source of delight, a guide for righteousness, and a standard for humanity (Psalm 119). The heart overflows with whatever has filled it. The third method of filling the heart is to train it by practicing constructive behaviors and habits that affect our inner character. The virtue of empathy, used as a lens on our behaviors, directs our attention toward attitudes and actions that effectively imitate Christ and develop personal character. The practices of formative presence and resilient trust are driven by empathic skills of reception, reflection, and response. These practices develop in us new habits of awareness, discernment, and accountability that replace old dispositions of selfishness, insularity, and complacency. Changing the heart, by any of these methods, requires commitment to the Creator and Sustainer of our lives. Influence is precious, and such a treasure is worth a lifetime to produce.

This chapter explores a few specific contexts of influence. First, I will discuss the context of a Christian educational ministry. Given the importance of networking and internet competence in today's world, the second setting for influence is the world of interconnectedness—both online and offline. The following section addresses those environments that have the potential for violent behavior, examining some approaches to being influential in the face of suffering or adversity. Finally, a discussion of the importance of truthfulness and how to discern truth in the presence of deceit is aimed at helping us maintain our integrity. At the end of each of these sections, some examples of real-life situations clarify how we can create an environment that nurtures our influence on each other.

INFLUENCE AND EDUCATION

The goal of a Christian teaching program is to grow in Christ. The methods of teaching and the forms of curriculum are important, but they are not the purpose of the gatherings. It is more important to respect people and to love them well than to present precise and persuasive lessons. God is the source of our love for each other, so his presence is both the incentive and foundation for effective learning and growth. The reason for having an educational program is to share the good news that the Lord offers abundant life. When people get a glimpse of a vision like this, they are invigorated to experience all that God offers them.

God's Spirit works within the learning participants, "making all things new" (Revelation 21:5). Christ has made change possible, the Holy Spirit produces the changes, and the engaged student commits to the promise of change. Therefore, the practices of education must emphasize Christ, the Holy Spirit, and personal engagement. Neither the teacher nor the educational structure is the central point of the teaching ministry. The teacher focuses on connecting people's hearts to Christ and with each other.

Forms of Education

A ministry of education in the church is much more than a collection of classrooms in which designated instructors facilitate the transfer of information. Ministry denotes service, and education as a service concerns the development of people rather than the establishment of a platform for debating issues or indoctrinating followers. Everyone has an influence in some way. God uses specific connections between people, together with his Spirit, to guide and transform his followers. Teaching is a matter of creating connections in which people are open to each other and to everyone's growth. These connections are characterized by empathy. People learn from each other by sharing and examining thoughts, feelings, behaviors, intentions, and values.

An empathic learning environment is composed of a network of hearts connected by love. All of the participants have opportunities to foster the spiritual growth of both themselves and others. Therefore, a ministry of teaching, observed as a whole, looks like a broad network of people engaged in each other's lives and spiritual growth. The network may be structured in a variety of ways, and most models include one or more leaders who organize, motivate, and provide resources for the ministry. In those cases that employ a pastor as the educational leader, the dynamics between participants become more complex due to the positional authority of the pastor. Teachers may be drawn from either the lay or clerical constituencies of the congregation, consistent with the preferences of the group members and the leadership.

Educational formats vary according to the priorities and activities of the church. The late Maria Harris, an influential advocate for religious education, described several forms of teaching and influence in the church. Using New Testament terminology, she classified them as "*koinonia* (community), *leiturgia* (prayer and worship), *didache* (teaching), *kerygma* (proclamation), and *diakonia* (outreach)."[1] When a church gathers as a community for an event, everyone contributes equally to the group identity, and everyone enjoys the supportive benefits of belonging to the group. For example, fellowships, potlucks, parties, and celebrations are occasions for casual sharing of influence with one another. Gatherings for prayer and worship—including church services for worship, weddings, baptisms, funerals, and prayer meetings—are more formal than community meetings and are often led by a small number of officials in the church. Influence is primarily received from God, with some instruction and engagement between the leaders and the body of members. Teaching and instruction take place in various settings, and the way influence is shared between participants depends on how the session is led. Proclamation is a form of teaching in which a few individuals convey important messages and conduct key rituals with the larger group. In this case, influence usually proceeds from leaders to participants. When a church engages in outreach, it focuses outside itself, and the potential for interpersonal influence greatly increases. Service projects create many influential connections between church members and other people engaged in the work. All of these types of gatherings provide contexts for learning, influence, and the use of empathic skills.

Training in Education

People who are asked to lead, facilitate, demonstrate, instruct, collaborate, or connect must be willing participants. The best teachers are usually those who are interested in a subject and compassionate toward people—they know they want to learn. The worst teachers are often those who either believe they have great wisdom to share or those who do not take the role of teaching very seriously. Whenever I ask people to lead, I don't pressure them to accept the commitment. I offer whatever support and training they need, and I encourage them to decline if the task is too big. If they are free to say "no," then I know they are making an uncoerced commitment when they say "yes." Also, I find that large teacher-training sessions are useful for communicating information like policies and schedules, but the sort of preparation teachers need most requires one-on-one discussions and small groups. I work closely with teachers to provide them with some examples for how to conduct a class and some suggestions for connecting with Christ and other Christians.

The skills of empathic connection—reception, reflection, and response—are familiar concepts in education, even though the terminology associated with them varies. Educational consultant and professor Robert Pazmiño has succinctly summarized the significance of these components:

> Effective education occurs when people listen attentively and sensi-
> tively, raise questions based upon what they hear and discern, and share
> with integrity, as a gift to others, the wisdom they have gained. Such
> education assumes interpersonal interaction and willingness to dialogue.[2]

Receptivity is often embodied in attentive listening and accompanied by the skill of reflective questioning and discernment. Pazmiño eloquently frames responsiveness as a *gift to others*, sharing integrity and wisdom. The following paragraphs offer some suggestions and applications regarding how

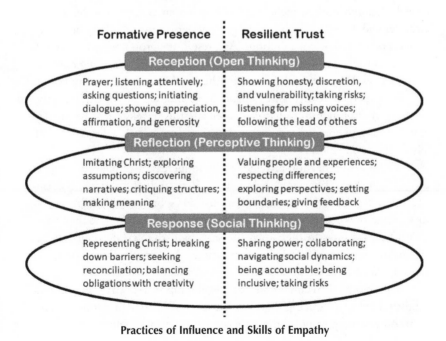

Practices of Influence and Skills of Empathy

these skills contribute to the practices of formative presence and resilient trust.

All teachers and students begin with the skill of reception—listening to Scripture and paying attention to God in prayer. Reception is developed by spending time with people and listening to their passions and hurts; it also helps to watch and follow what the Spirit is doing. As the people around us become more comfortable with dialogue and prayer and drawing insights from Scripture, they are not only being influenced—they are developing receptive skills that will help them become influential.

A key feature of the receptive environment is fearless communication. This can only occur when people work together to create trust and respect in a safe space shared by people who are searching for truth and facing struggles together. Church leaders create such an environment by making effective listening a high priority. It begins with genuine interest, curiosity, honesty, and discretion—qualities that are contagious within a group when sincerity and trustworthiness are evident. Receptive teachers respectfully draw upon the insights and experiences of their students. Reception is effective when people are asking questions, seeking challenges, broadening perspectives, and contributing with excitement.

Developing the skill of reception is often a difficult hurdle for people because it requires behaviors and attitudes focused on others rather than oneself. Church leaders, including teachers, set an example for the group's attitudes and expectations by valuing every person for who they are rather than merely for their contributions. As a result, the group behavior eventually moves toward mutual attention and encouragement. Learning becomes an act of reaching out and connecting hearts. Expressions of compassion, vulnerability, generosity, and collaboration indicate an open, receptive teaching environment. Leaders can accelerate this development by personally engaging in apprenticeships and learning from people who aren't usually called upon to lead.

The skill of reflection provides a way to increase awareness of people's thoughts, feelings, behaviors, habits, intentions, and assumptions. Reflecting upon their observations, realizations, and connections helps people make sense of what has been said, heard, seen, and felt. Then, as they apply new understandings to their own life situations, they create opportunities for making meaning out of these reflections. As a result, we become like (reflect) that which we ponder most (reflect on).

The model I recommend for developing a reflective educational ministry consists of small groups exploring some challenging topics with a focus on revealing some of the associated assumptions, beliefs, and norms.

These forums should not indulge complaints or gossip, but should focus on identifying assumptions. Some assumptions are uncomfortable to discuss—such as power relations and exclusionary behaviors—so the facilitators of this process must emphasize the importance of building trust and respect.

People who engage together in perceptive dialogue, especially when they focus on common concerns, will often develop friendships with one another. In addition to the power of examining assumptions together, friends have opportunities to offer constructive feedback to each other—potentially nurturing growth in areas other people cannot approach. Church leaders of all types need friends who can discern their character qualities and regularly speak truth to them. Teachers benefit from having friends—other teachers or insightful students—who will help them be accountable and responsible in their teaching. Our friends are often our key resource for understanding our own gifts and for making sense of our lives.

Reflection leads to response, helping us understand our attitudes toward people and events. As we interpret what we think are the intentions and causes of our behavior, we are sorting through layers of our own emotions, past experiences, future expectations, and health. All of this contributes to how we characteristically interact with others, and this self-scrutiny is an effective exercise in expanding our capacity for empathy and understanding the choices we make regarding our attachment to social groups.

People who develop the skill of empathic response will be honest about their accountabilities, knowing to whom they are responsible. Being responsible to God places one in the position of acting in a priestly manner between the things of heaven and earth. Being responsible to the community means supporting groups that seek to establish dignity and respect for all people. It also means encouraging churches to have an open table of fellowship that bridges cultural divisions. Some teachers have official church positions that give them a public voice, but the most effective educators are often the ones who personally join with people who are seeking direction from God and from connection with people.

Examples

One of the many challenges associated with church ministry is the task of enlisting volunteers to engage in various aspects of the work. Asking people for time and support exposes our vulnerability as leaders. Most of us don't like being dependent on other people's priorities and schedules. The problem is often exacerbated by the awkwardness present when individuals have to decline—especially if the person has to back out shortly before the scheduled event. There are three ways I use my personal influence to allevi-ate the stress of making requests. First, I contact specific people directly, and initially I use the most comfortable medium for me—like email or texting rather than a phone call. I observe by people's responses which media they frequently use, and I try to respect their preferences and continue contact-ing them in that manner. Sometimes I will also offer a general summons for volunteers in order to reach everyone. The second way I reduce the anxiety of asking for help (for both myself and the other person) is by mak-ing the request as clear as possible. It's better to communicate frequently than to risk losing the person's interest in serving. I want the person to be aware of the context of what will happen—the environment, the time constraints, and other actions scheduled before and after theirs. If they will need preparation, such as providing a microphone or accessing presentation material, I follow up with those details. The third way I help volunteers is to continually reinforce my principle that anyone can decline any request. I let people know that "no" is a satisfactory answer. In fact, the sooner a person can decline, the easier it is for me to ask someone else. In sum-mary, I try to communicate frequently with volunteers while managing the anxiety and awkwardness of volunteering. People often feel connected and empowered by requests, especially if the requested role involves some kind of leadership.

Another example of using empathic influence in an educational min-istry concerns the training of potential teachers. Generalized teacher train-ing sessions can be an effective means to revitalize those who already have teaching experience, but people with little experience need someone to walk alongside them in their preparation. Beginners benefit from sample study materials and some instruction in handling discussion classes. I initiate conversations with them about what happens in a typical group setting and how they can make the most of their presentations and interactions with the class. To get them started with thinking about teaching, I provide them with a copy of Karen Lee-Thorp's insightful book, *How to Ask Great Ques-tions*. After helping them identify a subject that interests them, I may also provide them a study guide on that topic. These materials provide examples of how they might structure their presentations and discussions, and having suitable examples usually reduces their anxiety about teaching. The most essential part of their preparation is their own spiritual development, and I encourage them to adopt specific spiritual disciplines like prayer, medita-tion, and reading Scripture. In one particular case, I was helping a young man prepare to teach a series of lessons on Paul's letter to the Philippians, and I suggested he read the book several times, taking notes during each reading. Shortly afterward, he approached me with excitement about what he learned each time he read it through. He was so motivated by the Spirit's guidance that he decided to read the book of Philippians every day during the two months he was leading the class. My influence opened a path to the Spirit's influence, with the result that a novice teacher developed a deeper love for reading and teaching God's Word.

INFLUENCE AND INTERCONNECTIVITY

Networking is not a new phenomenon. People have always interacted with other people in order to accomplish tasks and develop their own humanity. Corporate employees have long understood the value of connecting with a wide variety of people spanning industry groups and levels of management. Community organizations partner and collaborate with other groups in order to multiply their efforts. Church members serve and encourage one another and also reach into the community for opportunities to help. Most educational models are built upon the notion that learning takes place when collections of students are effectively placed in contact with collections of instructors and guides. Networking has always been important. The characteristic of networking that has been changing in recent decades is the nature and necessity of personal proximity—the meaning of being face-to-face.

At one time, most interconnectivity took place with all participants physically in the presence of one another. The advent of telephones allowed conversations to become remote, and television provided a means for broadcasting from a distance. Computing and communication technologies have come together over a few decades to give individuals a range of options for networking. Today, many people are more attuned to their preferred online networks than to their local offline community organizations. Even our spiritual formation, which has traditionally been cultivated between people in physical proximity, now progresses more often in virtual meeting environments.[3] The 2020 coronavirus pandemic accelerated this advance, with many churches offering worship, classes, and fellowship in online formats. Christian influence now takes place in more contexts than ever before, less limited by time and distance. We can arrange these interactions as one-on-one meetings, one-to-many conferences and webinars, or many-to-many livestreaming events. Combinations of these options are also possible, providing opportunities for people participating in large online gatherings to break out into focused discussions.

Benefits and Challenges

One of the benefits of networked relationships—regardless of whether they are online or offline—is that people who are not in official leadership positions are often the ones who make the contacts and share their influence. Church groups whose members network together for interpersonal learning help everyone become a spiritual influence. An interconnected church structure that relies on Christians joining specific discussions is less dependent on centralized organization than are more traditional church structures. The interconnected approach can focus on learning and mutual growth rather than on the implementation of specific procedures and programs. In many cases, lay people without official positions are leading these groups. This sharing of authority nurtures trust and transparency between members, and it helps everyone develop responsibility to each other and accountability for the influence they share.

Online community offers both benefits and challenges relative to offline assemblies. The internet brings a wide range of people into close contact, creating the possibility for a listening, supportive, progressive community. These shared spaces give the participants an experience of solidarity. However, without the physical proximity, some opportunities for people to be heard become occasions to bluster complaints. Anyone who has used social media has experienced those times when an ostensibly helpful or refreshing idea was bitterly mocked or condemned by some relatively unknown individuals. The nature of social media amplifies rather than clarifies messages that may or may not have been intended. Sherry Turkle, an expert in the sociology and psychology of human-technology interactions, points out that people need genuine conversation, yet the online environment tempts us to take control in a way that diminishes the value of communication.[4] Each of us who would like to be an influence should consider how we can pursue both online and offline activities that foster supportive communication. The following section offers some suggestions for applying empathic skills in networked environments.

Training for Interconnectivity

Preparation for becoming influential in a networked environment draws upon the same skills I presented in the previous section on education. The skill of reception is exhibited in paying attention to people, regardless of whether we are in the same room. We can be curious and honest in any context, engaging in conversations that help others open up and share. An online environment separates the participants into distinct spaces, and the screen in front of each person operates like a window into each one's space. Sometimes we have to intentionally enter these spaces in order to draw a person into the conversation.

Openness requires that we risk our own vulnerability while holding each other's privacy and confidence in a trustworthy manner. Neither gossip nor any other disparaging criticisms can be allowed in a learning space if we desire people to become more receptive. All of the engaged participants—not only the facilitator—must be ready to gently terminate destructive talk, and it can be accomplished by quickly redirecting the discussion. However, some comments should be called out as biased or inappropriate—such as racist, sexist, or ableist slurs. We build trust by respecting each other, so some responses are necessary in public in order to model respectful attitudes and mutual learning. In general, corrective responses are often more effective when handled privately. In order to encourage questions, ideas, and alternative views, the group should establish some rules for jumping into the discussion or backing off to let others speak. Leaders try to model the behaviors they want to see in the meeting.

The skill of reflection is challenging in an online environment because people assume someone must be talking most of the time. The model I recommended for education is still useful in small online groups—focused on exploring assumptions and beliefs about topics or texts. Most people don't mind a bit of online reflective silence when the assignment or question is clear. There will always be some in a group who are quicker to respond, so the facilitator may have to find creative ways to encourage everyone to join in with a comment or question. Since online sessions can easily be recorded and shared, the participants can reflect further on the discussion between meetings. The purpose of the reflection is to examine different perspectives and make connections with what people share. Whether the sessions are online or offline, the members of the group should be encouraged to connect with each other outside the meetings. The process should be an adventure rather than an analysis.

The skill of response develops as the group members express accountability to one another and to the larger community outside the online sessions. Meeting electronically serves as a good vehicle for most group contact, but individuals sometimes need personal attention. Just as in-person meetings occasionally break into smaller, casual conversations, the members of an online group will need one-on-one sessions to help each other with personal concerns. The networked group can also offer a springboard for other activities that include more people. I have observed that some people will not participate in online conferencing, so their need for connection must be considered in other ways.

How might we determine the extent of our influence? The best measure of influence is whether people are fulfilling their potential within the particular narrative that guides them. The primary goal of developing influence is not whether a person is conforming to specific cultural patterns like consumer behaviors, religious doctrines, or patriotic expectations. Empathic networked relationships require everyone to be transparent about their connection to each other. Occasionally students and apprentices recognize that their guiding narrative is not aligned with their goals for living abundant lives, and they look for a different narrative. As people grow in their sense of responsibility, they may need to replace their self-serving perspective with a more biblical, outward-focused narrative. Sometimes a learner decides to step into a role with more responsibility, and the influential Christian encourages the learner to explore various paths and consequences without coercion. Cultivating new leadership requires standing with people rather than over them. Influential online facilitators offer the participants time to think and respond in order to develop the group's confidence and competence. Regardless of whether an interaction is online or offline, our aim is to encourage everyone to live responsibly with each other and with God.

Examples

One example of interconnectivity is the collaboration between partner churches and affiliated organizations to serve a network of disadvantaged people. Triune Mercy Center in Greenville, South Carolina, is a nondenominational church that includes and assists people who are experiencing homelessness. Local nonprofits and charity organizations work closely with Triune staff to offer financial assistance, legal counsel, senior care, food and clothing, GED preparation, medical and prescription help, housing assistance, and employment opportunities. For some of these organizations, Triune Mercy Center provides office and meeting space to facilitate the nonprofit operations. The churches and service organizations in Greenville have collaborated to create resources for finding affordable housing, recovering from addiction, transitioning out of incarceration, and healing from sexual exploitation. Volunteers help with worship services, art and music activities, Support Circles, and food distribution. The interconnectivity of services ensures that empathic influence is available for people who need assistance and also for the local population who want opportunities to serve.

Another example of using influence in an interconnected environment is the handling of disruptive elements in a meeting or class. Disturbances occur in both online and offline gatherings, but social media and virtual conferencing tend to magnify the kinds of disruptions that are handled more easily in person. Responding to distractions and interference requires more patience and attention in an electronic environment. For example, people can easily talk over one another in a conference, so the host must find ways to gently inform them that they are monopolizing the meeting. I find that people will sometimes stop dominating when they feel heard, so the leader can use active listening skills—briefly repeating or summarizing what was said—to affirm the person's comment. In general, the leader should refrain from interjecting in a dialogue between participants, and all participants should be given opportunities to share in the discussion. Every participant can be an influence when everyone is encouraged to join in.

INFLUENCE AND NONVIOLENCE

We live in a violent society, and violence has taken many forms. I consider violence to be any physical, mental, or emotional harm inflicted against people either directly or indirectly. It can also be an imposition of social limitations, such as discrimination based on race, gender, age, or ability. When these forms of violence take place in the context of personal relationships, domestic abuse may result. Many forms of violence are instigated by people who are serving their own desires or fears at the expense of others. Blame and retribution are often contributing factors—the violent person experiences trouble, fear, anger, or pain and believes that others have caused it. The violent party often attributes the cause of a problem to the wrongness or inferiority of the other person or group without examining the assumptions and emotions underlying such accusations. The violent act may be as casual as an angry retort or as organized and extensive as international conflict. Violence is often used as a means to manipulate or provoke an outcome, but it seldom influences people to change. It is an action devoid of empathy for the victims, and it cannot resolve or reconcile differences.

The history of violence between people began with the first human children. Cain was the first son of Adam and Eve, and his name expresses their joy of *obtaining* or *producing* a son (Genesis 4:1). The second boy was called Abel, a name that refers to a shallow, fleeting breath—an expression of *mortality* and *futility*. The story of these two sons is a narrative of the ongoing conflict between success and vulnerability—between our obsession with controlling others and our desire to live sacrificially ourselves. Cain was angry because God accepted Abel's sacrifice and not his. The jealous rage Cain exhibited is reflected in every clash between people who do not want other people to advance ahead of them. It is the conflict between White culture and people of color in America. It is the conflict between men and women, between the middle class and the poverty classes, between identities considered "normal" and all other identities. Cain murdered his brother, Abel, because he could not reconcile the idea that someone he regarded as weak and inferior might receive a reward instead of him. Cain refused to accept that he was responsible for his brother's life. Even after his sentencing, Cain continued to deny accountability by complaining to God that his punishment was unfair (Genesis 4:13–15).

We continue the legacy of Cain when we deny our responsibility to the person who is different—the one who is the object of our jealousy and disdain. When people rise up in solidarity to express their value and their uniqueness, we who put them down and try to control their behavior are the murderous ones. We refuse to tell the truth about our abusive, exploitative behaviors because our admission would require that we do something about it. What will we say when God asks us, "Where is your brother?" Can we accept a nonviolent path forward?

In contrast to the destructive influence of violent behaviors, non-violence consists of positive action for human benefit, using constructive methods that do as little harm as possible. Jesus pointed out in his Sermon on the Mount (Matthew 5–7) that his new kingdom responds to violence with acts of nonviolence. Jesus struck at the heart of the strict Mosaic restraint on vengeance ("eye for an eye," commanded in Exodus 21:23–25) and said his disciples should not attack an evildoer. Jesus was not prescribing passive acquiescence to an aggressor but instead the refusal to return or initiate violence against the one who threatens. It is the exercise of a choice rather than the despair of having no choice. He asserts that agency and dignity are more influential than intimidation, and he says it is better to be wronged than to become another oppressor. This is indeed how Jesus answered the threats against himself: "When he was abused, he did not return abuse; when he suffered, he did not threaten; but he entrusted himself to the one who judges justly" (1 Peter 2:23).

Sharing in Suffering

In order to break the cycle of violence and vengeance, we will have to do something different than we have been doing. We must behave in a way that diminishes evil. In a well-known statement, Martin Luther King Jr. explained that we must bring light and love to each situation we encounter:

> Through violence you may murder the liar, but you cannot murder the lie, nor establish the truth. Through violence you may murder the hater, but you do not murder hate. In fact, violence merely increases hate. So it goes. Returning violence for violence multiplies violence, adding deeper darkness to a night already devoid of stars. Darkness cannot drive out darkness: only light can do that. Hate cannot drive out hate: only love can do that.[5]

The apostle Paul provides us an example for our new behavior (Acts 16:16–40). When he and Silas were arrested in the city of Philippi, they were severely beaten, humiliated, and locked up in a prison cell under a watchful guard. Their response was to pray and sing, knowing that all of the prisoners could hear them. At about midnight an earthquake shook the prison so intensely that the doors flew open and all of the prisoners' chains were broken. Did Paul take that as a sign of God wanting him out of there? No. He and the other inmates stayed put. The jailer was about to kill himself because he knew he would have to answer with his own life for any escapees, but Paul assured the jailer that no one was missing—he consoled his oppressor! By attending to the needs of his enemy, Paul influenced a prison official to become a Christian. He refused to inflict further suffering, but he held the authorities accountable to their own principles of Roman citizenship. Paul interpreted his circumstances in light of Jesus's sacrifice on a cross, and as a result, God's kingdom prevailed through empathy and compassion.

We have opportunities to be influential with people whenever there is a crisis. We may be the ones in an urgent predicament, or we may be witnesses to a violent event. Lisa Barnes Lampman, the founder of Neighbors Who Care, a Christian ministry supporting crime victims and their families, lists some critical goals for helping people who are going through a crisis: "(1) to provide immediate relief from pain, (2) to provide time for problem solving, (3) to help the individual regain old coping skills and/or develop new ones, and (4) to help the individual return to a healthy level of functioning and regain feelings of self-worth and confidence."[6] Lampman goes on to describe three stages of crisis, which align with the three empathic skills of influence. The initial stage, *impact*, is when the shock of the event is still fresh and victims need supportive contact with people. The second stage, *recoil*, is a period of confusion and insecurity in which the sufferers need to express their emotions, tell their story, and feel validated. During the third stage, *reorganization*, people in crisis need to cultivate positive cop-ing skills. When Christians practice formative presence, sufferers, witnesses, and caring supporters can build nurturing relationships to assist in healing and recovery.

Demonstrating Formative Presence

The essential model Jesus presents for all Christian influence is incarnation. God reconciled all people to himself through Jesus's presence in life, death, and resurrection. Christians are saved by identifying with Christ, which leads to a life that imitates his pattern of self-sacrificing influence. Our relationship with God motivates us to be intentionally *with* people, even when they cause violence and suffering. The apostle Paul suggested that our enemies may be the proving ground for our development of influence (Romans 12:14–21).

> Bless those who persecute you; bless and do not curse them. Rejoice with those who rejoice, weep with those who weep. Live in harmony with one another; do not be haughty, but associate with the lowly; do not claim to be wiser than you are. Do not repay anyone evil for evil, but take thought for what is noble in the sight of all. If it is possible, so far as it depends on you, live peaceably with all. Beloved, never avenge yourselves, but leave room for the wrath of God; for it is written, "Ven-geance is mine, I will repay, says the Lord." No, "if your enemies are hungry, feed them; if they are thirsty, give them something to drink; for by doing this you will heap burning coals on their heads." Do not be overcome by evil, but overcome evil with good.

We join with our adversaries at the table God prepares, and it is there that our cup overflows (Psalm 23:5). We are influential when we are fully pres-ent with them.

The skill of reception is about developing relationships that focus on the value of other people. The modern world tends to view most relation-ships in terms of selfish achievement, but the influential person is attentive to the other person's struggles and worries. The eyes and ears that Jesus told his followers to develop (Matthew 13:16) are locked onto hearts that are broken. Parker Palmer says, "One of the hardest things we must do sometimes is to be present to another person's pain without trying to 'fix' it, to simply stand respectfully at the edge of that person's mystery and misery."[7] Job's friends did well for seven days (Job 2:13), simply sitting with Job and acknowledging his pain. They began with good intentions, but the remainder of their time with Job made him more miserable. Like the people we know who are hurting, Job needed personal connection and encouraging support. His friends just wanted to change him so that all the troubles would then disappear and they could be comfortable again. Instead, they were the ones who had to change, and they had to be brought to the point of recognizing Job as the one who could influence them.

In the same way, becoming an influence for others requires that I seek to be influenced by those whom I would not normally expect to advise me. Constructive dialogue reduces violence. Discussing our experiences of fear and pain with each other closes the gap between us and heals our broken relationships. Receptive presence means opening our hands and hearts to people we may have pushed away.

The skill of reflection guides us in understanding what lies in the heart of both the oppressor and the oppressed—both the offender and the victim. Susan Wendell, an expert in the fields of ableism and psychosomatic dis-abilities, describes four perspectives from which violence and victimization may be observed.[8] Two of the perspectives—that of the victim and of the oppressor—are intuitive. Neither of these viewpoints can clearly see the whole picture of the violence because they are too close to it. Oppressors are usually perplexed about the problem and their contributions to it, even as they attempt to cover their culpability by imposing their view on the larger society. The victim often assigns blame and does not expect to have to change. The perspectives of both the oppressor and the victim have limited choices and unclear responsibilities. Two additional perspectives are available for both the victim and the oppressor to consider. The third per-spective is that of a responsible actor, who is clear about who or what has responsibility and what choices are available. This person is action-oriented and focused on the future. The fourth perspective on oppression is that of the observer/philosopher, who is able to overcome self-deception by focusing on the past and making accurate judgments. Individuals may move from one perspective to another as they recover and grow.

In order to illustrate how perspectives can change, consider the case of women trapped in sex trafficking and drug addiction. These women are victims of abuse, living in a narrative that says they are nothing more than "throwaways" in the community—no one cares about them. However, their perspective as victim is not the only way they see the world. Many acquiesce to the perspective of their oppressors and blame themselves for their plight. They believe the false image of community fostered by their dealers and pimps because no one has ever persuaded them that a bet-ter life is possible for them. They're often caught in a downward spiral of incarceration and hospitalization, with very few people offering help. When I spoke with Beth Messick, the executive director for the nonprofit organization Jasmine Road, she explained that these women need healthy relationships in order to find a way out of their situation. Trust-building takes a long time because they have been disappointed so often by people close to them. Eventually some of the women realize that they cannot continue on the same path. Their perspective shifts in the direction of the observer/philosopher, and they are able to examine the larger reality of their situation beyond the victim-oppressor relationship. They may not yet be ready to seek help because they are focusing on understanding the past and present rather than the future. Some of the women begin to realize that their lives have value and that the future could be better. Then they may move toward the perspective of the responsible actor. With the help of a loving community, they learn to build new lives.

The influential Christian can help oppressors and victims understand their perspectives by reflecting with them on their assumptions and on other possible perspectives. Blame should be eliminated from the discussion, since it reinforces the victim-oppressor relationship. It is helpful for both parties to look at the past with clarity and to imagine a more hopeful future. Wendell summarizes, "The perspective of the observer/philosopher is the best perspective from which to see the full distribution of power and responsibility in an oppressive situation. The perspective of the responsible actor is the best one from which to act to end oppression."[9]

Most people look for meaning in events but lack a complete set of tools for finding it. So the influential person perceptively helps people discover and acknowledge value where they have not looked before. A pastor friend of mine, Curtis Stamps, used to remark many years ago that "people without meaning become mean." People are often not aware of all the beliefs, suppositions, and interpretations that form their sense of themselves and others, and if they lack the ability to make sense of their world, they may use violence as a way to strike back at their confusion, anxiety, and distress. Initiating a dialogue about assumptions can be uncomfortable because most people don't like holding up a mirror to their behavior. We, as influential people, must be both perceptive and gracious, demonstrating how to see both sides of an issue and modeling a willingness to submit our own thinking to critical examination.

The skill of response entails a mature discernment of how God is working and how we as his children can participate. The apostle Paul understood the church's role as being responsible to God by working as ambassadors of reconciliation (2 Corinthians 5:20). Christ is the one who is reconciling the world to himself—and uniting people with each other—so the practice of formative presence is about breaking down barriers between people and addressing patterns of inequity and exclusion. Since God wants to reconcile the world, no one is beyond God's grace. The inclusiveness of a group's language and conduct is evidence of skillful responsiveness. Ultimately, the Christian's presence resembles what God's Spirit does—equipping, guiding, strengthening, and advocating for his purposes.

There is risk in being responsive. Martin Luther King Jr. was accused of being impatient for change, and people today who work for nonviolent reconciliation will likely be accused of "rocking the boat." However, King understood the urgency of helping his neighbors. In his last sermon before his assassination, he preached about the parable of the good Samaritan (Luke 10:25–37), considering the questions that might be in the minds of the parable's characters as they approached a wounded man on the road. The priest and the Levite knew they were in a dangerous area and possibly wondered, "If I stop to help this man, what will happen to *me*?" However, a Samaritan came by and reversed the question: "If I do not stop to help this man, what will happen to *him*?" King was thankful to be in Memphis on that occasion to support the sanitation workers' strike, even with the knowledge that his life might be imperiled.[10] The influential person chooses to live alongside the powerless and to risk insults rather than to live comfortably beyond the pain of his or her neighbors.

Samantha Power, who served as United States ambassador to the United Nations from 2013 to 2017, coined the term *upstanders*, referring to people who take a stand on behalf of others. She explained that "every day, almost all of us find ourselves weighing whether we can or should do something to help others. We decide, on issues large and small, whether we will be bystanders or upstanders."[11] Ultimately, our influence is judged by where we have chosen to stand. It is not our strength, but God's strength, that will prevail. And God stands close to those who are in distress.

Examples

On August 20, 2013, in an elementary school in Georgia, a mentally disturbed man entered the school with an AK-47 assault rifle and five hundred rounds of ammunition. The school clerk, Antoinette Tuff, began talking with him while she was also on the phone with the police. The twenty-year-old man said he had nothing to live for, and she responded that no one needed to die. She had been through great pain herself, and yet she was able to be respectful, calm, and loving toward this young man—even so far as offering herself as a human shield as he went out to the police. When he gave himself up, she said she was proud of him.[12] This is how people demonstrate living like Jesus—imitating the Lord in showing mercy and hope to those who seek our harm. Antoinette Tuff responded to aggression the way Jesus did—with loving influence.

An example of proactively supporting nonviolence was shown in a church's response to the suicide of one of its members. Holland Park Church in Simpsonville, South Carolina, organized a series of forums in 2016 to help church members and the community understand when people have such great burdens that they cannot manage their lives without help. Several community experts were invited to speak about some difficult social topics such as mental health, substance abuse and recovery, reconciliation in relationships, victimization and injustice, poverty and financial stability, suicide prevention, and grief support. Counselors and health specialists explained how to notice particular issues and to respond constructively. The series began with an exploration of Psalm 69, demonstrating that even the great King David felt overwhelmed in times of crisis. The psalm describes the fear and weariness of sinking to a place where God seems to be absent—where shame and despair are ever-present. The psalm concludes with God rescuing the needy and the oppressed, and all creation praises him. Each session in the series prepared the participants to be good neighbors who pay attention to people's pain and offer supportive help. Violence and suffering are constant realities affecting every one of us, and the church has opportunities to walk with people in their adversity and to offer hope.

INFLUENCE AND TRUTH

Truth and violence are related, due perhaps to the unwavering commitment people have to particular views and beliefs. One of those staunchly held views is that there is no absolute truth at all, which would suggest that everyone can generate their own truth, creating even more opportunities for conflict. Nevertheless, the way we handle truth determines how we respond to deception, conflict, and violence. Theologian and ethics professor Stanley Hauerwas stated, "A leadership which cannot stand the force of truth must always rely on armies."[13] Most people, including Christians, usually aren't interested in talking about truth unless it's a discussion of what will make their lives better and happier. What works is more important to the average person than what's true. When an individual in our society perceives that their truth is different from someone else's, there is seldom an initiative to listen and reflect on the difference. Most people either drop the discussion as futile or use some form of authority to justify their disregard for the other view. This lack of resolution often leads to either separation or conflict. Truth is too often a conversation stopper.

When Jesus, the King of Israel, stood before Pontius Pilate, the governor of Judea, he explained that he had come into the world in order to testify to the truth and that anyone who associates with the truth listens to his voice. Pilate's response indicated he may have been impatient, weary, cynical, or perplexed about Jesus (John 18:37–38). He asked, "What is truth?" Jesus had earlier told his disciples, "I am the way, and the truth, and the life" (John 14:6). Now Pilate was making his decision in the presence of the one who embodied truth, yet he was pondering truth as an abstract concept. The trial Jesus had just been through should have been a search for truth, but Jesus's accusers sought only condemnation. Both the Jewish and Roman authorities were interested in maintaining their power, and the truth was mostly irrelevant to them. Several centuries before the judgment upon Jesus, the prophet Isaiah proclaimed that Israel had abandoned truth: "Justice is turned back, and righteousness stands at a distance; for truth stumbles in the public square, and uprightness cannot enter" (Isaiah 59:14). The condition still exists today—truth is largely ignored in the public square. In order to understand truth, we must first be interested in finding it.

Contrary to the world's notion that truth is a concept people possess and apply as they see fit, the biblical view is that the living Christ embodies truth. Palmer explains our relationship with truth as a personal matter:

> Where conventional education deals with abstract and impersonal facts and theories, an education shaped by Christian spirituality draws us toward incarnate and personal truth. In this education we come to know the world not simply as an objectified system of empirical objects in logical connection with each other, but as an organic body of personal relations and responses, a living and evolving community of creativity and compassion. Education of this sort means more than teaching the facts and learning the reasons so we can manipulate life toward our ends. It means being drawn into personal responsiveness and accountability to each other and the world of which we are a part.[14]

Truth is much more than our subjective ideas about how to have better lives. Truth is a divine person who takes over our lives for his kingdom. We are not influential merely because we have the best life hacks, but rather as the result of Christ living in us. Our influence is his truth manifested in our identity and integrity.

Truth Makes Us Free

Once when Jesus was speaking to a group of Jews who believed his message, he told them that if they continued to follow him, they would know the truth, and the truth would make them free (John 8:32). They missed the point of knowing truth and were incensed that Jesus thought they were slaves. Full of their own hubris, these Jews were doing what we still do today—ignoring the power of what binds us and refusing to see the way to true freedom. Jesus could have reminded them that the Roman Empire currently held them in servitude much like the Egyptians had done during the time of Moses. Yet he spoke to them about a more significant enslavement. Jesus said, "Everyone who commits sin is a slave to sin" (8:34). He explained that a slave is not a family member, but God's Son gives sinners the opportunity to become God's children. His Jewish audience wasn't happy with this message either because they wanted to continue believing they were children of Abraham without any other obligation.

The dilemma the Jews faced is similar to a problem people in our society have today: We want to be free, and we want to think we *are* free, but we don't want to admit that we must give up our current servitude to sin in order to be truly free. Most of us would rather follow our own subjective notion of truth than confess we don't have all truth. Bound to our own perspective, we experience only a narrow portion of truth and cling to it obsessively. We also surround ourselves with people who are ideologically connected to the same truth, and together we create an idolatrous allegiance to both the group and our truth. Many truths we hold dear—such as life, liberty, and the pursuit of happiness—have been recast into idols because people treat them as destinations instead of signposts to greater truth. If we choose to remain in our bondage to sin, we will have little to offer the world, and we will have limited influence on the world. In order to be a Christian influence, we must be influenced by Christ. Only his truth can set us free.

God makes his truth known to those who are faithful to him. The psalmist David sought God with his whole heart, and he wrote, "Teach me your way, O LORD, that I may walk in your truth; give me an undivided heart to revere your name" (Psalm 86:11). David prayed for an undivided heart so that he could be fully committed to the one who gives truth. God's Word—his message, instruction, and guidance, as well as his incarnate Son—offers us salvation and freedom from sin and death. Jesus is our exemplar in following God's plan, but Jesus wasn't merely showing us how to find God. In Jesus, "the Word became flesh and lived among us" (John 1:14). God is *with us* in Christ. As *Immanuel,* God has come to be with his people so that his truth lives in those who know and trust him. The influential Christian depends upon God's presence for truth, and the practice of resilient trust connects us with people who are willing to be led by God's truth.

Demonstrating Resilient Trust

The practice of resilient trust is fundamentally a practice of expressing steadfast commitment to truthfulness and love in order to imitate Christ and increase solidarity among believers. Trust is cultivated in the soil of faithfulness, and it grows in people's hearts as they learn to be open and honest. The resilience in this practice stems from an expectation that God is long-suffering and continually offers grace for our unfaithfulness; therefore, we can return to him for help with the difficult experiences that hinder our integrity.

The skill of reception is exemplified in the openness of people to truth coming to them from outside their own experience, reasoning, and emotions. The wholeness and integrity of others—especially in group settings—becomes more important than protecting or honoring oneself. The practice of resilient trust is embodied in acts of welcoming, hearing, and respecting others as they express truth. Empathic Christians focus on *hearing* truth more than speaking it, and they listen in conversations for who is not being represented. They seek opportunities to elevate others and learn from them. In a context of Christian influence, the source of truth is understood to be the Lord who is both inside and above all of the participants. With the skill of reception, we discover how the Spirit touches each of us for the benefit of all of us.

When we build trust among people, we do more than recognize truth. As Palmer explains, "Truth also brings us to life by finding and naming us."[15] Truth is bigger than we are, and as the Lord opens our hearts to truth, he also cleans out the prejudices and pride that once held us captive to ourselves. Eventually we come to recognize that our influence is really not ours at all. We simply mirror the one we trust to influence us.

The skill of reflection helps us gain a better perception of how we are using the truths guiding our behavior. For example, I may be assuming I have the whole truth, and in reality I only see a piece of it. Furthermore, I may assume that the language I use to describe that truth is understood the same way by everyone. Conflicts between people or groups who ostensibly share the same truth are generally caused by each group imagining and professing that their perspective is the whole story. Robert Kegan, a developmental psychologist and research professor at Harvard, asserts that people have a "tendency to pretend to completeness when we are in fact incomplete."[16] Truth is usually more complex than any one group's version of it, and conflicts arise because of the gaps between people's perspectives.

Group reflection—especially in a diverse group—is helpful in driving out untruths and biased perspectives. Most stories are selective in what they present—storytellers and audiences have specific worldviews and particular assumptions related to those worldviews. Once when I was using an elliptical machine at my local YMCA, I noticed there were two television screens showing simultaneous newscasts on different channels. I was amazed at how the same events could be presented so differently, even though both networks claim to be unbiased. Networks spin the news by selecting which details to include and how to present them. Several independent media channels offer biased commentary posing as news and preying on devoted consumers. The current popularity of conspiracy theories indicates the extent to which many people are latching on to manipulative opinions rather than discerning truthful principles. Part of our responsibility as Christians is to reflect on how we are influenced by the world and how we can model effective approaches to determining what is true.

The skill of response is expressed by people in the way they foster a community of trust—an environment in which people are willing to take risks for one another. Resilient trust responds to problems of injustice by emphasizing agency rather than blame and by promoting a shared responsibility for collective structural issues. A trustful environment handles change and conflict by empowering people to act with integrity. The Lord equips his people with gifts and resources that foster collaboration rather than judgment, gratitude rather than rivalry, and love rather than bitterness. This relationship between people operates as a sort of kinship by choice, born out of commitment to one another. The characteristic behavior of empathic responsiveness is to give honor to people as they are, recognizing that what matters most is honoring God and accepting his mercy. We start with our responsibility to God and reach out responsively to others.

Examples

There are many ways we can value the experiences and stories of different people. Seeing ourselves in the context of other perspectives highlights the peculiarities of our behaviors while also building trust between diverse communities. An excellent approach to reflecting on faith practices is demonstrated in cross-cultural religious dialogue. My community, like many others, has occasional opportunities for members of different faith groups to participate together in cultural or educational events. Muslims, Hindus, Jews, Buddhists, and Christians invite each other to meals or discussions that encourage learning from each other. One of the local Islamic Centers in Greenville, South Carolina, has conducted dinner discussions in which they open their facility to the public. Hearing explanations of Muslim principles expressed by their own members helps non-Muslims relate to similar principles in their own traditions. Another approach to engaging with other faiths is to invite representatives of various groups to speak about their groups and answer questions. Holland Park Church conducted an educational series in 2017 that included some fascinating discussions with local leaders from Muslim, Hindu, Sikh, Buddhist, Mormon, and Jewish groups. We asked them to talk about their faith and practices, followed by an opportunity for questions and dialogue. These conversations allowed us to see our common ground as well as our different perspectives.

Brené Brown offers an example of working with someone on a project and recognizing that they had very different perspectives. She demonstrates respect for truth that is seen in a different context and through different experiences:

> Perspective taking requires becoming the learner, not the knower. Let's say that I'm talking to a colleague on my team who is twenty-five, African American, gay, and grew up in an affluent neighborhood in Chicago. In our conversation we realize that we have completely different opinions about a new program we want to develop. As we're debating the issues, he says, "My experiences lead me to believe this approach will fall flat with the people we want to reach." I can't put down my straight, white, middle-aged, female lens and just snap on his lens to see what he sees, but I can ask, "Tell me more—what are you thinking?" and respect his truth as a full truth, not just an off version of my truth.[17]

The practice of resilient trust creates an environment where it's safe to explore truth and ask difficult questions. Meetings may produce conflict, but a community of trust can turn disagreement into productive dialogue.

INFLUENCE AND LOVE

The apostle Paul dealt with churches two millennia ago that were much like churches today, and he told some of them that they were focusing on the wrong things. In a letter to the Corinthian church, Paul described their members as clamoring to impress each other with their knowledge and their spiritual gifts. Acting like they had a hotline to God, the Corinthian Christians were impressed with their ability to speak heavenly things. They thought they could influence anyone with their self-assurance and persuasive speech. But they had missed something. All those spiritual strengths amounted to nothing without love as the foundation, and their behavior contradicted the basic character of love. They thought their works were good, but they had ignored the reason for doing them. So Paul reminded them what love looks like (1 Corinthians 13:4–7):

> Love is patient; love is kind; love is not envious or boastful or arrogant or rude. It does not insist on its own way; it is not irritable or resentful; it does not rejoice in wrongdoing, but rejoices in the truth. It bears all things, believes all things, hopes all things, endures all things.

Paul began his description of love with a couple of God's attributes— patience and kindness (compare Romans 2:4). Then he proceeded to contrast the nature of love with his earlier descriptions of the Corinthians. They had been envious and boastful and arrogant. They had been seeking their own advantage at the expense of others.

The way we influence people is directly related to the way we understand God's influence on us. Do you truly believe that God is patient and kind? Is his love a present reality in your life? If we believe that God is a judgmental bully, then we may either become oppressors ourselves or reject God entirely. We may buy in to the world's view that influence is about imposing our beliefs on other people. The Christians in Corinth had behaved so badly that Paul had to explain to them that love doesn't act shamefully or selfishly, that it isn't easily angered or unjust. They didn't notice that they had missed what love is about. We fail to notice that we miss it, too. Yet love rejoices in truth, so God must be longing to celebrate our integrity and to welcome the development of our character to include endurance, faith, and hope. God endures everything for us. He proved that by becoming human in order to rescue us. Therefore, Jesus is the ultimate image of God's empathy and influence.

A Christian's purpose is to imitate Christ and to help others do the same. As Christ is incarnate within us, so we represent his identity in the world as a formative presence. Furthermore, as Christ embraces all truth and trustworthiness, we also demonstrate his integrity in our expressions of resilient trust. The most influential people are not always those who are the best talkers; influence means engaging people in a learning experience, which takes many forms. Ministry is sustained by the network of people who have observed that their own growth has been accelerated by the spiritual preparation God provides them. The Spirit of God equips and supports those who are willing to share God's grace and truth.

Developing influence grounded in empathy requires a transformation of the heart. Our heart—the core of our personal character and the center of our thoughts, emotions, beliefs, and desires—is influenced by love. We are to love the Lord with our whole hearts, and we are to love our neighbor as ourselves (Matthew 22:34–40). Lasting influence is the product of generous, trustworthy, and persistent love. It is the evidence that God is present, for "if we love one another, God lives in us, and his love is perfected in us" (1 John 4:12).

QUESTIONS FOR GROUP DISCUSSION

The implications of becoming an influence are demonstrated in the story about Paul being thrown into prison in Philippi. Read Acts 16:16–40 with your group and discuss how your group members relate to this story.

1. Describe the kind of influence you want to have on people's lives.
2. Why do you need to be influenced by others?
3. What sort of things fill your heart? How do you put things in your heart?
4. What are some environments in which people influence one another?
5. Explain how technology has affected the influence you receive from others and your ability to influence others.
6. What are some things you do in order to diminish violence? What are some things you do that contribute to acts of violence?
7. Read Job 11 (Zophar's argument to Job) and discuss what Job's friends could have done that would have been more supportive.
8. What are some ways we can stand with people who are in distress?
9. What causes you to avoid engaging with truth?
10. How does truth make us free? (John 8:32).
11. What resources are available to help us perceive what is true in current events?
12. How do the characteristics of love make you a better influence?

NOTES

INTRODUCTION

1. Craig Dykstra, *Growing in the Life of Faith: Education and Christian Practices* (Louisville, KY: Westminster John Knox Press, 2005), 56.

CHAPTER 1

1. John Lewis, *Across That Bridge: Life Lessons and a Vision for Change* (New York: Hyperion, 2012), 14.

2. Jay E. Adams, *How to Help People Change: The Four-Step Biblical Process* (Grand Rapids, MI: Zondervan, 1986), 194.

3. Simon Sinek, *Start with Why: How Great Leaders Inspire Everyone to Take Action* (New York: Penguin Books, 2011), 17.

4. Curt Thompson, *Anatomy of the Soul: Surprising Connections between Neuroscience and Spiritual Practices That Can Transform Your Life and Relationships* (Carol Stream, IL: Tyndale House, 2010), 65.

5. Thompson, 156.

6. Parker J. Palmer, *To Know As We Are Known: Education as a Spiritual Journey* (San Francisco: HarperOne, 1993), 101.

7. Paulo Freire, *Pedagogy of the Oppressed*, trans. Myra Bergman Ramos (New York: Continuum, 1981), 162.

8. Paulo Freire, *Pedagogy of Freedom: Ethics, Democracy, and Civic Courage*, trans. Patrick Clarke (Lanham, MD: Rowman & Littlefield, 1998), 30–31. Italics are original.

9. Henri J. M. Nouwen, *Reaching Out: The Three Movements of the Spiritual Life* (Garden City, NY: Image Books, 1986), 20.

CHAPTER 2

1. Brené Brown, *Daring Greatly: How the Courage to Be Vulnerable Transforms the Way We Live, Love, Parent, and Lead* (New York: Avery, 2015), 145.

2. Brené Brown, *Dare to Lead: Brave Work, Tough Conversations, Whole Hearts* (New York: Random House, 2018), 126.

3. Mary Gordon, *Roots of Empathy: Changing the World Child by Child* (New York: The Experiment, 2009), 30.

4. Edward Bradford Titchener, *Lectures on the Experimental Psychology of the Thought-Processes* (New York: Macmillan, 1909), 21.

5. C. Daniel Batson, *Altruism in Humans* (New York: Oxford University Press, 2011), 12–19.

6. For example, Marco Iacoboni, *Mirroring People: The Science of Empathy and How We Connect with Others* (New York: Picador, 2009), 268; Roman Krznaric, *Empathy: Why It Matters, and How to Get It* (New York: Perigee, 2015), 10, 21–26; J. D. Trout, *Why Empathy Matters: The Science and Psychology of Better Judgment* (New York: Penguin Books, 2010), 233, 29–31.

7. Karla McLaren, *The Art of Empathy: A Complete Guide to Life's Most Essential Skill* (Boulder, CO: Sounds True, 2013), 55.

8. John Dickson, *Humilitas: A Lost Key to Life, Love, and Leadership* (Grand Rapids, MI: Zondervan, 2011), 24.

9. Andrew Murray, *Humility: The Beauty of Holiness* (London: Nisbet, 1896), 12.

10. Robert N. Bellah et al., *Habits of the Heart: Individualism and Commitment in American Life* (Berkeley, CA: University of California Press, 1996), 153.

11. Henry Cloud and John Townsend, *Boundaries: When to Say Yes, When to Say No, to Take Control of Your Life* (Grand Rapids, MI: Zondervan, 1992), 35–40.

12. Stanley Hauerwas, *A Community of Character: Toward a Constructive Christian Social Ethic* (Notre Dame, IN: University of Notre Dame Press, 1981), 111.

13. Pirkei Avot, "Ethics of the Fathers: Chapter Two," Chabad Classic Texts, accessed November 28, 2020, https://www.chabad.org/library/article_cdo/aid/2011/jewish/Chapter-Two.htm.

14. Aristotle, *Nicomachean Ethics*, trans. Martin Ostwald (Indianapolis: Bobbs-Merrill, 1962), 49–50 (§1109a19–24).

15. Adam Smith, *The Theory of Moral Sentiments* (New York: Augustus M. Kelley, 1966), 6, 10.

16. Paul Bloom, *Against Empathy: The Case for Rational Compassion* (New York: Ecco, 2018), 37.

17. The following resources address the pitfalls of manipulative empathy: Robert D. Lupton, *Toxic Charity: How Churches and Charities Hurt Those They Help, and How to Reverse It* (New York: HarperOne, 2012); Steve Corbett and Brian Fikkert, *When Helping Hurts: How to Alleviate Poverty without Hurting the Poor . . . and Yourself* (Chicago: Moody Publishers, 2012).

18. Freire, *Pedagogy of the Oppressed*, 28–29.

19. Stephen R. Covey, *The Seven Habits of Highly Effective People: Powerful Lessons in Personal Change* (New York: Simon and Schuster, 1990), 236–37.

20. James C. Kaufman, "The Charlie Brown Theory of Personality: The Five Factor Model of Personality, Exemplified by Charlie Brown Characters," *Psychology Today* (blog), March 3, 2010, accessed November 28, 2020, http://www.psychology today.com/blog/and-all-jazz/201003/the-charlie-brown-theory-personality.

21. McLaren, *The Art of Empathy*, 22. McLaren refutes the claims of British psychopathologist Simon Baron-Cohen that autistic people are neurologically unempathic, citing studies by Swiss and Israeli neuroscientists that propose a theory describing autism in terms of hypersensitivity. McLaren, 290n7.

22. Thomas Lickona, "Developing the Ethical Thinker and Responsible Moral Agent," in *Toward Human Flourishing: Character, Practical Wisdom, and Professional Formation*, eds. Mark L. Jones, Paul A. Lewis, and Kelly E. Reffitt (Macon, GA: Mercer University Press, 2013), 41.

23. Stanley Hauerwas and Charles R. Pinches, *Christians among the Virtues: Theological Conversations with Ancient and Modern Ethics* (Notre Dame, IN: University of Notre Dame Press, 1997), 68.

24. Cyril of Alexandria, *Commentary on John, Vol. 2, John IX–XXI*, trans. Thomas Randell (London: Walter Smith, 1885), Book XI, Chapter 11, accessed November 28, 2020, http://www.tertullian.org/fathers/cyril_on_john_11_book11.htm.

CHAPTER 3

1. Gregory Boyle, *Tattoos on the Heart: The Power of Boundless Compassion* (New York: Free Press, 2011), 72.

2. Alasdair MacIntyre, *After Virtue: A Study in Moral Theory* (Notre Dame, IN: University of Notre Dame Press, 2007), 187, 191, 203.

3. Dykstra, *Growing in the Life of Faith*, 66.

4. Richard J. Foster, *Celebration of Discipline: The Path to Spiritual Growth* (San Francisco: Harper & Row, 1988), 3, 7.

5. Everything DiSC, "DiSC Profile," Personality Profile Solutions LLC, accessed November 28, 2020, https://discprofile.com/what-is-disc/overview/. Everything DiSC is a registered trademark of John Wiley & Sons, Inc. Note that there are similar tools using the same letters with somewhat different labels, but *influence* seems to be a consistent category.

6. Covey, *The Seven Habits of Highly Effective People*, 81–88.

7. Robert Banks, *Reenvisioning Theological Education: Exploring a Missional Alternative to Current Models* (Grand Rapids, MI: Eerdmans, 1999), 111. Italics are original.

8. William H. Willimon, *Pastor: The Theology and Practice of Ordained Ministry* (Nashville: Abingdon Press, 2016), 288. For this particular point, Willimon cites

Donald E. Miller, *Reinventing American Protestantism: Christianity in the New Millennium* (Berkeley, CA: University of California Press, 1997).

9. Parker J. Palmer, "The Heart of a Teacher," *Change* 29, no. 6 (December 1997): 17. Italics are original.

10. Freire, *Pedagogy of Freedom*, 108.

11. William A. Kahn, "Psychological Conditions of Personal Engagement and Disengagement at Work," *Academy of Management Journal* 33, no. 4 (December 1990): 692–724.

12. Laura Weaver and Mark Wilding, *The 5 Dimensions of Engaged Teaching: A Practical Guide for Educators* (Boomington, IN: Solution Tree Press, 2011), 2–6, 21, 41, 57, 69, 87.

13. Boyle, *Tattoos on the Heart*, 187.

14. Nouwen, *Reaching Out*, 154.

15. Sara Little, *To Set One's Heart: Belief and Teaching in the Church* (Atlanta: John Knox Press, 1983), 89. Also see Gert J. J. Biesta, *The Beautiful Risk of Education* (Boulder, CO: Paradigm Publishers, 2014), 44.

16. Scott Simon and Emma Bowman, "Making the Best of Virtual Learning: Some Advice from the Founder of Khan Academy," NPR.org, accessed November 28, 2020, https://www.npr.org/2020/08/22/904652858/making-the-best-of-virtual-learning-some-advice-from-the-founder-of-khan-academy.

17. Carol S. Dweck, *Mindset: The New Psychology of Success* (New York: Ballantine Books, 2006), 11.

18. Parker J. Palmer, *The Courage to Teach: Exploring the Inner Landscape of a Teacher's Life* (San Francisco: Jossey-Bass, 1998), 57.

19. Boyle, *Tattoos on the Heart*, 72. Italics are original.

20. Palmer, *The Courage to Teach*, 13.

21. Brown, *Dare to Lead*, 224–33. The "Anatomy of Trust" video is available at Brené Brown, "The Anatomy of Trust," *SuperSoul Sessions* (blog), accessed November 28, 2020, https://brenebrown.com/videos/anatomy-trust-video/.

22. Eric Greitens, *Resilience: Hard-Won Wisdom for Living a Better Life* (New York: Houghton Mifflin Harcourt, 2015), 22–25.

23. Brennan Manning, *Ruthless Trust: The Ragamuffin's Path to God* (New York: HarperCollins, 2000), 4.

24. Miroslav Volf, *Free of Charge: Giving and Forgiving in a Culture Stripped of Grace* (Grand Rapids, MI: Zondervan, 2006), 43.

25. Gregory Boyle, *Barking to the Choir: The Power of Radical Kinship* (New York: Simon & Schuster, 2017), 168.

26. Nouwen, *Reaching Out*, 31.

27. Arbinger Institute, *Leadership and Self-Deception: Getting Out of the Box* (Oakland, CA: Berrett-Koehler Publishers, 2015), 101, 111, 159.

28. Palmer, *To Know As We Are Known*, 89.

29. Henri J. M. Nouwen, *The Wounded Healer* (New York: Image Books, 1979), 72.

30. Circles programs are offered in Greenville County, South Carolina, through Triune Mercy Center and Buncombe Street United Methodist Church. The latter is affiliated with Circles USA (https://www.circlesusa.org/).

31. Sally Ann Flecker, "When Fred Met Margaret." *Pitt Med Magazine* (Publication of the University of Pittsburgh School of Medicine; Winter 2014). Quoted in Maxwell King, *The Good Neighbor: The Life and Work of Fred Rogers* (New York: Abrams Press, 2018), 138–39.

CHAPTER 4

1. Palmer, *To Know As We Are Known*, 8. Italics are original.

2. Palmer, *The Courage to Teach*, 41.

3. Elena Aguilar, *Art of Coaching: Effective Strategies for School Transformation* (San Francisco: Jossey-Bass, 2013), 33.

4. Miroslav Volf, *Exclusion and Embrace: A Theological Exploration of Identity, Otherness, and Reconciliation* (Nashville: Abingdon Press, 1996), 100.

5. Stephen R. Covey, *The 7 Habits of Highly Effective Families* (New York: Golden Books, 1997), 13–14.

6. Hans-Georg Gadamer, *Truth and Method*, trans. W. Glen-Doepel, Joel Weinsheimer, and Donald G. Marshall (New York: Bloomsbury Academic, 2013), 369.

7. Michael P. Nichols, *The Lost Art of Listening: How Learning to Listen Can Improve Relationships* (New York: The Guilford Press, 1995), 63.

8. Dominic F. Ashkar, *Road to Emmaus: A New Model for Catechesis* (San Jose, CA: Resource Publications, 1993), 70–71.

9. Reuel L. Howe, *The Miracle of Dialogue* (New York: The Seabury Press, 1966), 37.

10. Brown, *Dare to Lead*, 37.

11. C. Clifton Black, "Augustinian Exegesis and the Nature of Christian Inquirers," in *Inquiring after God: Classic and Contemporary Readings*, ed. Ellen T. Charry (Malden, MA: Blackwell Publishers, 2000), 226. Black is referring to Augustine's sermons on 1 John (specifically Homilies 7 and 8).

12. Dallas Willard, *Hearing God: Developing a Conversational Relationship with God* (Downers Grove, IL: InterVarsity Press, 2012), 256. Italics are original.

13. Timothy Keller, *Prayer: Experiencing Awe and Intimacy with God* (New York: Dutton, 2014), 48.

14. Nichols, *The Lost Art of Listening*, 109. Italics are original.

15. Edward T. Hall, *Beyond Culture* (New York: Anchor Books, 1977), 105–16.

16. Martin L. Hoffman, *Empathy and Moral Development: Implications for Caring and Justice* (New York: Cambridge University Press, 2000), 294.

17. Jane Vella, *Training Through Dialogue: Promoting Effective Learning and Change with Adults* (San Francisco: Jossey-Bass, 1995), 180.

18. Michael Marquardt, *Leading with Questions: How Leaders Find the Right Solutions by Knowing What to Ask* (San Francisco: Jossey-Bass, 2005), 71–72. Also see Karen Lee-Thorp, *How to Ask Great Questions: Guide Your Group to Discovery with These Proven Techniques* (Colorado Springs, CO: NavPress, 1998).

19. Nouwen, *Reaching Out*, 74–75.

20. Frederick Buechner, *Listening to Your Life: Daily Meditations with Frederick Buechner* (New York: Harper Collins, 1992), 2.

21. Evan B. Howard, *A Guide to Christian Spiritual Formation: How Scripture, Spirit, Community, and Mission Shape Our Souls* (Grand Rapids, MI: Baker Academic, 2018), 242.

22. Laurent A. Daloz, *Effective Teaching and Mentoring: Realizing the Transformational Power of Adult Learning Experiences* (San Francisco: Jossey-Bass, 1990), 212–13. Also see Laurent A. Daloz, *Mentor: Guiding the Journey of Adult Learners* (San Francisco: Jossey-Bass, 1999), 206–9.

23. Etienne Wenger, Richard McDermott, and William M. Snyder, *Cultivating Communities of Practice* (Boston: Harvard Business Review Press, 2002), 233n1.

24. Ronald A. Heifetz, *Leadership without Easy Answers* (Cambridge, MA: The Belknap Press of Harvard University Press, 1996), 99–100, 128.

25. Henri J. M. Nouwen, "Bearing Fruit in the Spirit," *Sojourners* 14, no. 7 (July 1985): 30. Quoted in James M. Childs Jr., *Faith, Formation, and Decision: Ethics in the Community of Promise* (Minneapolis: Fortress Press, 1992), 41.

26. Steve Saccone and Cheri Saccone, *Protégé: Developing Your Next Generation of Church Leaders* (Downers Grove, IL: IVP Books, 2012), 32. The authors refer to envy, self-reliance, overconfidence, and entitlement as the "four deadly sins of emerging leaders."

27. The following is a list of resources for apprenticing initiatives: Ruby K. Payne, Philip E. DeVol, and Terie Dreussi Smith, *Bridges Out of Poverty: Strategies for Professionals and Communities* (Highlands, TX: aha! Process, Inc., 2009); Lisa Barnes Lampman, ed., *Helping a Neighbor in Crisis: How to Encourage When You Don't Know What to Say* (Wheaton, IL: Tyndale House, 1997), 151–224; Soong-Chan Rah, *Many Colors: Cultural Intelligence for a Changing Church* (Chicago: Moody Publishers, 2010), 174–76; Brown, *Daring Greatly*, 85–91.

28. Brown, *Dare to Lead*, 201.

29. This exercise is condensed from Earl Koile, *Listening As a Way of Becoming* (Waco, TX: Calibre, 1977), 87–91.

30. bell hooks, *Teaching Critical Thinking: Practical Wisdom* (New York: Routledge, 2010), 53.

CHAPTER 5

1. Peter M. Senge, *The Fifth Discipline: The Art & Practice of the Learning Organization* (New York: Doubleday Business, 1994), 277–78.

2. Senge, 191.

3. Maria Harris, *Teaching and Religious Imagination: An Essay in the Theology of Teaching* (San Francisco: HarperSanFrancisco, 1991), 25–40, 163.

4. Daniel T. Willingham, "Critical Thinking: Why Is It So Hard to Teach?," *Arts Education Policy Review* 109, no. 4 (April 2008): 21.

5. Fred A. J. Korthagen, "In Search of the Essence of a Good Teacher: Towards a More Holistic Approach in Teacher Education," *Teaching and Teacher Education* 20, no. 1 (January 2004): 79–81. Also see Fred Korthagen and Hildelien S. Verkuyl, "Do You Encounter Your Students or Yourself? The Search for Inspiration As an Essential Component of Teacher Education," in *Enacting a Pedagogy of Teacher Education: Values, Relationships and Practices*, eds. Tom Russell and John Loughran (New York: Routledge, 2007), 114.

6. Robert Kegan and Lisa Laskow Lahey, *How the Way We Talk Can Change the Way We Work: Seven Languages for Transformation* (San Francisco: Jossey-Bass, 2001), 68. Italics are original.

7. For more help with reflective methods, see Keith R. Anderson and Randy D. Reese, *Spiritual Mentoring: A Guide for Seeking and Giving Direction* (Downers Grove, IL: IVP Books, 1999), 133–35, 146–47; Jennifer Osmond and Yvonne Darlington, "Reflective Analysis: Techniques for Facilitating Reflection," *Australian Social Work* 58, no. 1 (March 2005): 10–11; Carolin Kreber, "Critical Reflection and Transformative Learning," in *Handbook of Transformative Learning: Theory, Research, and Practice*, eds. Edward W. Taylor and Patricia Cranton (Hoboken, NJ: John Wiley & Sons, 2012), 330.

8. Thomas E. Hill, *The Concept of Meaning* (New York: Routledge, 2013), 59, 95–96, 178.

9. Some examples of ambiguous images include *Rubin's Vase* and the image of the young or old woman. Centre for the Study of Perceptual Experience, "Explore Illusions," *The Illusions Index*, accessed November 28, 2020, https://www.illusions index.org/illusions.

10. Jennifer Riel and Roger L. Martin, *Creating Great Choices: A Leader's Guide to Integrative Thinking* (Boston: Harvard Business Review Press, 2017), 39.

11. Raymond J. Wlodkowski, *Enhancing Adult Motivation to Learn: A Comprehensive Guide for Teaching All Adults* (San Francisco: Jossey-Bass, 1999), 69–81.

12. N. T. Wright, *Paul and the Faithfulness of God* (Minneapolis: Fortress Press, 2013), 487. Italics are original.

13. Karl Barth, *The Word of God and the Word of Man* (New York: Harper & Brothers, 1957), 39, 43.

14. Stephen Preskill and Stephen D. Brookfield, *Learning As a Way of Leading: Lessons from the Struggle for Social Justice* (San Francisco: Jossey-Bass, 2009), 16.

15. Eviatar Zerubavel, *Social Mindscapes: An Invitation to Cognitive Sociology* (Cambridge, MA: Harvard University Press, 1999), 3, 24, 81, 87, 90, 112.

16. William H. Whyte Jr., "Groupthink," *Fortune*, March 1952, 114–17. Whyte derived the term from George Orwell, *Nineteen Eighty-Four: A Novel* (London: Secker & Warburg, 1949).

17. Volf, *Exclusion and Embrace*, 213. Italics are original. Volf emphasizes that it is possible to simultaneously stand within a given tradition and also to learn from other traditions.

18. Randy Pausch and Jeffrey Zaslow, *The Last Lecture* (New York: Hyperion, 2008), 112.

19. Barbara Brown Taylor, *Holy Envy: Finding God in the Faith of Others* (New York: HarperOne, 2019), 88.

20. Megan Boler, *Feeling Power: Emotions and Education* (New York: Routledge, 1999), 178, 181, 186, 193.

21. Aristotle, *Nicomachean Ethics*, 218–20 (§1156a5–1156b32), 229 (§1159a26–27).

22. Boyle, *Tattoos on the Heart*, 27.

23. L. Gregory Jones, "Discovering Hope through Holy Friendships," Faith & Leadership, *Christian Leadership* (blog), June 18, 2012, accessed November 28, 2020, https://faithandleadership.com/l-gregory-jones-discovering-hope-through-holy-friendships.

24. L. Gregory Jones, *Embodying Forgiveness: A Theological Analysis* (Grand Rapids, MI: Eerdmans, 1995), xii.

25. Volf, *Exclusion and Embrace*, 125.

26. Martin Luther King Jr., *Strength to Love* (Philadelphia: Fortress Press, 1982), 49.

27. Edwin H. Friedman, *A Failure of Nerve: Leadership in the Age of the Quick Fix* (New York: Church Publishing, 2017), 18–21, 183–84, 209; Cloud and Townsend, *Boundaries*, 31–50.

28. Palmer, *To Know As We Are Known*, 104.

29. This activity and the next are adapted from Stephen Brookfield, *Becoming a Critically Reflective Teacher* (San Francisco: Jossey-Bass, 1995), 72–77.

CHAPTER 6

1. H. Richard Niebuhr, *The Responsible Self: An Essay in Christian Moral Philosophy* (Louisville, KY: Westminster John Knox Press, 1999), 61.

2. "The Epistle to Diognetus," in Michael W. Holmes, ed., *The Apostolic Fathers*, trans. J. B. Lightfoot and J. R. Harmer (Grand Rapids, MI: Baker Book House, 1992), 299 (§6:1). Also see Alan Kreider, *The Patient Ferment of the Early Church: The Improbable Rise of Christianity in the Roman Empire* (Grand Rapids, MI: Baker Academic, 2016), 99.

3. Iris Marion Young, *Responsibility for Justice*, Oxford Political Philosophy (New York: Oxford University Press, 2011), 11.

4. Young, 26. Italics are original.

5. Dietrich Bonhoeffer, *Ethics*, trans. Neville Horton Smith (New York: Simon & Schuster, 1995), 249.

6. Charles Duhigg, *The Power of Habit: Why We Do What We Do in Life and Business* (New York: Random House, 2012), 145. Italics are original.

7. Hauerwas, *A Community of Character*, 10.

8. John Rawls, *A Theory of Justice* (Cambridge, MA: Harvard University Press, 2003), 6.

9. Also titled "Letter from Birmingham Jail" and "The Negro Is Your Brother," the letter was published in *Liberation Magazine* (June 1963), *The Christian Century* (June 12, 1963), *The New Leader* (June 24, 1963), and the *Atlantic Monthly* (August, 1963). The version I am using is an early pamphlet (May, 1963) and includes the clergy statement to which King was responding: Martin Luther King Jr., *Letter from Birmingham City Jail* (Philadelphia: American Friends Service Committee, 1963). For an online version, see Martin Luther King Jr., "Letter from a Birmingham Jail," African Studies Center, University of Pennsylvania, April 16, 1963, accessed November 28, 2020, https://www.africa.upenn.edu/Articles_Gen/Letter_Birmingham.html. For the letter that prompted King's response, see A Group of Clergymen, "Letter to Martin Luther King," Teaching American History, April 12, 1963, accessed November 28, 2020, https://teachingamericanhistory.org/library/document/letter-to-martin-luther-king/.

10. King, *Letter from Birmingham City Jail*, 12. This metaphor also appears in King, *Strength to Love*, 19.

11. King, *Strength to Love*, 31.

12. Jonathan Sacks, *To Heal a Fractured World: The Ethics of Responsibility* (New York: Schocken Books, 2005), 45–46. Italics are original.

13. Jonathan Sacks, *The Dignity of Difference: How to Avoid the Clash of Civilizations* (New York: Continuum, 2003), 60.

14. Martin Luther King Jr., *Where Do We Go from Here: Chaos or Community?* (New York: Harper & Row, 1967), 181.

15. King, *Letter from Birmingham City Jail*, 13.

16. Niebuhr, *The Responsible Self*, 49, 51, 55, 56, 89, 126, 162.

17. Carol Gilligan, *In a Different Voice: Psychological Theory and Women's Development* (Cambridge, MA: Harvard University Press, 1982), 166–67, 174.

18. Sacks, *The Dignity of Difference*, 149.

19. On the beloved community, see Charles Marsh, *The Beloved Community: How Faith Shapes Social Justice, from the Civil Rights Movement to Today* (New York: Basic Books, 2005), 53–54; Martin Luther King Jr., *Stride Toward Freedom: The Montgomery Story* (New York: Ballantine Books, 1961), 82; King, *Strength to Love*, 139.

20. Tertullian, "Apology," in *The Ante-Nicene Fathers*, ed. Alexander Roberts and James Donaldson, vol. III (Grand Rapids, MI: T & T Clark, 1997), 46 (§39.7–10).

21. Matt McCullough, "Wendell Berry and the Beauty of Membership," *The Gospel Coalition* (blog), June 25, 2013, accessed November 28, 2020, https://www.thegospelcoalition.org/article/wendell-berry-and-the-beauty-of-membership/. In this blog, McCullough specifically cites Wendell Berry, *Jayber Crow* (Washington, D.C.: Counterpoint, 2000).

22. Lewis, *Across That Bridge*, 159.

23. King, *Letter from Birmingham City Jail*, 3.

24. Emmanuel Katongole and Chris Rice, *Reconciling All Things: A Christian Vision for Justice, Peace and Healing* (Downers Grove, IL: IVP Books, 2008), 84.

25. Corbett and Fikkert, *When Helping Hurts*, 218.

26. This list is an expansion of the "principles of equitable civic engagement" provided in Kirwan Institute for the Study of Race and Ethnicity, "Race in Conversation. Equity in Practice," Annual Report 2017/2018 (Columbus, OH: The Ohio State University, 2018), 33.

CHAPTER 7

1. Maria Harris, *Fashion Me a People: Curriculum in the Church* (Louisville, KY: Westminster John Knox Press, 1989), 25.

2. Robert W. Pazmiño, *So What Makes Our Teaching Christian? Teaching in the Name, Spirit, and Power of Jesus* (Eugene, OR: Wipf & Stock, 2008), 86.

3. Howard, *A Guide to Christian Spiritual Formation*, 164.

4. Sherry Turkle, "Connected, But Alone?," TED: Ideas Worth Spreading, February 2012, accessed November 28, 2020, https://www.ted.com/talks/sherry_turkle_alone_together.

5. King, *Where Do We Go from Here*, 62–63.

6. Lampman, *Helping a Neighbor in Crisis*, 10.

7. Parker J. Palmer, *Let Your Life Speak: Listening for the Voice of Vocation* (San Francisco: Jossey-Bass, 2000), 63.

8. Susan Wendell, "Oppression and Victimization: Choice and Responsibility," *Hypatia* 5, no. 3 (Autumn 1990): 21–43.

9. Wendell, 43.

10. Martin Luther King Jr., "I've Been to the Mountaintop," in *A Call to Conscience: The Landmark Speeches of Dr. Martin Luther King, Jr.*, eds. Clayborne Carson and Kris Shepard (New York: Grand Central Publishing, 2002), 219. The hypothetical quotations presented here are paraphrased from King's sermon.

11. Samantha Power, *The Education of an Idealist: A Memoir* (New York: Dey Street Books, 2019), 132.

12. Antoinette Tuff and Alex Tresniowski, *Prepared for a Purpose: The Inspiring True Story of How One Woman Saved an Atlanta School Under Siege* (Bloomington, MN: Bethany House, 2014). The CNN interview (August 23, 2013) is available at http://www.cnn.com/2013/08/22/us/georgia-school-shooting-hero/index.html.

The NPR interview (January 31, 2014) is available at http://www.npr.org/2014/01/31/268417580/.

13. Hauerwas, *A Community of Character*, 31.

14. Palmer, *To Know As We Are Known*, 14–15.

15. Palmer, 60.

16. Robert Kegan, *In Over Our Heads: The Mental Demands of Modern Life* (Cambridge, MA: Harvard University Press, 1994), 319.

17. Brown, *Dare to Lead*, 144.

BIBLIOGRAPHY

Adams, Jay E. *How to Help People Change: The Four-Step Biblical Process.* Grand Rapids, MI: Zondervan, 1986.

Aguilar, Elena. *Art of Coaching: Effective Strategies for School Transformation.* San Francisco: Jossey-Bass, 2013.

Anderson, Keith R., and Randy D. Reese. *Spiritual Mentoring: A Guide for Seeking and Giving Direction.* Downers Grove, IL: IVP Books, 1999.

Arbinger Institute. *Leadership and Self-Deception: Getting Out of the Box.* Oakland, CA: Berrett-Koehler Publishers, 2015.

Ashkar, Dominic F. *Road to Emmaus: A New Model for Catechesis.* San Jose, CA: Resource Publications, 1993.

Banks, Robert. *Reenvisioning Theological Education: Exploring a Missional Alternative to Current Models.* Grand Rapids, MI: Eerdmans, 1999.

Belenky, Mary Field, Blythe McVicker Clinchy, Nancy Rule Goldberger, and Jill Mattuck Tarule, eds. *Women's Ways of Knowing: The Development of Self, Voice, and Mind.* New York: Basic Books, 1986.

Bellah, Robert N., Richard Madsen, William M. Sullivan, Ann Swidler, and Steven Tipton. *Habits of the Heart: Individualism and Commitment in American Life.* Berkeley, CA: University of California Press, 1996.

Biesta, Gert J. J. *The Beautiful Risk of Education.* Boulder, CO: Paradigm Publishers, 2014.

Boler, Megan. *Feeling Power: Emotions and Education.* New York: Routledge, 1999.

Bonhoeffer, Dietrich. *Ethics.* Translated by Neville Horton Smith. New York: Simon & Schuster, 1995.

Boyle, Gregory. *Barking to the Choir: The Power of Radical Kinship.* New York: Simon & Schuster, 2017.

———. *Tattoos on the Heart: The Power of Boundless Compassion.* New York: Free Press, 2011.

Brookfield, Stephen. *Becoming a Critically Reflective Teacher.* San Francisco: Jossey-Bass, 1995.

Brown, Brené. *Dare to Lead: Brave Work, Tough Conversations, Whole Hearts*. New York: Random House, 2018.

———. *Daring Greatly: How the Courage to Be Vulnerable Transforms the Way We Live, Love, Parent, and Lead*. New York: Avery, 2015.

Childs, James M., Jr. *Faith, Formation, and Decision: Ethics in the Community of Promise*. Minneapolis: Fortress Press, 1992.

Cloud, Henry, and John Townsend. *Boundaries: When to Say Yes, When to Say No, to Take Control of Your Life*. Grand Rapids, MI: Zondervan, 1992.

Corbett, Steve, and Brian Fikkert. *When Helping Hurts: How to Alleviate Poverty without Hurting the Poor . . . and Yourself*. Chicago: Moody Publishers, 2012.

Covey, Stephen R. *The Seven Habits of Highly Effective People: Powerful Lessons in Personal Change*. New York: Simon and Schuster, 1990.

Daloz, Laurent A. *Effective Teaching and Mentoring: Realizing the Transformational Power of Adult Learning Experiences*. San Francisco: Jossey-Bass, 1990.

Dweck, Carol S. *Mindset: The New Psychology of Success*. New York: Ballantine Books, 2006.

Dykstra, Craig. *Growing in the Life of Faith: Education and Christian Practices*. Louisville, KY: Westminster John Knox Press, 2005.

Foster, Richard J. *Celebration of Discipline: The Path to Spiritual Growth*. San Francisco: Harper & Row, 1988.

Freire, Paulo. *Pedagogy of Freedom: Ethics, Democracy, and Civic Courage*. Translated by Patrick Clarke. Lanham, MD: Rowman & Littlefield, 1998.

———. *Pedagogy of the Oppressed*. Translated by Myra Bergman Ramos. New York: Continuum, 1981.

Friedman, Edwin H. *A Failure of Nerve: Leadership in the Age of the Quick Fix*. New York: Church Publishing, 2017.

Hall, Edward T. *Beyond Culture*. New York: Anchor Books, 1977.

Harris, Maria. *Fashion Me a People: Curriculum in the Church*. Louisville, KY: Westminster John Knox Press, 1989.

———. *Teaching and Religious Imagination: An Essay in the Theology of Teaching*. San Francisco: HarperSanFrancisco, 1991.

Hauerwas, Stanley. *A Community of Character: Toward a Constructive Christian Social Ethic*. Notre Dame, IN: University of Notre Dame Press, 1981.

Hauerwas, Stanley, and Charles R. Pinches. *Christians among the Virtues: Theological Conversations with Ancient and Modern Ethics*. Notre Dame, IN: University of Notre Dame Press, 1997.

Heifetz, Ronald A. *Leadership Without Easy Answers*. Cambridge, MA: The Belknap Press of Harvard University Press, 1996.

Hill, Thomas E. *The Concept of Meaning*. New York: Routledge, 2013.

Hoffman, Martin L. *Empathy and Moral Development: Implications for Caring and Justice*. New York: Cambridge University Press, 2000.

Howard, Evan B. *A Guide to Christian Spiritual Formation: How Scripture, Spirit, Community, and Mission Shape Our Souls*. Grand Rapids, MI: Baker Academic, 2018.

Howe, David. *Empathy: What It Is and Why It Matters*. Basingstoke, Hampshire: Palgrave Macmillan, 2013.

Howe, Reuel L. *The Miracle of Dialogue*. New York: The Seabury Press, 1966.

Jones, L. Gregory. *Embodying Forgiveness: A Theological Analysis*. Grand Rapids, MI: Eerdmans, 1995.

Katongole, Emmanuel, and Chris Rice. *Reconciling All Things: A Christian Vision for Justice, Peace and Healing*. Downers Grove, IL: IVP Books, 2008.

Kegan, Robert, and Lisa Laskow Lahey. *How the Way We Talk Can Change the Way We Work: Seven Languages for Transformation*. San Francisco: Jossey-Bass, 2001.

Keller, Timothy. *Prayer: Experiencing Awe and Intimacy with God*. New York: Dutton, 2014.

King, Martin Luther, Jr. *Letter from Birmingham City Jail*. Philadelphia: American Friends Service Committee, 1963.

———. *Strength to Love*. Philadelphia: Fortress Press, 1982.

Koile, Earl. *Listening As a Way of Becoming*. Waco, TX: Calibre, 1977.

Lampman, Lisa Barnes, ed. *Helping a Neighbor in Crisis: How to Encourage When You Don't Know What to Say*. Wheaton, IL: Tyndale House, 1997.

Lee-Thorp, Karen. *How to Ask Great Questions: Guide Your Group to Discovery with These Proven Techniques*. Colorado Springs, CO: NavPress, 1998.

Lewis, John. *Across That Bridge: Life Lessons and a Vision for Change*. New York: Hyperion, 2012.

Little, Sara. *To Set One's Heart: Belief and Teaching in the Church*. Atlanta: John Knox Press, 1983.

Lupton, Robert D. *Toxic Charity: How Churches and Charities Hurt Those They Help, and How to Reverse It*. New York: HarperOne, 2012.

MacIntyre, Alasdair. *After Virtue: A Study in Moral Theory*. Notre Dame, IN: University of Notre Dame Press, 2007.

Manning, Brennan. *Ruthless Trust: The Ragamuffin's Path to God*. New York: HarperCollins, 2000.

Marquardt, Michael. *Leading with Questions: How Leaders Find the Right Solutions by Knowing What to Ask*. San Francisco: Jossey-Bass, 2005.

McLaren, Karla. *The Art of Empathy: A Complete Guide to Life's Most Essential Skill*. Boulder, CO: Sounds True, 2013.

Moran, Gabriel. *A Grammar of Responsibility*. New York: Crossroad Pub. Co, 1996.

Murray, Andrew. *Humility: The Beauty of Holiness*. London: Nisbet, 1896.

Nichols, Michael P. *The Lost Art of Listening: How Learning to Listen Can Improve Relationships*. New York: The Guilford Press, 1995.

Niebuhr, H. Richard. *The Responsible Self: An Essay in Christian Moral Philosophy*. Louisville, KY: Westminster John Knox Press, 1999.

Nouwen, Henri J. M. *Reaching Out: The Three Movements of the Spiritual Life*. Garden City, NY: Image Books, 1986.

———. *The Wounded Healer*. New York: Image Books, 1979.

Palmer, Parker J. *The Courage to Teach: Exploring the Inner Landscape of a Teacher's Life*. San Francisco: Jossey-Bass, 1998.

———. *To Know As We Are Known: Education as a Spiritual Journey*. San Francisco: HarperOne, 1993.

Pazmiño, Robert W. *So What Makes Our Teaching Christian? Teaching in the Name, Spirit, and Power of Jesus*. Eugene, OR: Wipf & Stock, 2008.

Phelps, Joseph. *More Light, Less Heat: How Dialogue Can Transform Christian Conflicts into Growth*. San Francisco: Jossey-Bass, 1998.

Preskill, Stephen, and Stephen D. Brookfield. *Learning As a Way of Leading: Lessons from the Struggle for Social Justice*. San Francisco: Jossey-Bass, 2009.

Riel, Jennifer, and Roger L. Martin. *Creating Great Choices: A Leader's Guide to Integrative Thinking*. Boston: Harvard Business Review Press, 2017.

Saccone, Steve, and Cheri Saccone. *Protégé: Developing Your Next Generation of Church Leaders*. Downers Grove, IL: IVP Books, 2012.

Sacks, Jonathan. *The Dignity of Difference: How to Avoid the Clash of Civilizations*. New York: Continuum, 2003.

———. *To Heal a Fractured World: The Ethics of Responsibility*. New York: Schocken Books, 2005.

Senge, Peter M. *The Fifth Discipline: The Art & Practice of the Learning Organization*. New York: Doubleday Business, 1994.

Sinek, Simon. *Start with Why: How Great Leaders Inspire Everyone to Take Action*. New York: Penguin Books, 2011.

Smith, Adam. *The Theory of Moral Sentiments*. New York: Augustus M. Kelley, 1966.

Taylor, Barbara Brown. *Holy Envy: Finding God in the Faith of Others*. New York: HarperOne, 2019.

Thompson, Curt. *Anatomy of the Soul: Surprising Connections between Neuroscience and Spiritual Practices That Can Transform Your Life and Relationships*. Carol Stream, IL: Tyndale House, 2010.

Vella, Jane. *Training Through Dialogue: Promoting Effective Learning and Change with Adults*. San Francisco: Jossey-Bass, 1995.

Volf, Miroslav. *Exclusion and Embrace: A Theological Exploration of Identity, Otherness, and Reconciliation*. Nashville: Abingdon Press, 1996.

———. *Free of Charge: Giving and Forgiving in a Culture Stripped of Grace*. Grand Rapids, MI: Zondervan, 2006.

Wadell, Paul J. *Friendship and the Moral Life*. Notre Dame, IN: University of Notre Dame Press, 2009.

Weaver, Laura, and Mark Wilding. *The 5 Dimensions of Engaged Teaching: A Practical Guide for Educators*. Boomington, IN: Solution Tree Press, 2011.

Wenger, Etienne, Richard McDermott, and William M. Snyder. *Cultivating Communities of Practice.* Boston: Harvard Business Review Press, 2002.

Willard, Dallas. *Hearing God: Developing a Conversational Relationship with God.* Downers Grove, IL: InterVarsity Press, 2012.

Wlodkowski, Raymond J. *Enhancing Adult Motivation to Learn: A Comprehensive Guide for Teaching All Adults.* San Francisco: Jossey-Bass, 1999.

Young, Iris Marion. *Responsibility for Justice.* Oxford Political Philosophy. New York: Oxford University Press, 2011.

Zerubavel, Eviatar. *Social Mindscapes: An Invitation to Cognitive Sociology.* Cambridge, MA: Harvard University Press, 1999.

SCRIPTURE INDEX

BIBLE PASSAGES

17:2	84
17:10–12	78, 102
17:16–34	78
17:17	84
20:7–12	84

Romans

2:4	190
8:12–27	87
12	73
12:1	46
12:3–8	24
12:14–21	180

1 Corinthians

2:4	6
4:17	124
4:20	157
12	47
12:12–26	150
13	47
13:4–7	190

2 Corinthians

2:17	55
5:17	16
5:17–21	149
5:18–19	51
5:20	182

Galatians

3:27–29	154
6:2	60
6:5	60

Ephesians

1:3–14	153
2:13–18	147
3:14–21	73

OTHER JEWISH WORKS

INDEX

Smith, Terry, 5
social connection model, 139
social influencers, 1
socialization, 111–12
social media, 110, 174, 175
social thinking, *169*; change and, 161;
    community and, 142–48, 159–62;
    empowerment and, 142–43,
    146, 160–61; fear and, 161–62;
    inclusivity and, 160; initiative and,
    144–46; justice and, 8, 142–48,
    149–50, 159–62; love and, 147–48;
    marginalized communities and,
    159–62; power and, 146–47;
    recognizing patterns of inequity,
    159–60; response and, 142–48,
    159–62
Soteria Community Development
    Corporation, 13–14
spiritual change, 9–10
spiritual development, 7–8, 87; heart
    and, 16, 166; meaning and, 9–10;
    reflection and, 107, 114–15
spiritual practices, 45–47
Stamps, Curtis, 118–19, 182
Starbucks, 141
status, 122
Steadiness style personality, 48, 49
stories, 101, 113–14
success, 122, 130
suffering, 178–81, 183–84
support, 93–95, 96–97, 179–80
Support Circles program, 71, 84,
    96, 128
sympathy, 17–18, *18*

Taylor, Barbara Brown, 121–22
teaching: Bible on, 43–44; empathy
    and, 31–32, 33, 37; engagement
    and, 110–11; formative presence
    and, 57–59; friendship and, 129;
    influence and, 43–44, 56, 168; by
    Jesus Christ, 50–51, 57–58; learning
    and, 43–44; love and, 71, 129; by
    Paul, 51, 58–59, 61; reflection and,
    129, 135–36; response and, 158–59;
    training and, 168–73

team dynamics, 84, 125
teenage pregnancy, 103
Tertullian, 153–54
Thomas Aquinas, 124
Timothy, 4, 7, 58–59, 61, 124
Titchener, E. B., 17
Titus, 58
Townsend, John, 127
toxic charity, 31
tradition, 200n17
training: for interconnectivity, 174–76;
    leadership, 5; teaching and, 168–73
transformation. *See* change
trauma, 13, 41–42, 103
Triune Mercy Center, 103, 119,
    146–47, 176
trust: anatomy of, 63–64; in Bible, 65;
    BRAVING Inventory and, 63–64,
    67; change and, 67–68; empathy
    and, 13–14; empowerment and,
    160; faith and, 64–65, 69–70;
    friendship and, 125–26; in God,
    54–55, 63, 64–65, 69–70, 122–23;
    influence and, 3–4, 63–70; love and,
    71–72; in marriage, 70; openness
    and, 84; race and, 72; reception
    and, 187; reflection and, 187–88;
    in relationships, 69–70, 75–76;
    resilient, 3, 53–54, 63–70, 75–76,
    187–88; truth and, 66–68, 187–88;
    vulnerability and, 64, 69
truth: Bible on, 185–87; engagement
    and, 111; examples of influence in,
    188–89; freedom and, 186–87; God
    and, 44, 51, 68, 159, 186–87; grace
    and, 4, 159; influence and, 184–89;
    Jesus Christ and, 185–86; openness
    and, 84; Paul on, 66; response and,
    188; trust and, 66–68, 187–88;
    violence and, 184
Tuff, Antoinette, 183–84
Turkle, Sherry, 174
2001: A Space Odyssey (film), 15

United Ministries, 140
upstanders, 183

BIOGRAPHY

Michael W. Andrews has directed adult education for over ten years at Holland Park Church in Simpsonville, South Carolina, and he has taught and preached in several churches for over three decades. He is a member of the board of directors for Triune Mercy Center, a nondenominational church in Greenville, South Carolina, that reaches out to people who are displaced or disadvantaged. He and  his wife, Beth, have lived in South Carolina for fifteen years. Mike retired from the telecommunications industry in 2001, after twenty-five years of managing international research and development projects for Bell Laboratories, AT&T, and Lucent Technologies. During his engineering career, he received five U.S. Patents for innovations in telecommunications products and processes. He holds degrees in electrical engineering from Tennessee Technological University (1977) and the University of California (1978). He also has a Master of Divinity from Erskine Theological Seminary (2012) and a Doctor of Ministry from the Divinity School at Duke University (2020). He is an ordained minister affiliated with the Churches of Christ and has served as an interim minister/pastor in both New Mexico and South Carolina.

752970LVX00117B PERFECT	9780715110935 5.83X8.27	The PCC Members Essential Guide 98 MATTE (1)
752970LVX00118B PERFECT	9781848258686 5.00X8.00	Daily Prayer with the Corrymeela Commu 94 MATTE (4)
752970LVX00119B PERFECT	9781471723001 5.83X8.27	Cose da grandi: Fantasia, critica e adultità 94 MATTE (1)
752970LVX00120B PERFECT	9781617208966 6.00X9.00	The Time Machine 92 MATTE (1)
752970LVX00121B PERFECT	9781614274513 6.00X9.00	Confusion de Confusiones [1688]: Portio 68 MATTE (1)
752970LVX00122B PERFECT	9781614276517 6.00X9.00	Magic: A Treatise on Natural Occultism 62 MATTE (1)

CPSIA information can be obtained
at www.ICGtesting.com
Printed in the USA
LVHW042121200723
752970LV00002B

752970LVX00096B PERFECT	9780985427603 5.50X8.50	The Sniper's Wife: A Joe Gunther Novel 232 MATTE	(1)
752970LVX00097B PERFECT	9780979861338 5.50X8.50	St. Alban's Fire: A Joe Gunther Novel 228 MATTE	(1)
752970LVX00098B PERFECT	9781475843248 6.00X9.00	Seen and Not Heard : Why Children's Voi 224 MATTE	(1)
752970LVX00099B PERFECT	9780985427641 5.50X8.50	The Second Mouse: A Joe Gunther Novel 222 MATTE	(1)
752970LVX00100B PERFECT	9780979861314 5.50X8.50	Tucker Peak: A Joe Gunther Novel 222 MATTE	(1)
752970LVX00101B PERFECT	9781627554442 6.00X9.00	The Shadow of Doctor Syn 218 MATTE	(1)
752970LVX00102B PERFECT	9780985427610 5.50X8.50	The Surrogate Thief: A Joe Gunther Novel 216 MATTE	(1)
752970LVX00103B PERFECT	9781608932825 6.00X9.00	Moving to Maine: The Essential Guide to 216 MATTE	(1)
752970LVX00104B PERFECT	9781493032143 6.00X9.00	Myths and Legends of Yellowstone: The T 216 MATTE	(1)
752970LVX00105B PERFECT	9780762760466 6.00X9.00	They Call Me Doc: The Story Behind The 216 MATTE	(2)
752970LVX00106B PERFECT	9780979861345 5.50X8.50	Gatekeeper: A Joe Gunther Novel 208 MATTE	(1)
752970LVX00107B PERFECT	9781493040087 6.00X9.00	Michigan Myths and Legends: The True 208 MATTE	(1)
752970LVX00108B PERFECT	9780762760718 6.00X9.00	Black Cowboys of the Old West : True, Se 202 MATTE	(2)
752970LVX00109B PERFECT	9781632994035 5.50X8.50	Retirement Stepping Stones 188 MATTE	(2)
752970LVX00110B PERFECT	9781618952738 6.00X9.00	Homage to Catalonia 174 MATTE	(6
752970LVX00111B PERFECT	9781614274865 6.00X9.00	The Problems of Philosophy 168 MATTE	(1
752970LVX00112B PERFECT	9780762761289 6.00X9.00	It Happened in Illinois: Remarkable Even 146 MATTE	(1
752970LVX00113B PERFECT	9781087903606 6.00X9.00	Clutter-Free Home: How to Declutter, Or 144 MATTE	(1
752970LVX00114B PERFECT	9781617209833 6.00X9.00	The Further Adventures of Doctor Syn 136 MATTE	(1
752970LVX00115B PERFECT	9781614274117 6.00X9.00	Negroes with Guns 130 MATTE	(1
752970LVX00116B PERFECT	9781773692302 6.00X9.00	What in the World is DNA? 118 MATTE	(1

752970LVX00075B PERFECT	9781614274384 6.00X9.00	The Light of Egypt; Or, the Science of the 492 MATTE	(1)
752970LVX00076B PERFECT	9781728206141 5.50X8.25	Boyfriend Material 434 MATTE	(1)
752970LVX00077B PERFECT	9781728260730 5.00X8.00	Game of Fate 418 MATTE	(1)
752970LVX00078B PERFECT	9780979812224 5.50X8.50	Scent of Evil: A Joe Gunther Novel 360 MATTE	(1)
752970LVX00079B PERFECT	9781493052493 6.00X9.00	Brave Hearts : Indian Women of the Plains 354 MATTE	(1)
752970LVX00080B PERFECT	9781493033607 6.00X9.00	Buckular Dystrophy : A Woods Cop Myste 354 MATTE	(1)
752970LVX00081B PERFECT	9780762780303 5.50X8.50	Jackpot : High Times, High Seas, And Th 330 MATTE	(2)
752970LVX00082B PERFECT	9781944967550 5.50X8.50	The Religion of the Apostles: Orthodox C 322 MATTE	(3)
752970LVX00083B PERFECT	9780979812293 5.50X8.50	Occam's Razor: A Joe Gunther Novel 316 MATTE	(1)
752970LVX00084B PERFECT	9780979812255 5.50X8.50	The Dark Root: A Joe Gunther Novel 310 MATTE	(1)
752970LVX00085B PERFECT	9780300187120 5.50X8.50	Realm of the Nebulae 288 MATTE	(1)
752970LVX00086B PERFECT	9780979812200 5.50X8.50	Open Season: A Joe Gunther Novel 286 MATTE	(2)
752970LVX00087B PERFECT	9780979812262 5.50X8.50	The Ragman's Memory: A Joe Gunther N 278 MATTE	(1)
752970LVX00088B PERFECT	9780979812217 5.50X8.50	Borderlines: A Joe Gunther Novel 276 MATTE	(1)
752970LVX00089B PERFECT	9780979812248 5.50X8.50	Fruits of the Poisonous Tree: A Joe Gunth 262 MATTE	(1)
752970LVX00090B PERFECT	9781402284557 5.50X8.25	I Have a Bad Feeling about This 258 MATTE	(1)
752970LVX00091B PERFECT	9781538151730 6.00X9.00	The Influential Christian : Learning to Lea 248 MATTE	(4)
752970LVX00092B PERFECT	9780985427658 5.50X8.50	Chat: A Joe Gunther Novel 244 MATTE	(1)
752970LVX00093B PERFECT	9780979812279 5.50X8.50	Bellows Falls: A Joe Gunther Novel 234 MATTE	(1)
752970LVX00094B PERFECT	9780979812286 5.50X8.50	The Disposible Man: A Joe Gunther Novel 234 MATTE	(1)
752970LVX00095B PERFECT	9780979861307 5.50X8.50	The Marble Mask: A Joe Gunther Novel 232 MATTE	(1)

Printed at: Thu Jul 20 21:16:25 2023 on device lvhp04-80

75297 0LV

Promise Date: 20-JUL-23 (T!

Batch Location _____

Shipping _____

Cutting _____

Binding _____

Printing _____

Department   Operator's Name (Please print)

BOOK
STBC19_SM   CONTAINS: MONO

75297 0LV00002B

[7529 70LVX0007 5B - 75297 0LVX00122B [48 : 66]

PT4:BLACKSTD
PERFECT ** MATTE **

7529 70LV00002B/3